Windows® 7 Tweaks

Windows® 7 Tweaks

A Comprehensive Guide to Customizing, Increasing Performance, and Securing Microsoft® Windows 7

Steve Sinchak

Wiley Publishing, Inc.

Windows® 7 Tweaks

Published by
Wiley Publishing, Inc.
10475 Crosspoint Boulevard
Indianapolis, IN 46256
www.wiley.com

Copyright © 2010 by Wiley Publishing, Inc., Indianapolis, Indiana

Published simultaneously in Canada

ISBN: 978-0-470-52591-3

Manufactured in the United States of America

10 9 8 7 6 5 4 3 2 1

For general information on our other products and services please contact our Customer Care Department within the United States at (877) 762-2974, outside the United States at (317) 572-3993 or fax (317) 572-4002.

Wiley also publishes its books in a variety of electronic formats. Some content that appears in print may not be available in electronic books.

Library of Congress Control Number: 2009937282

This book is dedicated to my wife Stephanie and my family.

About the Author

Steve Sinchak is an entrepreneur who has started several technology-related businesses. Steve is currently running a web development firm, known as Advanced PC Media LLC, that owns and operates several web sites geared toward computer enthusiasts. Aside from writing for his web sites and running Advanced PC Media LLC, he works as a Systems Engineer for a large financial services company.

Steve has been working with computers for more than 18 years. Starting with a desktop that had a 286-based processor, 1 MB of RAM, and Windows 3.1, he taught himself how to make Windows run faster on the slow hardware. Driven by a strong curiosity to understand how it works, he spent countless hours researching and experimenting with the inner workings and features of Windows. Over the years, he has worked closely with all versions of Windows. Every year since 2005 Microsoft has honored him with the Most Valued Professional (MVP) award for his work with Windows and his contributions to the Windows community.

Credits

Acknowledgments

Writing this book required a lot of time and compromises, so I want to thank my wife Stephanie for her love and help taking care of me.

I want to thank my family, relatives, coworkers, and friends who have motivated and inspired me throughout my life.

I also want to thank everyone involved in this book at Wiley for their help and advice.

Contents at a Glance

Contents

Introduction

Fewer than three years after Windows Vista was completed, Microsoft finished work on the most significant release of Windows in years. The development of Windows 7 was very different from its predecessor because the development team was under new management: Windows division president Steven Sinofsky. New features were kept secret until a quality benchmark was met and Microsoft was certain that the features would make it into the final product. Public deadlines were never provided. When asked when Windows 7 would be completed, Microsoft would only provide a vague two to three years after Windows Vista, followed up by, "When it's ready."

Clearly, a response to the public relations problem caused by the numerous features dropped and deadlines missed with Windows Vista, the change in style also allowed the developers to focus on writing high quality code rather than rushing to get new features into the release. Microsoft was very focused on reliability and performance data provided by every pre-release version of Windows 7. The millions of beta and release candidate installations provided an enormous amount of valuable data, such as how long it takes your computer to start, what applications are crashing, what device drivers are missing, and how you perform common tasks. Microsoft knew exactly what code needed to be optimized, what drivers were not performing well, and even where to improve the user interface to make Windows easier to use.

The end result is an operating system that was developed with quality performance as the goal. Windows 7 is fast, reliable, and easy to use. No wonder many are calling Windows 7 the best version of Windows to date.

Having said all that, Windows 7 is not 100% perfect. There are over one billion Windows users and a wide range of unique hardware configurations.

While the majority of users may prefer to do a task one way, others may prefer a completely different way. The same goes for the appearance of the user interface. Everyone has different preferences and likes different things. This is where Windows 7 Tweaks will help you customize Windows 7 so it is tuned just for you. I show you how to customize almost every aspect of Windows. By the time you are finished with this book, your Windows 7 will look and feel as if Microsoft designed it just for you.

As I mentioned earlier, performance has been greatly improved in Windows 7, driven by performance data and focused optimization. The result provides a much better experience than Windows Vista, but there are still many features that you may not use that contribute to slower performance, depending on how you use your computer. This book is going to help you cut the fat and help you improve the performance of Windows 7 even further. I guide you through speeding up Windows 7 from the boot to the core Windows components.

Security is another important topic with Windows, in general. Windows XP had a horrible security track record when it was first released, with numerous viruses attacking and crippling the OS. I remember setting up a brand new Windows XP computer for a neighbor that was compromised within seconds of connecting to the Internet, before I could even run Windows Update on it. The major update known as Windows XP Service Pack 2 fixed a lot of the major security holes, but the OS was far from perfect. Windows Vista shifted the security pendulum far in the other direction aiming to increase security significantly, but at the cost of annoying so much that many simply turned off the security features. Learning from past mistakes, and also from data collected from the beta and RC users, Microsoft has found a good balance of security and annoyance in Windows 7. It's not perfect, but it is significantly better than Windows XP or Windows Vista. This book shows you how to use and configure Windows 7 security features and increase the security of your computer.

Are you ready to customize, speed up, and secure your Windows 7 computer? Read on to get started!

Who Should Read This Book

This book is intended for all Windows 7 users who are interested in customizing, improving the performance of, and using the latest security features and tools to secure Windows 7. Previous Windows experience is necessary for this book. Most of the topics in this book are geared toward a more advanced Windows user, but every section is written in a way that even beginner Windows users can understand and complete.

How This Book Is Organized

In this book you will find 19 chapters spread across four parts. Each part covers a different theme and each chapter is broken into sections supporting the chapter's topic.

Part I: Getting Started with Windows 7

Chapter 1 will begin with an introduction to the many versions of Windows 7 and will make sure that you select the right version. Chapter 2 will guide you through the different methods to install Windows 7 and Chapter 3 will show you how to tweak your computer safely using proper backup precautions.

Part II: Customizing Windows 7

The second part will help you customize the look and behavior of just about every component of Windows 7. Chapter 4 will begin showing you how to customize the startup of your computer. Chapter 5 covers customizing user navigation elements, such as the Start menu and the Taskbar. Chapter 6 shows you how to customize the desktop, and Chapter 7 guides you through using themes and skinning the interface. Chapter 8 will help you fine tune the Windows explorer interface, and Chapter 9 will customize Internet Explorer 8. Chapter 10 is all about customizing your Windows Media experience, including tweaking Windows Media Player and Media Center.

Part III: Increasing System Performance

The third part of *Windows 7 Tweaks* is all about increasing the power of your computer. Chapter 11 will help you analyze your system's performance and identify bottlenecks. Chapter 12 guides you through improving boot speed, and Chapter 13 will help with logon speed. Chapter 14 will target streamlining Windows Explorer, and Chapter 15 will cover optimizing the core Windows components, such as the file system and RAM. The attention turns to network performance in Chapter 16.

Part IV: Securing Your System

The final section will help you improve the security of your computer and maintain a secure operating environment. Chapter 17 guides you through actively protecting your data and also controlling one of the most talked about features, User Account Control. Chapter 18 will focus on Internet and network security, and Chapter 19 will help you protect your privacy by clearing history data from Windows 7.

What You Need to Use This Book

Windows 7 Ultimate is required to perform all tweaks and hacks mentioned in this book. You can use other versions of Windows 7, but you may find that certain sections do not work because that particular feature of Windows 7 is not in your version.

Conventions Used in This Book

In this book, you'll find two notification icons — Tip and Caution — that point out important information. Here's what the two types of icons look like:

TIP Tips provide small, helpful hints and related tweaks.

CAUTION Cautions alert you to possible hazards that can result from the tweak.

Code, commands, filenames, and executables within the text appear in a `monospace font`, whereas content you will type appears in **bold**.

The Book's Companion Web Site

For links and updates, please visit this book's companion web site at `http://Tweaks.com/books/win7tweaks`.

Windows® 7 Tweaks

Getting Started with Windows 7

In This Part

Selecting the Right Version

Similar to Windows Vista, Microsoft decided to offer Windows 7 in a number of editions for different markets and users. Specifically: Starter, Home Basic, Home Premium, Professional, and Ultimate/Enterprise. Of the five versions of Windows 7, only Home Premium and Professional are promoted heavily to consumers. The remaining versions are available only to specific markets. Sorting out what version of Windows 7 you need and can buy in your market can be very confusing. There are significant differences among all versions, so selecting the correct version is critical to your Windows experience.

In this chapter, I explain the various versions of Windows 7 so you can make an informed decision about what version you need. Then I show you how to upgrade Windows 7 to a better version with Anytime Upgrade.

Version Comparison

Why are there so many versions of Windows 7? That is exactly the question I asked when Microsoft announced the version details, and I always got the same "one size does not fit all" explanation. With more than a billion Windows users worldwide and thousands of individual markets, Microsoft decided to offer a variety of versions tailored to different markets. For most of the world, two main versions will be offered when you walk in to your local electronics store:

1. Windows 7 Home Premium
2. Windows 7 Professional

The remaining versions are for specific markets:

- Windows 7 Starter Edition is primarily for Netbooks
- Windows 7 Home Basic is for emerging markets
- Windows 7 Enterprise is for large enterprises
- Windows 7 Ultimate is for enthusiasts

In some countries some versions are not available. For example, in the United States, consumers can only purchase Home, Professional, and Ultimate versions. Starter Edition can only be purchased by computer manufacturers (OEMs) and Home Basic is not offered at all. Additionally, Enterprise requires enterprises to have a Volume License agreement with Microsoft to obtain that version.

Now that I have explained the different versions and what is available, it is important to understand the technical differences among the versions. Why should you buy Professional instead of Home? Do you really need Ultimate? These questions can be answered by looking at what features are offered in each version to match your needs. To help, look at the version matrix in Table 1-1 to see what features are in each version.

Table 1-1: Windows 7 Version Matrix

FEATURES	STARTER	HOME BASIC	HOME PREMIUM	PROFES-SIONAL	ENTERPRISE AND ULTIMATE
Max Processors	1	1	2	2	2
Max Cores	Unlimited	Unlimited	Unlimited	Unlimited	Unlimited
Max Ram 32-Bit Version	4GB	4GB	4GB	4GB	4GB
Max Ram 64-Bit Version	8GB	8GB	16GB	192GB	192GB
Max Running Application	Unlimited	Unlimited	Unlimited	Unlimited	Unlimited
Windows Search	X	X	X	X	X

Table 1-1: Windows 7 Version Matrix *(continued)*

FEATURES	STARTER	HOME BASIC	HOME PREMIUM	PROFES-SIONAL	ENTERPRISE AND ULTIMATE
Join a HomeGroup	X	X	X	X	X
Windows Media Player	X	X	X	X	X
Backup and Restore	X	X	X	X	X
Enhanced Media Playback	X	X	X	X	X
Action Center	X	X	X	X	X
Device Stage	X	X	X	X	X
Home Media Streaming	X	X	X	X	X
Bluetooth Support	X	X	X	X	X
Fax and Scan	X	X	X	X	X
Basic Games	X	X	X	X	X
Credential Manager	X	X	X	X	X
Live Taskbar Thumbnail Previews		X	X	X	X
Fast User Switching		X	X	X	X
Create ad-hoc Wireless Networks		X	X	X	X
Internet Connection Sharing		X	X	X	X
Multi-Monitor Support		X	X	X	X
Windows Mobility Center		X	X	X	X
Aero Glass			X	X	X

Continued

Table 1-1: Windows 7 Version Matrix *(continued)*

FEATURES	STARTER	HOME BASIC	HOME PREMIUM	PROFES-SIONAL	ENTERPRISE AND ULTIMATE
Advanced Windows Navigation			X	X	X
Windows Touch (Multi-Touch and Tablet Support)			X	X	X
Create a HomeGroup			X	X	X
Windows Media Center			X	X	X
Remote Media Streaming			X	X	X
DVD Playback			X	X	X
Premium Games			X	X	X
Snipping Tool			X	X	X
Sticky Notes			X	X	X
Windows Sideshow			X	X	X
Location Aware Printing				X	X
Domain Join and Group Policy Controls				X	X
Remote Desktop Host				X	X
Advanced Backup				X	X
Encrypted File System				X	X
Windows XP Mode				X	X
Windows Presentation Mode				X	X

Table 1-1: Windows 7 Version Matrix *(continued)*

FEATURES	STARTER	HOME BASIC	HOME PREMIUM	PROFES-SIONAL	ENTERPRISE AND ULTIMATE
Offline Folders				X	X
BitLocker Drive Encryption					X
BitLocker To Go					X
AppLocker					X
DirectAccess					X
BranchCache					X
MUI Language Packs					X
Enterprise Search Scopes					X
VDI Enhancements					X
Boot from VHD					X

Windows Anytime Upgrade

In Windows 7, users have the option to upgrade to a higher version at any time thanks to a feature called Anytime Upgrade. Users can move up from Home to Professional or even all the way to Ultimate. Did your Netbook come preinstalled with Starter? Any time Upgrade allows you to upgrade to Ultimate, just run the Windows Anytime Upgrade application and pay the upgrade fee and Windows will automatically unlock the new features without a reinstall. You don't even need your Windows 7 install DVD because all the files are already on your computer.

You have two options to purchase the upgrade to a higher version. Some local electronics stores sell upgrade keys in a box that looks similar to but smaller than the normal Windows 7 retail DVD box. You can also buy the upgrade directly from Microsoft through the Windows Anytime Upgrade application.

Upgrading is very simple. Just click the Start button, type in Windows Anytime Upgrade, and hit Enter. Then, follow the onscreen directions as shown in Figure 1-1. In less than 20 minutes your computer will be upgraded.

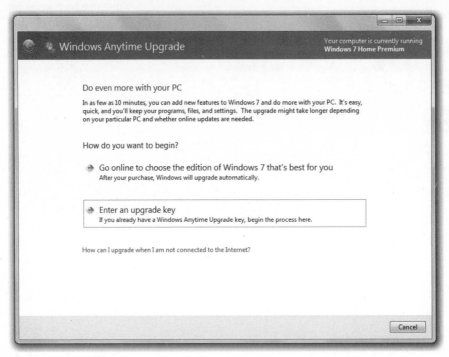

Figure 1-1: Windows Anytime Upgrade

Summary

This chapter was about clarifying the confusion around the various versions of Windows 7. As I mentioned in the preface, this book is written for all the features included in Enterprise/Ultimate so it is important to know what features are in each version. If a specific topic and feature covered in this book is not in your version, you can always upgrade with Windows Anytime Upgrade. In Chapter 2, I show you how to install Windows 7 a number of ways including complex installations such as dual booting.

Installing Windows 7

Now that you know about the various versions of Windows 7, you are almost ready to install Windows 7 on your computer. First it is important to understand the differences between 32-bit and 64-bit Windows 7 because both versions are provided by Microsoft when you buy a retail box. I show how to pick the right version for your computer hardware. Then I walk you through the installation steps and even show you some install tricks to get Windows 7 installed on computers without using an optical drive. In the end I show you how to configure advanced configurations such as dual-booting Windows XP and Windows 7 on the same computer.

Install Media

Included in every Windows 7 retail box are 32-bit and 64-bit media for two versions of Windows 7. The most common version used is still the 32-bit variant that has been around for ages, but recently the 64-bit version is becoming more popular for a number of reasons I'll get to shortly.

32-Bit or 64-Bit?

Making its debut in April 2005, the first version of 64-bit Windows was released as Windows XP Professional x64 Edition. Although the 64-bit edition was a true 64-bit OS, it was plagued by spotty driver support that limited its adoption. This was caused by the fact that the new 64-bit kernel required 64-bit drivers for all hardware devices. This vastly cut down on the number of compatible hardware devices. Hardware manufacturers had little incentive to rewrite drivers for the niche operating system. That all started to change with the release of Windows Vista that was the first Microsoft Windows release to come out in both 32-bit and 64-bit versions at the same time. Hardware manufacturers responded and 64-bit drivers are now available for almost all modern mainstream hardware.

The 64-bit Windows has started to mature and the number of Windows 7 64-bit installations will begin to grow much faster. What is the real difference between 32-bit and 64-bit Windows 7?

Aside from the obvious fact that you need a 64-bit CPU to run Windows 7 64-bit (which just about any new CPU you buy today supports), there are other differences, such as the ability to use more RAM, additional processing power, and extra security features.

The primary advantage of a 64-bit operating system is the ability to utilize the larger 64-bit registers that are a feature of the 64-bit CPU. This allows larger calculations to be performed with one cycle and also addresses and accesses significantly more RAM. With 32-bit Windows 7 the maximum number of memory addresses available is 2^{32}, which equals 4GB of RAM that can be used. 64-bit Windows 7 can use up to 192GB of RAM with the Professional, Enterprise, and Ultimate editions.

There are also features that are only included in the 64-bit version of Windows 7, such as PatchGuard. This is a helpful piece of technology that attempts to protect the kernel of the operating system from being patched by malicious and legitimate software. In my opinion, anything that tampers with the kernel is bad, because it can affect the stability of your system. Microsoft is trying to put a stop to this by implementing the PatchGuard feature and creating a new API for legitimate software to interact with the kernel in a safer way.

Some mathematic intensive applications such as rendering a 3D scene will also perform better on 64-bit Windows 7 when used with a 64-bit version of the rendering application. Encryption programs also seem to run faster on 64-bit Windows.

Now that you know the benefits of the 64-bit version of Windows 7, it is important to decide which is better for your hardware. For me, RAM and driver support are the main decision factors. I tend to use 32-bit Windows 7 on my older hardware for which no 64-bit drivers are available. I use 64-bit Windows 7 on my newer hardware, so I can take advantage of more than 4GB of RAM.

Alternative Install Media

The Windows 7 retail versions include installation software on a DVD. That works fine for the majority of users, but it is a big problem for those who own Netbooks or other computers without optical drives. If you don't have an optical drive on your computer, then you will need to take some extra steps to install Windows 7.

There are a few solutions to this problem, such as network booting to a Windows Deployment Server (feature of Windows Server 2008). However, the most popular and easiest to configure is a bootable USB flash drive. This is my personal preference as well, and is how I installed all the beta builds of Windows 7, so I could avoid wasting my DVD-R media. In fact, installing Windows 7 from a USB flash drive is actually much faster than installing from a DVD.

Preparing the USB Flash Drive

You will need a 4GB USB flash drive to have enough space to fit the entire Windows 7 installation code on the drive. I found that the 4GB SanDisk Cruzer Micro works well for booting the Windows 7 installation code and seems to be compatible with a wide range of computers. Before you can copy the code to the drive it is important to prepare the USB drive.

Insert the drive into a Windows computer and follow these steps:

1. After the drive has been recognized and installed on the computer, click the Start button and then click Computer.

2. Locate the USB flash drive on the Windows Explorer Computer window. Right-click the icon and select Format.

3. Make sure the File system is set to FAT32 (Default) and the Allocation unit size is 4096 bytes. Label the drive, uncheck Quick Format, and click Start, as shown in Figure 2-1.

Figure 2-1: Formatting the
USB flash drive

4. Click Yes on any confirmation screens, if shown.

5. Click OK on the format complete message box.

Copying the Installation Software

The final step, now that you have your USB flash drive prepared, is to copy the code. You can use a physical installation DVD as the code source in this step or you can use a DVD image that you downloaded from a MSDN, Technet, or Volume License subscription. Just make sure that you extract the ISO DVD image with a tool such as WinRAR (www.rarlabs.com) to a folder on your computer before following the next steps.

You can use some fancy xcopy commands for this step but I found a simple copy and paste works just fine. Navigate to the DVD drive or folder on your computer that has the Windows 7 installation files. Select all the files, as shown in Figure 2-2, and then right-click and select Copy.

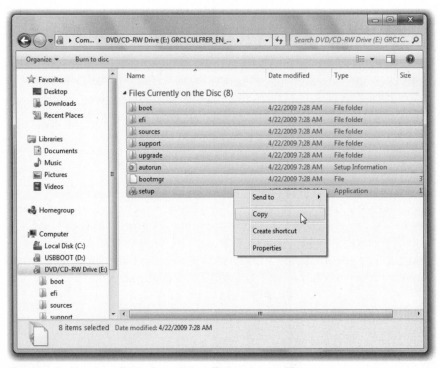

Figure 2-2: Copying all Windows 7 installation source files

Navigate to the root of the USB flash drive and select Paste. The file copy can take a number of minutes, but after it is finished you will be able to install Windows 7 fast and on machines that don't have an optical drive.

Full Install

The best way to install Windows 7 and minimize the chance for issues is to perform a clean full install. This will wipe your computer of all installed applications and data but is worth it in the long run. Upgrading from Windows Vista is supported and promoted by the Windows marketing group but just about any support person will tell you always to do a full install. Even a number of Microsoft employees on the support side I talked with recommend sticking with a full install.

Why do all the support guys suggest a full install? Because the upgrade process is not perfect. Along with your applications and data it will also migrate junk and, potentially, issues from your old computer. One of the first questions you will be asked if you contact Microsoft for support is whether you performed a full install or an upgrade. In some situations you may be asked to perform a full install to see if your issue still exists. In my opinion it is best to do it right the first time by choosing to perform a full install and avoid this scenario completely. Additionally, many applications have been updated to work better on Windows 7 and take advantage of the new features, so it is best to update and install new versions, anyway.

TIP **Although Microsoft allows users to buy the upgrade version of Windows 7, if you own any previous version of Windows the software only supports upgrading from Windows Vista. If you have Windows XP or older you can only perform a full install with the upgrade media.**

Now that you know the benefits of the full install, I will show you how to install Windows 7:

1. Insert the installation DVD or USB flash drive you created into your computer. Then reboot and select the boot menu key for your computer. On mine, I press F12 and then select the device I want to boot to as shown in Figure 2-3. If you are using a DVD, make sure to hit any key after you see "press any key to boot from CD or DVD" on your screen.

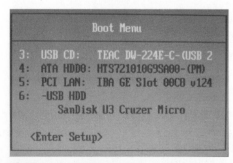

Figure 2-3: PC Boot Menu

2. You will now see a progress bar on the bottom of the screen followed by the Starting Windows animation. On the next screen, make sure that the language, time and currency format, and keyboard are set properly. Hit Next when ready, as shown in Figure 2-4.

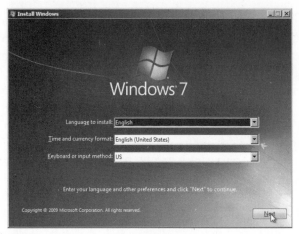

Figure 2-4: Windows 7 Install regional selection

3. On the next screen click Install now.

4. The screen will say Setup is starting, and it will examine your computer to see whether you have a previous version installed. Depending on your installation media, you may be presented with the next screen that allows you to select what version of Windows 7 you want to install, as shown in Figure 2-5. Click the version that you have a product key for, and click Next.

Figure 2-5: Selecting the operating system version

5. Click I accept the license terms and then click Next.

6. On the next screen you can select to Upgrade or Custom install. Don't even think about it; click Custom to perform a clean install as shown in Figure 2-6.

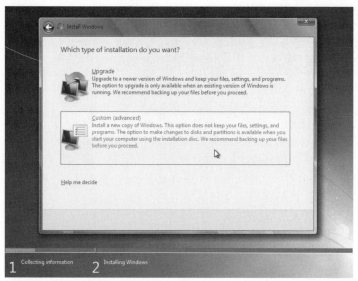

Figure 2-6: Custom install

7. The last manual step of the install is to select the drive to which you want to install. After I copy my data to a backup drive, I like to delete all the partitions on the drive on which I will be installing Windows 7. This can be accomplished by selecting the partition and then clicking Drive Options. Then just click Delete. Repeat for the other partitions on the drive, select the Unallocated Space, and then click Next, as shown in Figure 2-7. This will partition and format the drive automatically, and Windows will begin to install.

Setup is now fully automated. Files will be copied to the destination drive and the computer will reboot a few times. When the install is finished the computer will restart and after booting up will ask you for your username, computer name, password, and product key and other first-run information. Congratulations, Windows 7 is now installed and ready for tweaking.

Dual-Boot Windows XP

With virtualization becoming more popular, the need to run multiple operating systems on a computer has significantly decreased. Application compatibility was the main reason in the past that users installed multiple operating systems. Old Windows XP applications will not function in Windows Vista? Just restart and boot into Windows. Virtual machine applications such as VMWare Workstation, Sun Virtualbox, and Microsoft Virtual PC now allow you to boot the second operating system on top of your main OS, eliminating the need and hassle of rebooting into another OS. This solves the compatibility problem for most apps, but a virtual machine is not always perfect.

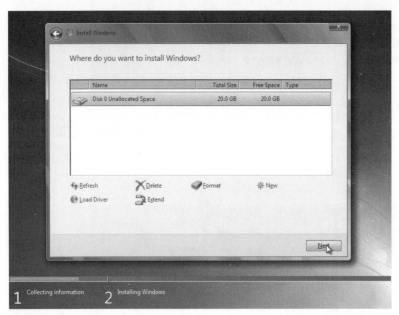

Figure 2-7: Install destination

Gaming is one area that remains a problem for virtual machines because 3D support and performance is just not good enough yet. Although Windows 7 has made many improvements in gaming performance, some old classic computer games are not compatible. If you are a gamer, then I will show you how you can dual-boot Windows XP and Windows 7 on the same PC to be able to play your old computer games without issue.

There are a number of ways to achieve a dual-boot system with both XP and Windows 7, but the easiest method that is nearly fully automated is the Windows XP first method. This is where you partition your hard drive in a certain way, or use multiple hard drives, and install Windows XP first on your computer. After you have XP up and running on the first partition you will install Windows 7 on the second partition. The Windows 7 installer will detect the Windows XP installation and automatically set up a boot menu to allow you to select which OS you want to use at power on.

Configuring HDD and Installing XP

Before you begin, make sure that you back up all important data on your hard drives because this procedure will completely wipe all data from your computer on your primary hard drive. To get started you need a Windows XP installation CD:

1. Boot up your computer to the XP CD drive, and choose to boot to the CD.

2. After setup loads, hit Enter to begin setup, and then hit F8 on the Windows XP License Agreement screen.

3. Next, I show you how to prepare the partitions on your hard drive. If partitions already exist on the drive, select them and hit D to delete the partition followed by L to confirm. Remember, this will delete any data on that partition. When all the partitions are deleted, as shown in Figure 2-8, you are ready to create the new partitions.

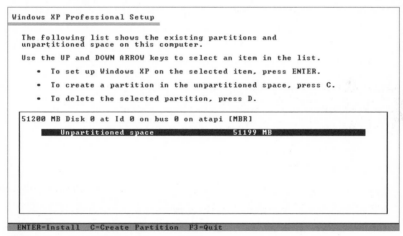

Figure 2-8: Hard drive with no partitions

4. Back on the drive and partition screen, select the Unpartitioned space on the drive on which you want to install your operating systems. Then press C to create a partition. Next, enter the size of the partition in megabytes. I like to use 20GB for XP and plenty of space for games which equals 20480MB. Enter the size and hit Enter as shown in Figure 2-9.

5. Next, select the Unpartitioned space again, and hit C to create the partition for Windows 7. This time, I suggest leaving the partition size as calculated, so it uses up the rest of the free space on your hard drive. Hit Enter to create the partition.

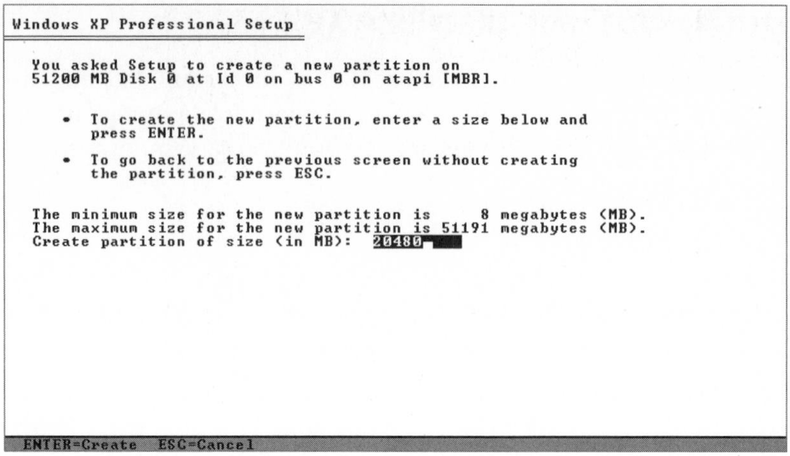

```
Windows XP Professional Setup

  You asked Setup to create a new partition on
  51200 MB Disk 0 at Id 0 on bus 0 on atapi [MBR].

       •  To create the new partition, enter a size below and
          press ENTER.
       •  To go back to the previous screen without creating
          the partition, press ESC.

  The minimum size for the new partition is      8 megabytes (MB).
  The maximum size for the new partition is 51191 megabytes (MB).
  Create partition of size (in MB):  20480

 ENTER=Create   ESC=Cancel
```

Figure 2-9: Setting XP partition size

6. When returned to the drive and partition screen you should see both of the partitions you created. Select Partition1 and hit Enter to install. Because the new partition does not yet have a file system you will need to format it with one. Select Format the partition using the NTFS file system (Quick) option on the top of the list and hit Enter.

From this point on, follow the normal Windows XP installation steps. After you have Windows XP fully installed and up and running, you are ready to install Windows 7.

Installing Windows 7

When you have Windows XP installed and configured, insert the Windows 7 install DVD into your computer, and then restart and boot to the DVD. Make sure to hit any key to boot to the DVD when asked.

Proceed through the install normally, but stop on the Which type of installation do you want? screen, shown in Figure 2-6, and follow these steps:

1. Select the Custom (advanced) option.

2. Select the second partition that you created during the Windows XP install, as shown in Figure 2-10, and click Next.

3. Continue to install as normal.

While Windows 7 is installed, a boot menu will be automatically configured and created that will allow you to switch between Windows XP and Windows 7 at boot.

Figure 2-10: Installing Windows 7 to Partition 2

After Windows 7 is fully installed and configured you can switch between Windows XP and Windows 7 by restarting your computer. Keep in mind that if you enable hibernation on either OS and hibernate instead of doing a full shutdown you will not see the boot menu when you turn on your computer. It is only shown when you restart or are on a full, normal startup.

Summary

In this chapter you learned the differences and the benefits of the 32-bit and 64-bit version of Windows 7. You learned how to install Windows 7 using a "clean install" from the DVD and how to install off a USB flash drive — a very useful trick. Then I jumped over to the world of dual-booting and demonstrated how to install both Windows XP and Windows 7 on the same computer.

In the next chapter you discover the basics of safely tweaking your computer by using the various backup and restore utilities that come with Windows 7.

Safe Tweaking

Now that you have Windows 7 installed, or your computer came with Windows 7 pre-installed, you are almost ready to start tweaking. This chapter first talks about the safe way to tweak and customize your computer. There are many tweaks, tips, and secrets that can create severe problems if you accidentally miss a step. That is why this is a good time to discuss some of the ways you should protect your computer, so you can easily undo any tweak that causes problems for your computer.

To get started, you will create Restore Points that allow you to take a configuration snapshot to easily jump back to a prior state. Then this chapter covers Windows Backup to protect your data, and Startup Repair to automatically fix issues that may prevent Windows 7 from starting up.

Using System Restore

System Restore has been in Windows for almost 10 years, but it has matured into something very valuable for any power user who tweaks his computer. Every time you make a change there is a risk that something could go wrong. Wouldn't it be nice if you could easily undo any change with just a few clicks? System Restore is the solution to that problem by allowing you to jump back in time to an earlier state.

In the next sections I show you how to create Restore Points before you tweak and then how to restore to a previous state if something goes wrong.

Creating Restore Points

Restore Points in Windows can be created a number of ways. Every time you install new software, Windows automatically creates a new Restore Point. You can also manually create Restore Points in Windows. This chapter will start first with the normal way and then show you how to create a desktop shortcut that allows you to jump directly to the Create Restore Point screen. To get started, do the following:

1. Click the Start button, type in **Create a Restore Point,** and then hit Enter.

2. This will load the System Properties System Protection tab as shown in Figure 3-1. This allows you to view your System Restore settings and create Restore Points.

Figure 3-1: System Restore Settings

3. Next, click the Create button near the bottom of the window.

4. On the next screen, type in a name for your Restore Point and click Create.

After you click the Create button the Restore Point will immediately begin taking a snapshot of your system. You will be shown a progress screen and notified when it is complete. In my experience it only takes a few minutes at most to create a Restore Point. Sometimes it takes less than a minute.

Next, I show you how to use the Restore Point to revert to an earlier point.

Reverting to a Previous State

The second half of using System Restore is using the Restore functionality to revert your computer to a previous state. This is with the System Restore utility that allows you to jump back to previous Restore Points.

Before proceeding, it is important to understand that System Restore will not delete any of your personal documents such as photos, music, and Microsoft Word documents when you revert to a previous state. However, all system changes made between points, such as installing new drivers and new software, will be wiped out. It is also advised to close all open applications before restoring your computer.

Now that you know what to watch out for, follow these steps to restore your computer to a previous Restore Point:

1. Click the Start button, type in **System Restore,** and hit Enter.

2. After the System Restore utility has loaded, click Next on the first screen.

3. You will now see a list with the date, time, and a description of each Restore Point. There is also a Show more Restore Points checkbox on the screen that I advise checking, so you can see all available System Restore Points.

4. When you have the Restore Point selected that you want to revert to, select it and click Next.

5. Check the confirmation page, and then click Finish.

6. Click Yes on the final confirmation screen.

Your computer will now log you off and start the System Restore process. When completed, your computer will restart.

One of the best parts of System Restore is that you can always undoing the recent restore if restoring your computer did not solve your problem or created new problems. You can undo the recent restore by starting up System Restore again. You will see the undo option on the opening screen after restoring to a previous point.

System Recovery Console

The System Recovery Console in Windows 7 is a great new feature that allows you to fix your computer if it ever gets stuck in a state where it will not boot properly. A number of tools are included, such as Startup Repair, System Restore, System Image Recovery, Memory Diagnostics and access to Command Prompt. I'll go into more detail about the tools available in the System Recovery Console shortly but first, let's dive into how to access the console.

Accessing the System Recovery Console

There are two ways to access the System Recovery Console. The most popular is to boot the hidden recovery partition that was set up when Windows 7 was installed on your computer. This is done by pressing F8 on your keyboard right after you turn on your computer and after the POST is complete. If you hit F8 at the right time, a special boot menu is shown that will give you the option to repair your computer. On my computer, I start hitting F8 multiple times as soon as POST is finished, to make sure I catch the short window in which the F8 key works before the computer loads Windows normally.

After you select the Repair your computer option you will see a progress bar as the System Recovery Console is loaded. When complete, you will see the System Recovery Console main screen as shown in Figure 3-2.

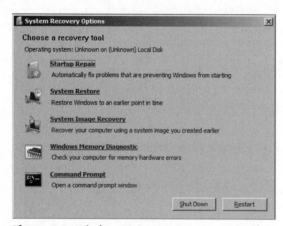

Figure 3-2: Windows 7 System Recovery Console

The previous method will work on the majority of Windows 7 installations, but it is dependent on the special hidden partition. If something happens to that partition, or Windows 7 was installed without creating that partition, then you will need to access the System Recovery Console with the System Recovery Console Boot CD.

If you have a Windows 7 installation DVD, then you can boot your computer with that and then select Repair my computer. However, if your computer came with Windows 7 preloaded, or if you lost your installation DVD, you can create your own System Recovery Console Boot CD/DVD within Windows 7.

On a Windows 7 computer with a CD/DVD burner, follow these steps to create a System Recovery Console CD/DVD:

1. Put a blank CDR/CDRW/DVDR/DVDRW in your CD/DVD burner drive.

2. Click the Start button, type in **Create System Repair Disc,** and then hit Enter.

3. Make sure the correct drive is selected and then click Create disc.

Now you can use your custom made System Recovery Console CD/DVD to access the same screen shown in Figure 3-2. Put the CD/DVD in when you turn on your computer and use the correct boot menu options for your computer to boot to the disc.

Using the System Recovery Console Tools

Now that you know how to access the System Recovery Console, I will go over the various tools available to fix your computer:

- Startup Repair — This tool inspects your Windows boot files and boot settings and tries to fix any problems that it detects that may prevent Windows from starting up properly.

- System Restore — This tool provides another way to restore to a previous Restore Point. If a tweak caused serious Windows problems, you can revert to an earlier Restore Point even if Windows will not load.

System Image Recovery — Here you can apply a backup image to your computer to restore everything on your computer including personal documents and files from a system image. I'll show you how to create a System Image in the next section.

- Windows Memory Diagnostic — This is a very useful memory test tool that helps you identify hardware problems with your memory. If you are experiencing random blue screens, try checking your memory. Bad memory is a common source of issues causing critical Windows components to crash.

- Command Prompt — The ultimate tool in any power user's toolbox.

As you can see, the System Recovery Console offers a wide array of valuable tools that can help you fix Windows in the event it will not start up. Next, I show you how to create a full system backup image.

Creating a Backup Image

Every computer user should create regular backup copies of the important data on their computer. Power users, including you, should create backup images of your computer so you can easily restore your entire computer to a perfect state from an image. Creating an image of your computer allows you to restore all your programs, personal data, and Windows settings without reinstalling Windows manually, reinstalling every application, and then copying your personal data back over.

When something bad happens, such as a hard drive failure or Windows being broken beyond repair, it is better to restore your computer from an image. That is why I suggest you follow the next section to create a backup image of your computer at least once a year.

Creating the Image

Windows 7 includes tools that help you create an image of your entire hard drive, burn it to a series of DVD discs, save it to a network share, or save it on another hard drive. I have a Windows Home Server in my home so I save backup images to that. If you don't have a network server available, you can always use writable DVD media or an external USB hard drive to store your backup. Regardless of the storage option you select, the steps are the same:

1. Click the Start button, type in **Backup and Restore,** and then hit Enter.

2. On top of the side menu, click Create a system image.

3. When the Create a system image utility loads, select where you want to store your image and click Next.

4. The following screen will confirm the settings. Click Start backup to begin, as shown in Figure 3-3.

When the backup starts, a progress screen will appear, as in Figure 3-4.

Figure 3-3: Creating a system image

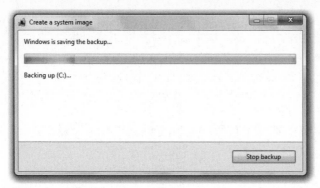

Figure 3-4: System image creation progress

When finished, store your backup data in a safe place. You will also be asked to create a System repair disk, but click No because you already did that in the last section.

Restoring a System Image

In the event you ever need to restore your backup system image, you will need to boot up into the System Recovery Console I covered earlier in this chapter. You can do that by pressing the F8 key right after the POST and after you turn on your computer and select Repair my computer. Alternatively, you can use the custom made System Recovery Console Boot CD/DVD that I showed you how to make, as well.

After you load the System Recovery Console, follow these steps:

1. Insert the last DVD of a backup set, or attach the external hard drive on which you stored the backup image.

2. Click System Image Recovery on the System Recover Options menu.

3. At this point the utility should find your backup (if you inserted the correct final DVD of a backup set or attached the correct external hard drive). If it doesn't, try clicking the Retry button. If you stored your backup on a network location, click Cancel on the Windows cannot find a system image on this computer screen.

4. Click Next on the initial welcome screen.

5. If you stored the image on a network share, click Advanced to locate the image on your network. Otherwise, skip this step.

6. When you see your image on the list, select it and click Next.

From this point on, follow the simple wizard to apply the image to your computer.

Summary

This chapter covered how to tweak your computer safely by protecting it with System Restore. It showed you how you can recover your computer with the System Recovery Console followed by creating and restoring a full system image.

You are now ready to begin tweaking the interface, performance, and security of Windows 7.

Customizing Windows 7

In This Part

Customizing the Startup

Windows 7 has a great new look, but after a while, the new look can get old. With the help of some cool tools and tricks, you can customize many components of Windows 7.

This chapter guides you through customizing the logon screen. This screen can be customized in several ways, such as customizing the user pictures and various settings that will allow you to increase your privacy and change the way the logon screen behaves. I even show you how to change your logon screen background.

Customizing the Logon Screen

Windows 7 includes a slightly improved logon screen similar to the one used in Windows Vista. Gone is the Windows NT–style classic logon screen with which many domain users are familiar (because it was included in the last several releases of Windows). The new Welcome screen, as I called it in Windows XP, is now your only choice for logging on. Not much changed except for a few visual enhancements that make the screen look more professional and make it fit in with the theme of the rest of the operating system.

New to Windows 7 and Vista is a more secure logon system that requires all components to be digitally signed by Microsoft. If any of the logon files are modified the digital signature is destroyed and you will no longer be able to log on. This prevents malicious software from hijacking the logon process, but it also makes it next to impossible for people like us who want to customize the logon screen; you can no longer just hack a system file and replace some resources in it.

The days of customizing every single element on the logon screen are over until someone writes an application that extends the logon screen or someone releases a patch that disables the digital signature requirement.

Is this the end of customizing the logon screen? Not at all! You can still do a lot of useful tweaks to the logon screen that will give it a personal touch, such as changing user pictures, hiding users, customizing the logon screen screen-saver, and more.

Changing User Pictures

Each user set up on your computer can associate an image that appears next to his or her name on the logon screen, as shown in Figure 4-1. By default, you have the option to select a picture for your account when you install Windows. However, the screen that allows you to pick an image offers only a small selection of the pictures available to you. In addition, if you do not like the images that Windows has to offer, you can select any image file.

Figure 4-1: The logon screen with an image next to the user's name

The process of changing a user's image is simple. Just perform the following steps, and you will have it changed in no time:

1. Click the Start button and then click your user picture, as shown in Figure 4-2.

Figure 4-2: Clicking your user picture to access your account settings

2. Select Change your picture from the middle of the list.

3. You will now be shown all available Windows user images. If you find one you like, click it, and then hit the Change Picture button.

4. If you prefer a different photo, click Browse for more pictures and use any image file on your PC.

5. After you have selected your new image, your setting change is instantly applied. You can now close User Accounts panel.

Your user image on the logon screen is now changed; you have also updated the image used on the Start menu.

Hiding Users on the Logon Screen

One of the features of the new logon screen is the list of all the user accounts on the computer. What if you created an account for running services? You do not want other users of your computer to have the option to log on to that account, because you designated it only to be used by applications running as a service. Maybe you have a secret user account that you don't want anyone to see. With the help of a simple registry tweak, it is possible to hide any account on the logon screen so no one will know it exists.

Hidden away in the registry is the feature that Microsoft used in the past to hide system accounts from the logon screen. In the next few steps, I show you how to re-create the missing registry code so that you can use this feature again to hide your accounts:

1. Click the Start button, type **regedit** in the Search box, and then press Enter.

2. When Registry Editor loads, navigate through HKEY_LOCAL_MACHINE, SOFTWARE, Microsoft, Windows NT, CurrentVersion, and Winlogon.

3. You must now create a new key. Right-click the Winlogon folder, select New, and then select Key. Name this new key **SpecialAccounts**.

4. Right-click the new SpecialAccounts key, select New, and then select Key. Call this new key **UserList**.

5. Now you are ready to add the name of the account that you want to hide. To add a name, right-click and select a new DWORD (32-bit) value, as shown in Figure 4-3.

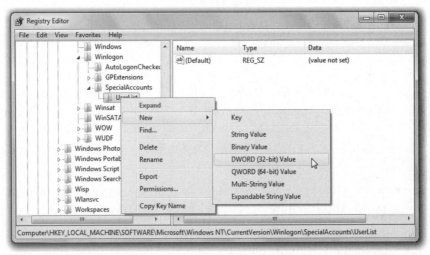

Figure 4-3: Using the Registry Editor to add another DWORD Value for the name of the account that will be hidden on the logon screen

6. When the new DWORD is created, enter the name of the user's account as the name of the DWORD. After you have done this, you can close the Registry Editor.

After you log off and back on or reboot, the user will not be displayed on the logon screen. If you want to hide all accounts and just have a User name and Password box, the next section is for you. If you opt for that method, you can hide all accounts and still log on to them. You just need to remember the username and the password because no accounts will be listed anymore.

If you ever change your mind and want the account to display on the logon screen again, just delete the DWORD that you made in the system registry, and everything will be back to the way it once was.

Clearing the Last User Logon

Every time you boot up your PC, all computer accounts and users who have logged on to it display on the logon screen. This can be a big security risk because it shows the usernames of all accounts that someone can try to use to break into the computer. In addition, the logon screen can become cluttered with many user accounts. Therefore, it might be a good idea to enable the Do not display last user name policy. In previous versions of Windows that used the classic logon screen, this policy would just clear the User name text box so that an attacker would have no clue about the last account used to log on. With the removal of the classic logon screen in 7, this policy behaves slightly differently by removing the Account list on the logon screen and turning on basic User name and Password boxes, as shown in Figure 4-4.

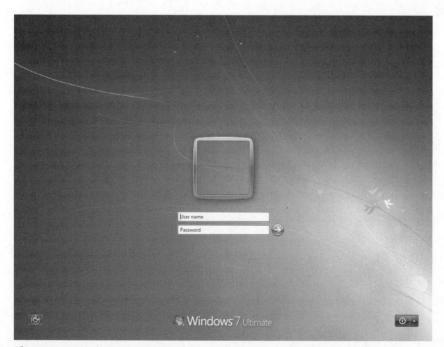

Figure 4-4: Basic User name and Password boxes on the logon screen

Using the policy is easy, if you choose to enable it. If so, just follow these steps:

1. Click the Start button, type **secpol.msc**, and press Enter.

2. When the Local Security Policy editor loads, navigate through Local Policies and then Security Options.

3. Locate the Interactive logon: Do not display last user name policy. Right-click it and select Properties.

4. On the Local Security Settings tab, select Enable, and then click OK.

5. Close the Local Security Policy editor and you are finished.

For those of you that don't have SecPol.msc in your version of Windows (only Professional version and higher) you will have to set the registry key manually:

1. Click the Start button, type in **Regedit**, and hit Enter.

2. Navigate through HKEY_LOCAL_MACHINE, SOFTWARE, Microsoft, Windows, CurrentVersion, Policies, then System.

3. Right-click dontdisplaylastusername and select Modify.

4. Set the value to 1 and click OK.

As soon as you log off or reboot, the new logon screen settings will be present.

Changing the Logon Screen Screensaver

If you turn on your computer and let it sit at the logon screen long enough, eventually the screensaver will appear. This setting can be tweaked so that the screensaver that you want to see instead is set and not the boring Windows default. Unlike changing your screensaver for your account when you are logged on, it is possible to change the logon screen screensaver setting only by using the registry. With the help of a few quick registry hacks, you can fine-tune the screensaver that is displayed and other settings, such as the screensaver Timeout value that determines how long before the screensaver is activated.

Follow these simple steps to customize your logon screensaver:

1. Start the Registry Editor. Click the Start button, type **regedit** in the box, and press Enter.

2. When the Registry Editor starts up, navigate through HKEY_USERS, .DEFAULT, Control Panel, and Desktop.

3. First, you need to tell Windows the logon screensaver is active. Right-click the Desktop key and select New and then String Value. Name the value **ScreenSaveActive**. Next, set the value to 1 by right-clicking it and selecting Modify. Enter 1 and click OK.

4. Set the amount of time the system waits after the last activity was detected before starting the screensaver. To do this, right-click the Desktop key and select New and then String Value. Name the new entry **ScreenSaveTimeOut**. Then, set the value to the number of seconds you want to wait before the screensaver starts by right-clicking the new value and selecting Modify. I like to set mine to 300 seconds for 5 minutes.

5. Now you need to set the screensaver you want to display. To do this, right-click the Desktop key again and select New and then String Value. Name this value **SCRNSAVE.EXE** and set its value to the full path to the .scr file. For example, I use `C:\windows\system32\Mystify.scr` for the Mystify screensaver. Refer to Table 4-1 for a list of Windows screensavers and the paths you can use.

6. Close Registry Editor. You are now finished. After a reboot, you will see your new screensaver.

Table 4-1: Windows 7 Screensavers

SCREENSAVER NAME	FULL PATH
Bubbles	`C:\Windows\System32\Bubbles.scr`
Mystify	`C:\Windows\System32\Mystify.scr`
Photos	`C:\Windows\System32\PhotoScreensaver.scr`
Ribbons	`C:\Windows\System32\Ribbons.scr`
Blank Screen	`C:\Windows\System32\scrnsave.scr`
3D Text	`C:\Windows\System32\ssText3d.scr`

Displaying a Security Message

Would you like to display a message to your users before they can log on? Are any instructions necessary for users of your computers, such as "Do not shut down this computer!" or possibly a security warning informing unauthorized users that they are breaking the law if they try to log on to your laptop? All these are possible with the help of Group Policy. With just a few clicks, you can easily display a message to your visitors, as shown in Figure 4-5.

Using the Local Security Policy editor, you can turn this feature on. Follow these steps to activate it on your PC:

1. Click the Start button, type **secpol.msc**, and press Enter.

2. When the Local Security Policy editor loads, navigate through Local Policies and then Security Options.

3. Locate the Interactive logon: Message title for users attempting to log on policy. Right-click it and select Properties.

4. On the Local Security Settings tab, type a title that you would like to use for your message, and click OK.

5. Locate the Interactive logon: Message text for users attempting to log on policy. Right-click it and select Properties.

6. On the Local Security Settings tab, type your message and click OK.

7. Close the Local Security Policy editor; you are finished.

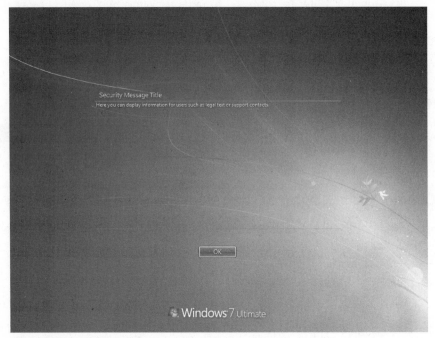

Figure 4-5: Security message on a Windows 7 logon screen

As soon as you log off or reboot, the security message settings will be activated.

Enabling Num Lock by Default

If you have a password that has both numbers and letters and you frequently use the number pad to enter part of your password, this hack is for you. I cannot count the number of times that I started to type my password and was then presented with a logon error telling me that my password was incorrect. I would sit there staring at the screen for a second before I realized that Num Lock on my keyboard was not on.

This is a great hack for every desktop computer with a full-size keyboard and a separate number pad. Turning on Num Lock by default on a laptop is not a good idea because most laptops do not usually have a separate number pad. Enabling this feature on a laptop will result in almost half your keyboard functioning as the number pad, and you would be much better off using the numbers instead of the letters. To get started, follow these steps:

1. Click the Start menu, type **regedit**, and press Enter.

2. When the Registry Editor loads, navigate through HKEY_USERS, .DEFAULT, Control Panel, and Keyboard.

3. Locate the InitialKeyboardIndicators entry, right-click it, and select Modify. To enable Num Lock, enter **2** into the box. If you want to disable it, enter 80000000 into the box with the Base set to Hexadecimal (80000000 is the hexadecimal equivalent of 2147483648 which is the system default value).

4. Then click OK to save the changes. That's it!

If you are on a laptop and you attempted to enable Num Lock — even though I told you not to — and need to fix your system, repeat the preceding directions but replace the value of InitialKeyboardIndicators with 80000000 to disable the feature.

Changing the Logon Screen Background

How would you like to customize the background image used on the logon screen just as easily as you change the background image on your desktop? I wrote a free utility called the Tweaks.com Logon Changer for Windows 7 that allows you to change your logon background with just a few clicks.

Microsoft included functionality to allow OEMs to customize the logon screen for the first time in Windows 7. Although there are restrictions on the file size (about 245KB), the wallpaper can be set with a registry key and file copy.

To set the screen manually, use an image editing program to compress your image and save it as backgroundDefault.jpg in `C:\Windows\system32\oobe\info\backgrounds\`. You will need to create that path if it does not already exist on your computer. Then open up Registry Editor and navigate through HKEY_LOCAL_MACHINE, SOFTWARE, Microsoft, Windows, CurrentVersion, Authentication, LogonUI, and Background. If Background does not exist right-click LogonUI, select New and then Key, and then name it Background. Now locate OEMBackground listed below (Default). If it does not exist right-click Background and select New and then DWORD and name it OEMBackground. Set the value of OEMBackground to 1. Test your changes by logging off.

To make changing the logon background simpler and much quicker, I created the Tweaks.com Logon Changer. My utility uses the same OEM functionality but completely automates the file copy, registry changes, and the image resize and compression so it fits within the max file size imposed by Microsoft. On top of these features, it also shows a live preview of what your new logon screen would look like.

Head over to `tweaks.com/software/tweakslogon/` and download a copy of the free utility. After you have it downloaded, simply extract it to any folder on your computer and run TweaksLogon.exe. When started, you will see the main preview screen displaying your current logon background, as shown in Figure 4-6.

Figure 4-6: Tweaks.com Logon Changer for Windows 7

Click Change Logon Screen and select a new background image. If the image you selected is larger than the size limit, the application will prompt you for action as shown in Figure 4-7.

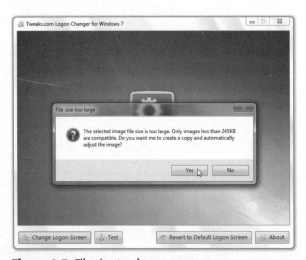

Figure 4-7: File size too large screen

Click Yes to have the utility automatically resize and recompress the image to fit under the limit. Alternatively, you can click No and resize and recompress the image on your own and then select the new file.

To see the new logon background in action, click the Test button. At any time you can click the Revert to Default Logon Screen button to undo any changes.

Summary

This first customizing chapter can be thought of as the first step in the complete customization of every possible aspect of your Windows 7 install. You started with tweaking the way the logon screen behaves and then made some major changes to the look by changing the background image.

The next chapter helps you customize the user navigation components of Windows 7. First, you learn all about customizing the Start menu. Then you learn how to customize the next most used component of Windows — the taskbar.

CHAPTER 5

Customizing User Navigation

Customizing user navigation is the next stop on the Windows 7 customizing road trip. In the previous chapter, with the help of some cool tweaks, you were able to change and improve the boot and logon screens. This chapter picks up where Chapter 4 left off and shows you how to customize and improve the visual navigation elements of Windows 7.

This chapter starts with customizing the look and the content of the cool new Start menu. The improved Start menu in Windows 7 has many useful new features, and I show how you can use them best. Then, I show you how you can customize the new program list and customize almost everything you see. If you don't like the new Start menu, you can get the old classic Start menu back. Then, you can improve and customize the classic Start menu with some cool hacks.

You also learn how to customize the taskbar on the bottom of your screen. The taskbar is an essential part of navigating your computer. I show you how to customize and improve its features and give you some new ideas about how you can use it to dramatically improve your experiences with Windows 7.

Customizing the Start Menu

First appearing in Windows XP, the new Start menu that replaced the classic program list has evolved into a comprehensive starting point for your PC. Improved for Windows 7, the Start menu offers the ability to search your programs and jump directly to various components of Windows Additionally, the Search box can launch commands similar to a traditional Run box. Everything can now be accessed from the Start menu.

Today, tools and hacks allow you to customize the Start menu. Almost everything on it is customizable. You can add and remove icons and shortcuts, and you can even change the way it looks. You can even change the way the features on it, such as the Search box, work.

After you finish reading these next few sections, you will have transformed your Start menu into something that works better for you and is much more useful for your everyday tasks.

Customizing Navigation Shortcuts

You will find many new navigation links on the Start menu that will help you navigate to various parts of Windows. All these shortcut buttons on the right side of the Start menu can be customized. Many can be removed completely, and others can be added. By default, you will see a button with your username followed by buttons for Documents, Pictures, and Music. All these buttons are shortcuts to your personal libraries. The next set — Games and Computer — are more functional navigation shortcuts that allow you to jump to the most common system components. The last four shortcuts offer you a way to access system configuration components such as Control Panel, Devices and Printers, Default Programs, and a convenient shortcut to Help and Support for new users.

Some shortcuts are not displayed, such as the classic Run button and Favorites. Other features, such as Display as a Menu which converts buttons into a nested menu, are also disabled. This feature can be very useful in some situations. For example, if you enable Display as Menu on the Computer button, you will see a list of drivers that you can jump directly to. This eliminates a few extra clicks that will help you get where you want to go faster.

All these features and shortcuts are customizable on one screen. Follow these steps to access the Start menu Customization screen:

1. Right-click the Start button and click Properties.

2. On the Start Menu tab, click the Customize button on the top right of the window. This loads the Customize Start Menu window, as shown in Figure 5-1.

3. Scroll through the list and make changes to the items as you see fit. Refer to the sections that follow for my recommendations.

4. When finished adjusting the options, click OK twice to close Taskbar Properties. Your changes will be live instantly.

Now that you know how to change the settings, the next few sections guide you through my recommendations for creating a clean and powerful Start menu.

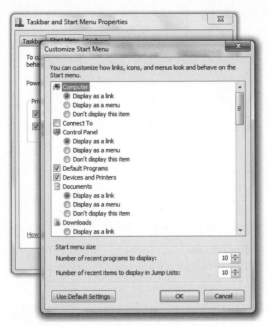

Figure 5-1: Customizing the Start Menu window

Hiding User Folders

Having all the user folders on the Start menu can be useful for some but not for me. You are already given a button that has your username on it. Through that button, you can access your music, pictures, and documents. Having these extra folders visible is just cluttering the Start menu and taking up real estate that could be better spent.

To clean up the user folders, set these options on the Customize Start Menu window (shown in Figure 5-1):

- **Documents:** Select Don't display this item.
- **Music:** Select Don't display this item.
- **Pictures:** Select Don't display this item.
- **Games:** Select Don't display this item. You can reach the games through the normal Start/All Programs menu.

Customizing Feature and Management Shortcuts

The feature shortcut and management buttons such as Help and Support also take up a lot of space on your Start menu. I rarely find myself using any of these buttons with the exception of Computer. The others I have pinned to my taskbar, or you can find them in the Notification area. Here are my recommendations for these two sections:

- **Connect To:** Clear the checkbox. You can access this in the Notification area.

- **Computer:** Set to Display as a menu.

- **Default Programs:** Clear the checkbox.

- **Help:** Clear the checkbox.

- **Network:** Clear the checkbox. You can access this in the Notification area.

- **Devices and Printers:** Check. The only other place you can get this is in Control Panel, which is inconvenient if you print a lot.

- **Run command:** Check if you like the old Run button. You can use the Search box now as a Run box, too, but some may still like the old Run box. I do!

You are now finished customizing your Start menu. If you followed my recommendations, your Start menu will now look similar to Figure 5-2.

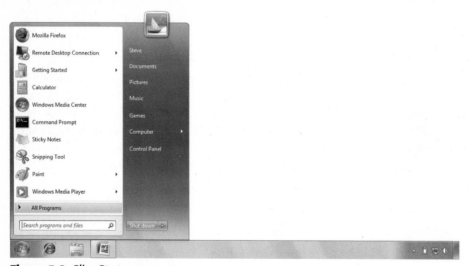

Figure 5-2: Slim Start menu

Customizing the Frequently Run Programs List

Every time you launch an application on your PC, Windows is watching. It keeps track of the applications you run to derive the list of frequently run programs. You can find the list of frequently run programs on the left side of the Start menu. This program list can be useful for quickly accessing your applications instead of navigating through the entire All Programs menu.

There are a few cool tweaks for the Frequently Run Programs list that will allow you to customize it to make it more useful for you. The next three sections show you how you can modify the icon size, change the number shown, hide applications from showing up, and pin applications to the list.

Customizing Icon Size

One way that I like to customize my Start menu is to decrease the size of the icons on the left so that I can fit more icons on the screen. Figure 5-3 shows the difference between a Start menu that has been switched to use small icons and the normal Start menu.

Figure 5-3: The difference between the two Start menu icon sizes

Changing the icons is easy. You just need to change one setting within the Start menu properties. To do so, follow these steps:

1. Move your mouse cursor over the Start button and right-click it, and then click Properties.

2. This brings up the Start Menu Properties menu that you used in the preceding section. Here you want to click the Customize button.

3. Scroll all the way to the bottom of the list and uncheck Use large icons.

4. Click OK to save your change and click OK again to finish.

You have now made some more room so that you can display more frequently run programs on the Start menu. When you click the Start menu, you may notice that there are not any more programs showing up. That is because you also have to adjust the number of programs that will appear. The next section shows you how to adjust how many program shortcuts are displayed.

Tweaking the Number Displayed

By now you have changed the icon size of the Frequently Run Programs list so that you can fit more icons on the screen. Now you can increase the number of programs that will be displayed so that your list of programs will become even more useful. If you decide that you do not want to change the size of the icons, don't worry. You can still change the number of programs that display; you just can't display as many.

Changing the number of programs depends completely on personal preference. Do you like having a huge Start menu that stretches from the taskbar to the top of the screen? Do you like a Start menu with a small footprint? The resolution settings of your screen determine the maximum number of programs that can be displayed. If you accidentally choose too many programs, Windows lets you know by giving you a friendly pop-up message when you try to click your Start menu after the change.

Now that you have an idea of the number of programs that your computer can display, you are ready to get started. To increase the number of programs, do the following:

1. Right-click the Start button and select Properties to bring up the Taskbar and Start Menu Properties settings.

2. Click the Customize button to show the Customize Start Menu options.

3. On this screen, locate the Start Menu Size section and the Number of recent programs to display box. You can adjust this value by clicking the up and down buttons or just by selecting all the text and entering in a new number.

TIP If you want to save even more room and never use the Internet Explorer and Mail client links on the top of the Frequently Run Programs list, clear all the boxes in the Show on Start menu box on the Customize Start Menu window.

4. After you have entered the number of programs you want displayed, click OK to save your changes.

5. Then click OK again and you are finished.

The best way to set the number of programs is to experiment with several different values until you get your Start menu looking the way you want it. After you find the value that is just right, you will have a much-improved Start menu.

Keeping Programs off the List

You have a top-secret program that you do not want anyone else to know you have. Every time you run a program on your computer, Windows 7 records it and places the shortcut on your Frequently Run Programs list. Sometimes this is not always a good thing and can cause a privacy or job-security problem.

For example, let's use the situation of a guy named Larry. Larry is a big Solitaire player. It is not the best game, but he likes it because it is an alternative to actually doing work. Every time Larry plays Solitaire, Windows 7 automatically adds the game to the Frequently Run Programs list. In this situation, program tracking creates a big problem for Larry. He is concerned that one of his fellow employees or manager might see his Frequently Run Programs list and discover where he spends his time. What should he do? First, Larry should buy a copy of *Windows 7 Tweaks*, and then he should follow these steps:

1. Click the Start menu and select Run. Type **regedit** and click OK to start the Registry Editor.

2. Expand the HKEY_CLASSES_ROOT folder.

3. Search through the list of folders until you find the folder called Applications and expand that, too.

4. Now you will see a list of every executable file for the programs installed on your computer. To hide a program from the Frequently Run Programs list, expand the folder that is the executable for the program. To hide Solitaire, expand the Solitaire.exe folder.

TIP If you do not know the name of the executable file that a program shortcut points to, you can easily look this up by right-clicking the shortcut and selecting Properties. In the Properties box, you will see a full path to where the file is located and the name of the file.

5. Can't find a folder called Solitaire.exe? That is because some Windows applications are not listed. If your application *is* listed, skip this step. Otherwise, you need to create a new registry key. To do so, select the Applications key within HKEY_CLASSES_ROOT. Right-click and select New, and then select Key. Type in the name of the executable for the name of the key. For Solitaire, name the key Solitaire.exe.

6. Now that you have found the folder for the application or have created one, expand it so that you can see all its values. Then right-click the executable's folder that you just created or found in the registry. Select New, and then select String value. Type **NoStartPage** as the name of the string variable, as shown in Figure 5-4.

7. Close the Registry Editor and then log off and then back on. You will never see Solitaire in your Frequently Run Programs list again.

Now Larry can play as much Solitaire at work as he wants without having to worry about it showing up in his Frequently Run Programs list.

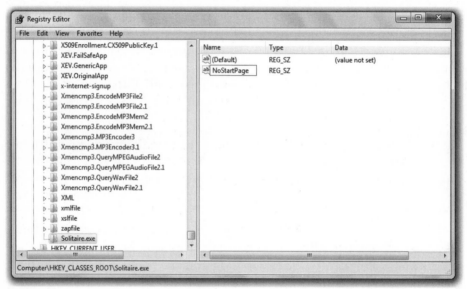

Figure 5-4: Using Registry Editor to hide applications from the Frequently Run Programs list

Pinning Programs

I use the Calculator application all the time when I am using my computer. My desk calculator is always lost, and I don't want to waste time looking for it when I just need to do a quick calculation. Every time that I want to use the Calculator application, I have to click the Start menu, select All Programs, and then navigate up through the Accessories menu until I can finally click the Calculator app. There is a much easier way to access this program.

Instead of navigating through the program listings, I can just pin the program to the Start menu. Pinning a program is a simple task that allows the program that you pin to appear on the Start menu just above the Frequently Run Programs list. If you pin a program shortcut, it appears on the top of the Start menu.

Navigating through the entire Start menu to launch a program you use all the time is a waste of time. Why waste your time? Pin your most commonly used programs today!

1. Start your pinning adventure by navigating through the Start menu as you normally do to launch a program. Navigate to a program that you use all the time, such as the Calculator application in the Accessories menu.

2. After you have highlighted the item, right-click the item and select Pin to Start menu. That's it. Your program will now appear directly on the Start menu.

Now, say that you got a little too excited and pinned too many applications and want to remove some. What should you do? Just click the Start button again to bring up the Start menu and highlight the program you want to unpin. Then right-click the item and select Unpin from the Start menu.

Pinning your favorite programs is a simple solution to speeding up access to your programs.

Customizing the Program List and Search

The actual program listings are the last component of the Start menu that you can customize. In Windows 7, users of the new Start menu have a new way of accessing the program list using the Search box. These next few sections show you how to customize the Search box feature of the new Start menu and show you tweaks for the way the program list displays in both the new Start menu and the classic Windows Start menu.

Adjusting Scope

The new Search box on the bottom of the Start menu in Windows 7 is an extremely versatile box where you can do everything from executing programs to searching your entire computer for a specific document. By default, when you search for some text, it will search all the indexed locations. When I am using this feature, I just want it to search for programs in my Start menu, not search all my e-mails and other documents all over my computer. Why? I like a clean-looking Start menu, and when the search scope is set to something very wide, the results can become cluttered with useless information. As I mentioned previously, when I search in the Start menu Search box, I expect it just to search the Start menu and nothing more. Thankfully, Microsoft has given a way for you to customize the scope of where this Search box searches. Follow these steps to customize your search scope:

1. Right-click the Start button and select Properties.

2. Click the Customize button on the Start Menu tab.

3. Scroll down the list of options until you get to the search settings, as shown in Figure 5-5.

4. Here, I like to select Don't search under Search other files and libraries.

5. Click OK to save and then OK again to close the Properties window.

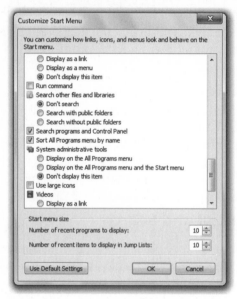

Figure 5-5: Start menu search options

After you are finished disabling the extra default search locations, you will notice that your search results are presented faster and are now less cluttered. Keep in mind that you can always still use the Search button on the right side of the Start menu to search for documents, favorites, communications, and files.

Disabling New Program Highlights

Program highlights was a great feature when I first started to use Windows XP. This feature would automatically highlight any new programs that you installed so that you could easily find them on the Start menu the first few times that you wanted to run the application. However, after I used this feature for a few months, I started to get annoyed with it. It never seemed to work correctly, and applications that I installed quite some time ago seemed as though they were going to be highlighted forever. Unfortunately, it is also included in Windows 7. So, as soon as I installed Windows 7 on my PC, I was haunted by the return of this once-great feature. Just follow these steps to get rid of those annoying highlights:

1. Right-click the Start button and select Properties.

2. Click the top Customize button for the Start menu.

3. Scroll through the list and uncheck Highlight Newly Installed Programs.

4. Click OK to save your changes.

5. Click OK once more to close the Properties window.

Now you will not have to worry about the programs that sometimes seem to be highlighted randomly.

Disabling Pop-Up Help

Ever notice that when you hover your cursor over a program listing in the Start menu a little help box pops up? This help feature is called Balloon Help. If you don't know what a program does, hold your cursor over the program for a second or so and a little message will fade in telling you what it is — if the programmer has set up this feature of the program. For programs that do not have this feature set up for their shortcut, the "balloon" just tells users where the program is located on their computer.

This feature can be useful for a beginning computer user. However, it can be another annoyance for more advanced users. If you don't need this feature, why not disable it? Follow these steps to get rid of this feature:

1. Click the Start menu and select Run, and then type **regedit** in the box and click OK.

2. After the Registry Editor has loaded, navigate through HKEY_CURRENT_USER, Software, Microsoft, Windows, CurrentVersion, Explorer, and Advanced.

3. Right-click the entry called ShowInfoTip and select Modify.

4. Set the value to 0 to disable this feature, and click OK.

5. Close the Registry Editor and log off and back on so that the feature can be removed.

You are now finished with the last section on customizing the Start menu and program listing. Now you can move on to customizing the classic Start menu.

Customizing the Taskbar

Windows 7 includes a brand new taskbar that was designed to give the user more control and more flexibility with what they do with their computer. What can be described as a giant Quick Launch bar, the new taskbar allows you to move applications around and pin applications so they remain on the taskbar even when closed. The first thing you will notice is the absence of labels by default on program listings. That creates a very clean look and allows Windows to cram a lot of open applications in a small amount of space.

On top of the visual changes, the taskbar includes new functionality such as Jump Lists, Aero Peek, and an improved Notification area. This section shows you how to customize these new features and more to personalize your taskbar.

Pinning Applications

The Quick Launch bar on the taskbar in previous versions of Windows was my favorite component to customize. I spent hours organizing and ordering short-cuts to numerous applications aiming to create the perfect setup. In Windows 7, Microsoft turned my world upside down by removing the Quick Launch toolbar from the taskbar. Thankfully, Microsoft realized the value of Quick Launch and built the same functionality into the new taskbar.

Now the taskbar is not just a place to view open applications, you can start applications from it too. This is done by pinning application shortcuts to the taskbar. Pinning will create a shortcut that permanently stays on your taskbar, just like an old Quick Launch shortcut. Different from previous versions of Windows is how the shortcuts appear. Open but not active applications have a border around them. Active, open applications have a border around them and a glass highlight effect. Closed, pinned applications just show up as an icon. All three types of applications are shown in Figure 5-6.

Figure 5-6: The new Windows 7 taskbar

The process of pinning an application can be done two ways:

- Drag any shortcut from your desktop or Start menu onto the taskbar.
- Right-click any open taskbar application and select Pin this program to taskbar.

Folders and drives that you attempt to pin will show up in the Explorer Jump List instead of an individual icon on the taskbar. This was a design decision made by Microsoft to clean up the taskbar and keep it organized.

Removing a pinned application is as simple as right-clicking the pinned application on the taskbar and selecting Unpin this program from the taskbar.

Modifying Icon Locations

The taskbar in Windows 7 was designed with *you* in mind. For the first time you can determine the location of each program. Even the location of programs you open yourself are currently open.

Moving your programs are very simple, just left-click and hold any icon and drag it where you want it to be. Applications that are not pinned will always start up by default at the end of the list, but you can move them again as soon as they load.

Tweaking Jump Lists

Jump Lists are a major component of the new taskbar. When you right-click an application, you are presented with a number of new options relevant to that application. Depending on the application, you are shown recent items, common tasks, and more. Most applications will show recently opened items, such as Word documents when you right-click Microsoft Word. Other applications such as Windows Messenger and Windows Media player have enhanced Jump Lists that allow you to do common tasks as shown in Figure 5-7. If you want to appear offline on Windows Messenger, just right-click the taskbar shortcut and you can quickly change your setting.

Figure 5-7: Windows 7 Jump Lists

Overall, Jump Lists are a great addition to the new taskbar because they allow you to jump to tasks faster than before. To make Jump Lists work better for you there is a tweak that will help you customize the feature.

Adjusting the Recent List

All applications that participate in the Windows MRU (most recently used) list automatically have a recent items component on their Jump List. Microsoft Word shows recent documents; Internet Explorer shows recent web sites; and Microsoft Paint shows recently opened pictures on their Jump Lists. By default, Windows shows the ten most recent used items. If you think that is too much or too little, I'm going to show you how to tweak that setting.

Windows sets a maximum of 60 recent items possible to show in the Jump List, although I never see that many even when I have it set to the max. I recommend that you set the value between 5 and 20 to keep the recent list useful. The setting to change the value is a little hard to find because it is not where you would expect it. Follow these steps to customize how many items are displayed in your recent lists:

1. Right-click the Start button and select Properties.

2. Click the Customize button on the Start Menu tab.

3. Under Start menu size, adjust the Number of recent items to display in Jump Lists box, as shown in Figure 5-8.

4. Click OK twice and you are finished.

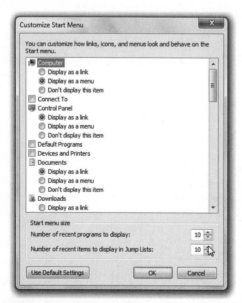

Figure 5-8: Adjusting the number of recent items to display

Enable Classic Taskbar Look and Behavior

The Windows 7 taskbar has a clean appearance with just the icons of opened and pinned applications grouped together by program. Microsoft realized that not all users would like the new look and grouping so they built in the ability to turn labels back on. The result is what I call the classic taskbar look and behavior as shown in Figure 5-9.

Figure 5-9: Windows 7 taskbar with labels turned back on

Similar to previous versions of Windows, the program label look and no application grouping is helpful for users that dislike the new taskbar and want a familiar look. Windows 7 offers three settings that allow you to configure the taskbar look and behavior:

- Always combine, hide labels — Default taskbar behavior
- Combine when taskbar is full — Labels are enabled
- Never combine — Labels are enabled

I don't recommend using the Never combine setting because it will make finding programs very difficult when you have a lot of windows and applications open. Instead, I would use Combine when taskbar is full as a good way to achieve the classic look and behavior.

To make the changes, follow these steps:

1. Right-click the Start button and select Properties.
2. Click the Taskbar tab.
3. Locate the Taskbar Buttons drop-down list and make your selection.
4. Click OK or Apply to see the new setting in action.

If you want the true classic look of small icons combined with the classic look and behavior, then the next section is for you.

Customize Taskbar Icon Sizes

I always like to customize the taskbar icon size on my laptop because it has a small screen. The large taskbar icons look great on my desktop LCD monitors that run at high resolutions but they take up too much space on the small screen of my laptop. Customizing this setting also allows you to fit many more pinned and open applications on the taskbar. As you can see in Figure 5-10, there is a big difference between small and large icons on the taskbar.

Figure 5-10: Comparison of taskbar icon sizes

Enabling small icons is set in Taskbar and Start Menu Properties:

1. Right-click the Start button and select Properties.

2. Click the Taskbar tab.

3. Check Use small icons located under Taskbar appearance.

4. Click OK or Apply to see the result.

Tweaking Taskbar Preview Delay

Taskbar previews have been improved in Windows 7 with Aero Peek that allows you to take a quick peek at a window by hovering over its taskbar preview. Also new to Windows 7 are previews of each tab open within Internet Explorer and other applications that support the new taskbar API. Instead of viewing only the currently open tab in IE, you can view all the tabs and jump directly to a specific tab.

All the new features add a lot to the new taskbar but my biggest complaint is the delay before the taskbar previews are shown. I want to use the new features but the amount of time I have to hover over a taskbar application is too long.

This can be tweaked with a simple registry hack:

1. Click the Start button, type in **regedit,** and hit Enter.

2. When Registry Editor is started, navigate through HKEY_CURRENT_USER, Software, Microsoft, Windows, CurrentVersion, Explorer and Advanced.

3. Right-click Advanced and select New and then DWORD (32-bit) Value. Name the new value ExtendedUIHoverTime.

4. Right-click the new ExtendedUIHoverTime value you just created and select Modify.

5. Enter the new value in milliseconds and click OK. The default value is 400, which is 400 milliseconds. I like to set mine to 100.

6. Reboot and test your new setting.

Restore Classic Quick Launch Bar

The classic Quick Launch bar was a great way to start your programs in previous versions of Windows. With the new taskbar in Windows 7, the Quick Launch bar was removed and replaced with the application pinning feature. The ability to pin an application to the taskbar is nice but it does not exactly replicate the old behavior of the Quick Launch bar.

Although the Quick Launch bar was removed in Windows 7, Microsoft left the ability to add more toolbars on the taskbar as in previous versions of Windows. We can exploit the toolbar feature to create a new toolbar pointing to the old Quick Launch location. Follow these steps to resurrect the Quick Launch bar:

1. Right-click the taskbar and select Toolbars and then New toolbar.

2. On the New Toolbar - Choose a folder screen, type in **%AppData%\Microsoft\Internet Explorer\Quick Launch** and click Select Folder, as shown in Figure 5-11.

Figure 5-11: Restoring the classic Quick Launch toolbar

3. The Quick Launch toolbar will be displayed on the far right of the taskbar, but you are not finished yet. Next, make sure that the taskbar is not locked so you can customize the toolbar that you just created. You can do that by right-clicking the toolbar and making sure Lock the taskbar is not checked.

4. After you have verified the taskbar is not locked or have unlocked the taskbar, you will be able to remove the Quick Launch toolbar label. Right-click the Quick Launch label and select Show title to disable that feature.

5. Right-click the new toolbar again and select Show Text to disable that feature as well.

6. The toolbar should begin to look familiar now. The last step is to position and size the Quick Launch bar to the location you want on the taskbar. You can resize it by left-clicking and holding on to the gripper bar on the left of the toolbar. Then, just drag left or right to resize. If you want to move it back to where it normally is, to the Start menu, right-click the gripper bar on the left of the normal taskbar and drag it right. That will make the new taskbar icons and the toolbar you just created switch locations.

If you want to replicate the full classic Windows taskbar look, I suggest you also follow the Customize Taskbar Icon Sizes tweak and Enable Classic Taskbar Look and Behavior tweak I mentioned earlier in this chapter. The combination of all three tweaks is a great help to users that like the old behavior and look of the Windows taskbar.

Modifying the Taskbar Location

The Windows taskbar is always seen on the bottom of the screen, but did you know that you can move it to any side you want? It is possible to move the task-bar and create a very different look in Windows 7. Figure 5-12 shows what your screen might look like if you move your taskbar to the left side of the screen.

Moving the taskbar is simple. There are just four basic steps:

1. Right-click the Start button and select Properties.

2. Click the Taskbar tab.

3. Locate the Taskbar location on the screen drop-down box and select the position you want to use.

4. Click OK or Apply and view your new location.

Customizing the Notification Area

Over the years the Notification area, previously known as the system tray, has become more and more cluttered. It seems as though just about every appli-cation you install wants to create a Notification area icon when it is running. In Windows 7, Microsoft finally decided enough is enough and cleaned up the Notification area by creating a new overflow container. Now when any applica-tion creates a Notification area icon it does not show up by default. Instead, you have to click the arrow on the end of the Notification area to view the overflow container. Then if you decide that the Notification area icon actually is useful, you can drag it from the overflow container to the main Notification area. Now you are in full control of your Notification area and can keep it nice and neat or cluttered depending on how you like it.

Figure 5-12: Windows 7 with the taskbar on the left side of the screen

In the next few sections I show you how you can fine-tune your Notification area by customizing the appearance and behavior.

Hiding Icons

As I mentioned earlier, the only additional icons that appear in your Notification area are icons that you personally drag into it. If you want to hide any of those icons, including the default system icons, you can simply drag them off it and they will fall in the overflow container. This works great most of the time, but there is another way to get more control:

1. Click the arrow to the left of the Notification area and then select Customize.

2. This will load the Notification Area Icons Control Panel screen where you can fine-tune each icon that ever attempted to load in the Notification area. Scroll through the list and select the behavior you want to use for

each icon. You can choose from Show icon and notifications, Hide icons and notifications, and Only show notifications.

3. After you have adjusted all your icons, click OK.

Removing System Icons and the Clock

Tweaking the system icons such as the Volume, Network, and Clock icons require an additional step. Follow these instructions to hide any of the default system icons:

1. Click the arrow to the left of the Notification area and then select Customize.

2. When the Notification Area Icons Control Panel screen loads, click Turn system icons on or off.

3. For each system icon toggle the drop-down list to turn each item on or off.

4. Click OK when you are finished.

Using Group Policy Editor to Customize the Start Menu and Taskbar

The Group Policy Editor is a great component of Windows that enables you to make dozens of advanced settings changes that are hidden from normal users. This works by defining various rules, called the *policy*, which tells Windows how to behave.

The collection of policies is what is known as Group Policy, of which there are two types: local and domain based. Local is when the policy resides in and is controlled on the local computer. Domain-based policy is when the policy resides on an Active Directory domain controller to which multiple computers are connected. Domain policy is primarily used only in businesses that need a way to control multiple computers from a central location. In this book, some tweaks use local Group Policy to configure the Start menu because most of you are customizing your home computer and do not have it connected to a domain controller. The actual policies and way you set them are the same for both types of group policies, so you can apply these same techniques to a domain policy if desired.

The policies are set and modified using the, you guessed it, Group Policy Editor. This is the tool that you will be using to set the policies to help you customize the Start menu. First, you learn how to use the policy editor, and then all the policies relevant to customizing the Start menu.

Setting Policies with the Group Policy Editor

Group Policy Editor is a lot like using the Registry Editor. It is based on a hierarchical structure of sections that all policies are organized within. All policies are divided into two sections: Computer Policies and User Policies. Computer Policies are settings that apply to components of Windows such as hardware and global feature settings. User Policies are settings that can vary between users on a computer. This is where most of the policies that you will use to customize the look of your interface are located.

Now that you know the basics of the Group Policy Editor, dive in and start using the policy editor:

1. Click the Start button, enter **gpedit.msc** in the Search box, and press Enter.

2. After the Group Policy Editor has loaded, you will see the hierarchical structure and Computer and User policies sections mentioned previously, as shown in Figure 5-13.

3. Navigate through User Configuration, Administrative Template, and then select Start Menu and Taskbar.

4. You will now see a list of all policies that you can configure. Right-click a policy that you want to configure and select Edit.

5. On the policy screen, select the option to turn on the policy or set the policy value, and then press OK, as shown in Figure 5-14.

6. Exit the policy editor and log off and back on. Some policy changes may require a reboot.

Figure 5-13: Using the Group Policy Editor

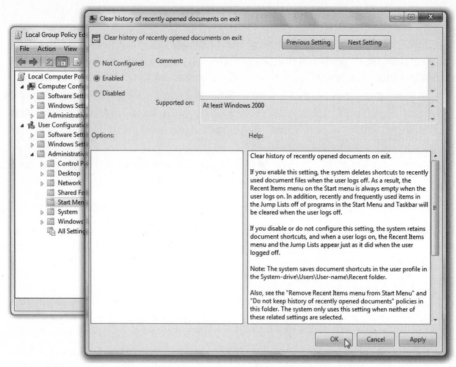

Figure 5-14: Configuring a policy in the Group Policy Editor

Now that you know how to use the Group Policy Editor, the next section shows you all the policies and briefly describes what they do.

Start Menu and Taskbar Policies

Table 5-1 shows a list of all the group policies that will help you customize the Start menu and the taskbar.

Table 5-1: Group Policy Settings to Configure the Start Menu and Taskbar

POLICY	DESCRIPTION
Add Search Internet link to Start menu	Allows you to search the Internet from the Start menu.
Clear history of recently opened documents on exit	Purges document history at logoff.
Clear the recent programs list for new users	Purges program history at logoff.
Add logoff to the Start menu	Controls the logoff option in the classic Start menu and Start menu.

Table 5-1: Group Policy Settings to Configure the Start Menu and Taskbar *(continued)*

POLICY	DESCRIPTION
Gray unavailable Windows Installer programs Start menu shortcuts	Provides users with a visual notification of applications that are not available.
Turn off personalized menus	Disables the feature that hides uncommonly run programs from the classic Start menu.
Lock the taskbar	Controls the locking state of the taskbar. A locked taskbar does not allow any changes to be made to it.
Add "Run in Separate Memory Space" check box to Run dialog box	Adds an additional setting for running programs with the Run box. I recommend enabling this setting.
Turn off notification area cleanup	Disables the ability to hide icons.
Remove Balloon Tips on Start menu items	Disables pop-up information when hovering over items in the Start menu.
Remove drag-and-drop and context menus on the Start menu	Disables the ability to use the drag-and-drop functionality in the Start menu.
Remove and prevent access to the Shut Down, Restart, Sleep, and Hibernate commands	Disables the user's ability to change the state of the machine. Useful for public computers.
Remove common program groups from Start menu	Allows only user-specific applications to appear in the Start menu.
Remove Favorites menu from Start menu	Hides Favorites shortcut.
Remove Search link from Start menu	Hides Search shortcut.
Remove frequent programs list from Start menu	Hides Frequently Run Programs list.
Remove Games link from Start menu	Hides Games shortcut.
Remove Help menu from Start menu	Hides Help shortcut.
Turn off user tracking	Disables all tracking of user programs and documents.
Remove All Programs list from Start menu	Removes the ability to search through the main part of the Start menu, All Programs.
Remove Network Connections from Start menu	Hides the Network Connection shortcut.
Remove pinned programs list from Start menu	Disables the ability to pin applications.

Continued

Table 5-1: Group Policy Settings to Configure the Start Menu and Taskbar *(continued)*

POLICY	DESCRIPTION
Do not keep history of recently opened documents	Disables the tracking of opening documents.
Remove Recent Items menu from Start menu	Hides the Recent Items shortcut.
Do not use the search-based method when resolving shell shortcuts	Disables the ability to search the computer when a shortcut is broken.
Do not use the tracking-based method when resolving shell shortcuts	Disables the ability to use NTFS tracking to try to fix a broken shortcut.
Remove Run menu from Start menu	Hides the Run shortcut.
Remove Default Programs link from Start menu	Hides Default Programs shortcut.
Remove Documents icon from Start menu	Hides Documents shortcut.
Remove Music icon from Start menu	Hides Music shortcut.
Remove Network icon from Start menu	Hides Network shortcut.
Remove Pictures icon from Start menu	Hides Pictures shortcut.
Do not search communications	Disables the ability to search e-mails from the Start menu search box.
Remove Search Computer link	Hides Search shortcut.
Remove See More Results/Search Everywhere link	Allows you to expand the Start menu search results.
Do not search files	Disables the ability to search for files that are in indexed locations from within the Start menu.
Do not search the Internet	Disables the ability to search the Internet from the Start menu.
Do not search programs and Control Panel items	Disables the ability to search the Start menu from the Start menu Search box. This will not make the Search box go away.
Remove programs on Settings menu	Prevents various settings' components from running, such as Control Panel and Network Connections.
Prevent changes to taskbar and Start menu settings	Locks taskbar and Start menu settings.
Remove Downloads link from Start menu	Hides Downloads link.

Table 5-1: Group Policy Settings to Configure the Start Menu and Taskbar *(continued)*

POLICY	DESCRIPTION
Remove Homegroup link from Start menu	Hides Homegroup link.
Remove Recorded TV link from Start menu	Hides Recorded TV link.
Remove user's folders from Start menu	Hides user folders.
Remove Videos link from Start menu	Hides Videos link.
Force classic Start menu	Disables the new Start menu and uses the Windows 2000–style Start menu instead.
Remove Clock from system notification area	Hides the clock.
Prevent grouping of taskbar items	Disables application grouping on the taskbar.
Do not display any custom toolbars in the taskbar	Disables third-party taskbars or user-made toolbars.
Remove access to the context menus for the taskbar	Disables capacity to right-click the toolbars in the taskbar.
Hide the notification area	Disables the entire notification area (system tray).
Remove user folder link from Start menu	Hides the User Folder shortcuts.
Remove username from Start menu	Hides the username from appearing on the Start menu.
Remove links and access to Windows Update	Hides the shortcuts to Windows Update.
Change Start menu power button	Allows you to change what the power button on the Start menu does. E.g. Shutdown/Hibernate/Sleep.
Show Quick Launch on taskbar	Enables the Quick Launch toolbar.
Remove the "Undock PC" button from Start menu	Hides the shortcut for undocking a laptop.
Add the Run command to Start menu	Provides the Run command on both the Start menu and the classic Start menu.
Remove Logoff on Start menu	Hides Logoff shortcut.
Remove the Action Center icon	Hides the Action Center icon in the Notification area.

Continued

Table 5-1: Group Policy Settings to Configure the Start Menu and Taskbar *(continued)*

POLICY	DESCRIPTION
Remove networking icon	Hides networking icon in the Notification area.
Remove battery meter	Hides power icon in the Notification area.
Remove volume control icon	Hides volume icon in the Notification area.
Turn off feature advertisement balloon notifications	Disables pop-up help about features.
Do not allow pinning items in Jump Lists	Disables adding items to Jump Lists.
Do not allow pinning programs to the taskbar	Disables adding applications to the taskbar.
Do not display or track items in Jump Lists from remote locations	Prevents recent documents from network shares from showing up in Jump Lists.
Turn off automatic promotion of notification icons to taskbar	Disables temporarily adding new Notification area icons to the Notification area before moving to overflow container.
Lock all taskbar settings	Locks the taskbar.
Prevent users from adding or removing toolbars	Disables the ability to add toolbars.
Prevent users from rearranging toolbars	Locks in the position of your toolbars (similar to locking the taskbar).
Turn off all balloon notifications	Disables pop-up help.
Remove pinned programs from taskbar	Disables and removes pinned applications on the taskbar.
Prevent users from moving taskbar to another screen dock location	Locks the position of your taskbar.
Prevent users from resizing taskbar	Locks the size of your taskbar.
Turn off taskbar thumbnails	Disables the application thumbnails that are shown when you move your cursor over taskbar items when running Aero Glass.

As you can see, there are dozens of useful group policies that will help you customize your desktop more than any other method. Additionally, these policies can be used in a domain policy that governs all Windows 7 computers connected to a domain.

Summary

This chapter walked you through the process of customizing the Start menu and then moved on to the taskbar. You customized your Start menu for the way you work and got rid of the extra clutter. Then you were shown how you can customize and improve how the taskbar works, followed by advanced tweaking via Group Policy.

The next chapter concentrates on customizing the desktop. You will find out how you can completely change the look of the interface and use other third-party applications to make the interface even better.

Personalizing the Desktop

Studies have shown that customizing your desktop will result in a 64 percent increase in productivity as well as a 248 percent increase in happiness levels of computer users. Whether or not this is true, customizing the desktop is still very beneficial.

This chapter shows you some cool tricks and tools to make your desktop look and work much better so that you can also benefit from a customized desktop. I show you how to remove icons, customize the size of icons, and replace icons on your desktop. Then I show you how you can customize your desktop way beyond changing your wallpaper. In the second half of this chapter, I show you how you can customize desktop gadgets as well as how you can create your own gadgets.

Customizing the Desktop Icons

Building on the icon improvements in Windows Vista, Microsoft has continued to refine the high-quality icons in Windows 7. These new high-resolution icons include various sizes, all the way up to 256 x 256 pixels. This allows the icons to look great at many different sizes and really shows off the quality and time that was spent creating the hundreds of new icons.

The next few sections show you how to take advantage of the new icons as well as how to trim down icons to use in other areas where they are considered more clutter than eye candy.

Removing All Icons from the Desktop

No matter how hard I try, I always end up with a lot of junk on my desktop. There is never an end to the war I fight with my desktop to keep it clutter-free — this is evident from the programs I download, documents that I am too lazy to save elsewhere, and new program links that seem to pop up from nowhere. I like to see my desktop wallpaper and not have my view of the wallpaper blocked by useless icons. One cool way to win the never-ending desktop war is to disable the desktop's ability to show the icons and instead pin the most common desktop icons — such as the Recycle Bin and other shortcuts — to the taskbar.

Disabling the icons on the desktop is actually a very simple task. Most people never know about this feature because it was placed where you would never expect it in previous versions of Windows. In Windows 7, just right-click your desktop, expand View, and then select Show Desktop Icons. Almost instantly, the icons disappear.

Don't worry because the icons and folders on your desktop were not deleted. If you ever want to turn the icons back on, just repeat the preceding steps again.

This is a very simple way to clean up the desktop quickly. It's sort of like sweeping dirt under a rug. The desktop clutter is still there, but you can't see it.

Customizing the Icon Drop Shadow Effect

The Drop Shadow effect makes the icons stand out from your wallpaper and makes them much easier to read when you are using a background such as a photo that has both light and dark spots. Depending on the wallpaper that you are using, you may like or dislike the feature. I really like the new effect, but if you are using a bright wallpaper, I recommend disabling it. Perform the following steps to turn the feature on or off:

1. Click the Start button, type **sysdm.cpl** in the Search box, and then press Enter to launch the System Properties window.

2. Click the Advanced tab, and then click the Settings button under the Performance section.

3. While on the Visual Effects tab, scroll to the bottom of the box.

4. Locate Use drop shadows for icon labels on the desktop, as shown in Figure 6-1, and check or uncheck the value, depending on what you would like to do.

5. Click OK to save your changes.

6. Click OK again to close the System Properties window.

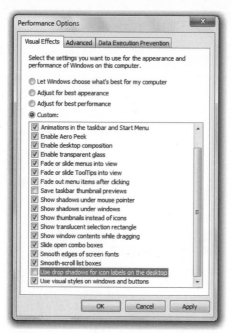

Figure 6-1: Turning the drop shadow effect on or off for icons on the desktop

Displaying Windows System and User Icons on the Desktop

In Windows 7, only one icon, the Recycle Bin, is on the desktop by default. Unlike previous versions of Windows, Microsoft is trying to keep the number of icons on the desktop to a minimum for a cleaner look. Nevertheless, if you like having the system and user icons on the desktop, such as Computer, Documents, Network, and others for convenience, it is possible to add those icons back to the desktop. Just follow these steps:

1. Click the Start button.
2. Right-click one of the items you would like to add back to the desktop, and then select Show on Desktop, as shown in Figure 6-2. For some icons you may need to right-click, select Send to and then Desktop (create shortcut).
3. Repeat Step 2 for each item you want to add back to the desktop.

You will see the icons on your desktop immediately after you complete the steps.

Figure 6-2: Adding Computer to the desktop

Adjusting the Size of Desktop Icons

Windows 7 uses a new desktop icon size that is slightly larger than in previous versions of Windows. This is one of the first things that I disliked immediately after installing Windows 7 on my computer. Why are the icons so large now? Well, everything seems to be bigger in Windows 7, but thankfully, as with other new features, it is very easy to adjust the size of the desktop icons.

You now have a choice between three different icon sizes on the desktop. Figure 6-3 shows the three icon sizes: small (classic), medium, and large.

Figure 6-3: Various desktop icon sizes

You can change the icon size by simply right-clicking the desktop, expanding View, and then selecting the icon size you prefer.

If you are a power user, there is a secret way to shrink or enlarge the icon sizes with a much wider range of sizes but you must have an external mouse with a scroll wheel. Just hold down the CTRL key on your keyboard and scroll up or down while on the desktop. You can create ridiculously large icons with this method as shown in Figure 6-4.

Figure 6-4: Very large icons with mouse scroll wheel trick

Renaming the Recycle Bin

To give my desktop a personalized touch, I like to rename my Recycle Bin to something different. In previous versions of Windows, this was only possible by editing the registry. In Windows 7, it is much easier. Just perform the following steps to rename your Recycle Bin:

1. Right-click the Recycle Bin on the desktop and select Rename.

2. Type a new name, such as Trash Compactor, and press Enter.

Removing the Shortcut Arrow from Icons on the Desktop

One thing that I always hate about Windows is the shortcut arrow. Sure, it is good to be able to tell if a shortcut is actually a shortcut, but I think that I know that the applications that I put on my desktop are already shortcuts. Also, the shortcut indicator that Windows uses does not look appealing, in my opinion. With a simple registry hack, it is possible to replace that shortcut icon overlay with any icon. This allows you to create your own icon using any popular icon editor and use it as an overlay on any shortcut.

I created a green arrow that I like to use as my shortcut icon overlay. You can grab it from the Windows 7 Tweaks web site at `Tweaks.com/books/win7tweaks`. Use the following steps to change the icon shortcut overlay:

1. Click the Start button, type **regedit** in the Search box, and then press Enter to start Registry Editor.

2. After Registry Editor has started, navigate through `HKEY_LOCAL_MACHINE\ SOFTWARE\Microsoft\Windows\CurrentVersion\Explorer`.

3. Right-click the Explorer folder, expand New, and select Key. Type **Shell Icons** as the name of the new key.

4. Right-click the new Shell Icons key, expand New, and select String Value. Type **29** as the name of the new String value.

5. Right-click the new string you just created and select Modify. Set the value to the icon path, a comma and the icon index number that starts at 0. For example, I use `c:\icons\myshortcut.ico,0` as shown in Figure 6-5. The icon index number specifies which icon you want to use in the file. (Some files can contain multiple icons, such as the `shell32.dll` file.) Press OK when you are finished.

6. Log off and back on, and you should see your new shortcut overlay. Figure 6-6 shows the before and after.

Customizing the Icons

Are you starting to get tired of the default icons in Windows 7? Sure, they are new and improved and have the new 7 look, but they can get old and dull after a while. If you are a hardcore desktop customizer, which you probably are if you have this book, then it is time to customize the Windows icons on the desktop.

To get started, you first need to find some great-looking replacement icons. Check out my favorite web sites and download icons for your desktop:

- **Iconaholic:** `www.iconaholic.com`
- **InterfaceLIFT:** `www.interfacelift.com`

- **VistaIcons:** www.vistaicons.com

- **VistaICO:** www.vistaico.com

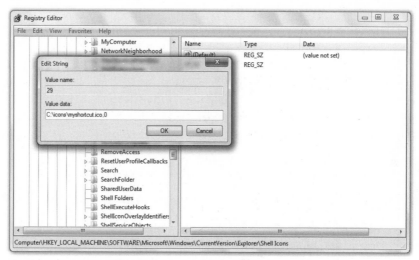

Figure 6-5: Setting the shell icon path and index

Figure 6-6: Before and
after shell icon overlays

Alternatively, you can use the library of Windows icons located in
%SystemRoot%\system32\SHELL32.dll.

Now, you can get started replacing icons on your desktop. Changing application shortcut icons is easier than system icons such as the Recycle Bin or
Computer. Changing system icons requires the help of an icon utility. First, I
show you how to change application icons and then how to change system icons.
Perform the following steps to change any application icons:

1. Right-click the item for which you want to change the icon and select
   Properties.

2. On the Shortcut tab, press Change Icon.

3. While on the Change Icon screen, press the Browse button and navigate
   to your new icon.

4. Select your new icon on the screen, as shown in Figure 6-7, and press OK.

5. Press OK again to exit and save your changes on the Properties screen.

Figure 6-7: Selecting a new icon

Now that you know how to change application shortcut icons, you can change system icons, such as the Computer shortcut or the Recycle Bin. It is best to use an icon utility to make these changes. My favorite utility for this is called Microangelo On Display, developed by Impact Software.

To get started, head over to `www.microangelo.us/free-icon-editor-download.asp` to get a free evaluation copy. After it is installed, follow these steps to customize your system icons:

1. After you have installed Microangelo On Display, right-click any system icon, such as the hard drive icon in Computer, and select Appearance. This brings up the Appearance window as shown in Figure 6-8.

2. Under the Display section, switch the option to Custom.

3. Browse and select your replacement icon and press OK.

4. Click Apply to save and see your changes and then press OK.

If you do not like your new icon and want to change it back to the default, right-click the icon again and this time select System Default under the Display section and press OK.

Now that you've finished customizing the look of your desktop and system icons, you can customize the desktop.

Figure 6-8: Changing an icon with Microangelo On Display

Customizing the Desktop

The desktop is a pretty simple part of Windows. Normally you can't do much to customize it besides changing the wallpaper. This section shows you how you can go further by utilizing some new wallpaper features in Windows 7 — such as automatic wallpaper changing and desktop gadgets.

Automatically Rotate Your Wallpaper

It seems as though this feature should have been in Windows many releases ago, but Microsoft has finally integrated an automatic wallpaper switcher into Windows. For the first time you can select a number of background images to use and an interval between changing the images. After the interval is hit you will see a smooth fade effect as the desktop background changes.

Configure multiple background images in the same place as you normally change your background. To get started, follow these steps:

1. Right-click your desktop background and select Personalize.

2. Click Desktop Background near the bottom of the window.

3. You should now see a thumbnail view of the default background images and any other images you added. Keep in mind you can always use the Browse button on the top to select more images. After you have your images you want to use identified, hover over each image and click the checkbox as shown in Figure 6-9. Repeat this for every other image you want to use.

4. When you have two or more images checked, the Change picture every drop-down list becomes activated. There you can choose to change the background every 10 seconds to once a day.

5. If you select a lot of images, I suggest leaving the Shuffle box checked so you see a variety of images because you never know what is coming up next.

Figure 6-9: Personalizing your desktop background

TIP One of my favorite places to find quality desktop images is `InterfaceLift.com`. It has a wide selection of every type of image you can think of in just about every size as well.

Using Desktop Gadgets

Formerly known as the Windows Sidebar, gadgets are exactly the same as in Windows Vista except the sidebar is gone and you can place them anywhere on the desktop. Additionally, they stick to your desktop so when you click the

Show Desktop button or just hover over it, Aero Peek is activated and you can easily take a quick look at all your gadgets. For those of you that skipped over Vista, gadgets can be thought of as miniature applications. They can do anything from displaying the current time, weather, and system information to offering simple games. The possibilities truly are endless and end users make new gadgets all the time.

So why would you want to use gadgets? Simple — it is a great way to customize your desktop with all sorts of useful utilities and even some eye candy.

Adding and Removing Gadgets

As I mentioned earlier, gadgets are basically miniature applications that can provide all sorts of information and functions. On my desktop I have a calculator, CPU and memory meter, the current weather, a battery meter, and my latest Outlook e-mails. Some of these gadgets came with Windows 7, whereas others I had to download. When you are finished with this section, you will know where to download more gadgets and add them to your desktop.

First, the basics: The process of adding and removing gadgets to your sidebar is very simple. To add, right-click the desktop and select gadgets. Then drag the gadget from the Gadget Gallery onto your desktop, wherever you want it. To remove, press the X button on the top-right side of the gadget, which is shown when you hover over it with your mouse.

Windows 7 only ships with a handful of gadgets that you can get tired of very quickly. The Windows Live Gadget Gallery is the best place to download new gadgets for your desktop. Right-click your desktop and then select Gadgets. When the Gadget Gallery is shown, click the Get more gadgets online link on the bottom-right of the screen. After you have selected and downloaded the gadget you want, simply open the .gadget file and click the Install button on the Security Warning screen shown in Figure 6-10.

Figure 6-10: Desktop Gadget Install
Security Warning

After you click Install, the gadget will show up on the Gadget selection screen and on your desktop immediately.

Customizing Gadgets

Most gadgets are interactive and allow you to customize the size and settings to personalize the gadget for your computer. Weather gadgets allow you to specify your location, and stock gadgets let you specify what stocks you want to watch. Additionally, some gadgets let you expand the size which can present much more information. For example, the default Weather gadget shows you the current weather conditions while in standard size. If you expand it to the large size it will show you a three-day forecast as well.

Both the size and the custom settings are controlled by the arrow and tool icons that are shown when you hover over a gadget on your desktop. Figure 6-11 shows the buttons on the Weather gadget starting with the Close button on the top followed by the Size button and then the Settings button on the bottom.

Figure 6-11: Desktop gadget buttons

To configure custom settings such as your zip code for the Weather gadget, hover over the gadget with your mouse and click the Tool icon which is on the bottom. If you want to enlarge the gadget, click the arrow button in the middle. I suggest trying the size button on all your gadgets — you may find some additional useful features.

Creating Your Own Gadgets

Now that you are an expert at using gadgets, you are ready to start creating your own. Creating a gadget is a lot like creating an interactive web page that uses JavaScript. Every gadget is powered by an HTML page that uses JavaScript with special APIs (application programming interfaces) to get access to interact with Windows or web services (two-way data feed similar to RSS).

Making a gadget can be simple or very complex depending on what you want the gadget to do. The JavaScript API, called the Windows Gadget Platform, is a very comprehensive library that provides access to all sorts of information and functions. To keep things simple, I'm going to show you how to create a simple gadget that will allow you to search a web site, such as `Wingeek.com`. This gadget will not be the best looking and will not use any of the advanced features of gadgets such as JavaScript. However, it will show you the basics of creating gadgets and the foundation necessary to start making more advanced gadgets.

Gadget Creation Overview

The three main steps to creating all gadgets are as follows:

1. Create an XML gadget information file that tells Windows information about your gadget: what it is called, who created it, and the main files it uses so that the sidebar application knows which files to read.

2. Create the HTML and JavaScript that makes the gadget user interface and adds the interactive element of a gadget. Create the interface in plain HTML and with the help of PNG images. Then add your JavaScript elements to the HTML to bring it to life. This is the most intensive part of the creation process.

3. The final step in the creation process is packaging the gadget into a Windows Gadget package. This allows you to easily install and distribute your gadget to multiple computers when you are ready.

Now you can start making your own gadget with the first step, creating the XML gadget information file.

Creating the XML Gadget Information File

As I mentioned earlier, the XML gadget file is what tells Windows the name of your gadget and which files it uses. To start the creation process, create a new folder somewhere on your computer to store all the gadget files that you create. Then, follow these steps to create the XML information file:

1. Open Notepad by clicking the Start button, typing **Notepad** in the Search box, and then pressing Enter.

2. You are now ready to start creating your XML gadget file. The following text shows the basic structure of the XML file:

```
<?xml version="1.0" encoding="utf-8" ?>
<gadget>
    <name>Search Gadget</name>
    <namespace>search.gadget</namespace>
    <version>1.0</version>
    <author name="Your Name">
        <info url="www.YourWebsite.com" />
    </author>
    <copyright>2007</copyright>
    <description>This gadget will search a website</description>
```

```
    <hosts>
        <host name="sidebar">
            <base type="HTML" apiVersion="1.0.0" src="search.html" />
            <permissions>full</permissions>
            <platform minPlatformVersion="1.0" />
        </host>
    </hosts>
</gadget>
```

The key parts of this XML file are the `name`, `description`, and `base type` sections, where the `src` (source) is set to `search.html` (the HTML file that has the gadget code). Type the preceding text into Notepad on your computer and replace the appropriate sections, such as `name`, `description`, and `author name` with your info. Make sure that you point the base `src` value to the name of the HTML file that you plan on using to store your gadget code — such as `search.html` for this example.

3. After you have your version of the gadget XML file typed into Notepad and you have checked it to make sure you typed it in the correct syntax, as shown in the preceding example code, you are ready to save it as an XML file. Click File and select Save As.

4. In the Save As window, change the Save As type to All Files.

5. Type **gadget.xml** as the filename. Your file must be called gadget.xml.

6. Navigate to the folder that you created to store all your gadget files and press Save.

After you have your `gadget.xml` file saved, you are ready to move on to creating the HTML code file the gadget will use.

Creating the HTML and JavaScript

Now that the XML information file is created, you are ready to create the main part of the gadget. For this step, you use some HTML to create a simple text box and button form that will post back to the `Wingeek.com` servers to display the search results.

1. Open Notepad again and enter the following HTML code:

```
<html>
<head>
    <style>
        Body
        {
            width:140;
            height:75;
        }
    </style>
</head>
```

```
<body>
    <form name="s" method="get" action="http://Wingeek.com/Search.aspx">
        <input type="text" name="q">
        <input type="submit" name="Search" value="Search">
    </form>
</body>
</html>
```

The preceding code is what draws the text box on the screen and the Search button as well as what creates the form that directs where to send the data when the Submit button is pressed. It starts off with a few formatting HTML commands, such as HTML and HEAD. Then it sets the width and height of the gadget that will be drawn on the sidebar. Finally, you get to the guts of the gadget: the code that specifies that this is a form and where it submits the data to, as specified by the action property.

2. After you have entered the preceding code, save it as search.html (because that is what you set in the gadget.xml file). Click File and select Save As.

3. In the Save As window, change the Save As type to All Files.

4. Type **search.html** as the filename.

5. Navigate to the folder that you created to store all your gadget files and press Save.

When you have your search.html file saved in the same folder as the gadget .xml file, you are ready for the final step.

Creating the Gadget Package

Now that you have your XML information file and search.html code file, you are ready to package your gadget into a single file format that the Windows Gadget Gallery can read. This is very easy to do because the gadget package file is just a compressed zip file with the extension changed from .zip to .gadget.

Perform the following steps to package your gadget so that you can easily install it:

1. Navigate to the folder that you created earlier and save both to the XML information file and the search.html code file.

2. Select both files in this folder.

3. Right-click one of the files while both are selected, expand Send To, and then select Compressed Folder. This will compress the two files into a zip file.

4. Name the file and change the file extension to .gadget from .zip. This can easily be done at a command prompt with the rename command if you have Show known file extensions turned off for Windows Explorer. Simply navigate to the path where you saved your zip file and then run rename file.zip file.gadget and hit Enter.

5. After you have the zip file renamed as `.gadget`, you will notice that the file icon changes. To test your new gadget, double-click the new package file. If you properly renamed the extension, you should see an install warning screen. Press Install and your new gadget will be installed and displayed on your sidebar.

You are now finished creating your first gadget!

As I mentioned earlier, this is an extremely basic gadget; however, it gives you an idea about how gadgets are made because they are all started in the same way. If you have a background in programming and would like to learn how to go to the next level with your gadget creation, check out `http://msdn.microsoft.com/en-us/library/aa906092.aspx` and read about Windows Sidebar. The gadget API did not change much from Windows Vista so you will find a lot of references to Windows Vista within.

I also recommend looking at some of the other gadgets that were created by Microsoft and other sidebar users; learning by example is very helpful. You can find those in `%localappdata%\Microsoft\Windows Sidebar\Gadgets` or `%programfiles%\Windows Sidebar\Gadgets` — just type in the path in any explorer window.

Summary

Throughout this chapter you have learned how to customize the icons on your desktop in many different ways to make the desktop much more personalized. I have even walked you through the steps of adding more gadgets to your computer and creating your own from scratch.

The next chapter is one of the most important of the customization chapters. I show you how to change the look of the entire Windows 7 user interface. Chapter 7 is a must for anyone who wants to customize the most visible part of Windows: the user interface.

Customizing the Appearance of the Windows Interface

In the last few chapters, you customized various parts of the operating system, starting with the logon screen. After customizing the Start menu and the taskbar, you spent some time customizing the desktop, too. This chapter shows you how to customize what the entire user interface looks like by changing the theme or visual style and fine-tuning settings of both.

In the sections that follow, you learn how to make major alterations in the way your computer looks (much more than you've learned so far). First, I explain the differences between a theme and a visual style, to clear up any possible confusion you might have. Then you learn how to create an advanced theme. Finally, you are able to tweak the Aero Glass look. This chapter ends with an easy way to give Windows 7 a completely different look with a third-party skinning utility called WindowBlinds.

Working with Themes

Themes have been a part of Windows for a long time. Ever since Windows 95 was released, themes made it possible to save the configuration of the fonts, colors, visual style, wallpaper, mouse cursors, and even the sounds that are used. Throughout the years, not a lot has changed in the theme world. Originally, you had to buy Microsoft Plus to use themes, but now the ability to use themes is included in all the latest Microsoft operating systems. In addition, when themes were first developed, they did not keep track of visual styles (because they didn't exist).

Why are themes still important to talk about even though they have been around so long? Because they provide a unique way to save all your computer visual settings and audio settings so that you can easily change all of them simultaneously. Additionally, Microsoft implemented some new secret features in themes that I cover.

Changing the Current Theme

When you install Windows 7, Microsoft includes a number of themes with different regional styles and visual styles. Changing themes is very simple, so I'm not going to spend much time on it. Just follow these steps:

1. Right-click the desktop and select Personalize.
2. Scroll through the list and click the theme you want to apply as shown in Figure 7-1. The theme will be previewed immediately.
3. When you have selected the theme that you want to use just close the Personalization.

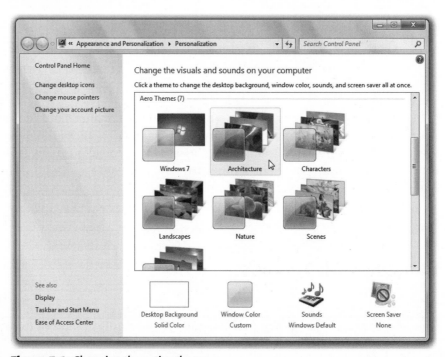

Figure 7-1: Changing the active theme

After you select the theme, the new theme is automatically applied. This process may take a few seconds if you select a theme with a different visual style such as Windows Classic or Windows 7 Basic.

Now that you know how to change a theme, it's time to make your own.

Downloading More Themes

There are a number of sites that will help you download more pre-made themes for Windows 7 complete with background images and sounds. Take a look at the following sites to find some more great themes:

- Microsoft: `http://windows.microsoft.com/en-US/windows7/downloads/personalize?T1=tab01`

- Tweaks.com: `http://tweaks.com/39413/`

When you find a theme you like online just download the .themepack file and double-click the file to install it. After it is installed it will show up below the included system themes in a new Installed Themes section.

Making Your Own Theme

Making your own theme enables you to back up your visual changes to Windows 7 easily so that you can distribute your settings to other computers or on the Internet. The most difficult part of the process is customizing all the little aspects of the visual elements that make up the user interface. The next few sections walk you through the process of fine-tuning the user interface and then show how you can save your changes and make your own theme file.

Modifying Window Metrics and Fonts

What exactly are window metrics? Well, it is a fancy way of talking about how big everything is. There are a lot of settings you can adjust to change the size of the user interface elements, such as window borders and buttons. It is also possible to tweak the fonts used and, more importantly, the size.

To get started, use Appearance Settings to make the changes:

1. Right-click the desktop and select Personalize.

2. Click Window Color on the bottom.

3. Then click Advanced appearance settings.

4. The Window Color and Appearance window should now be open. From here, you can change the size and the font for all the different aspects of a window. You can make changes in two different ways. The first is to

use the Item drop-down box. Just expand it and select the item that you want to modify. The other is to click the object that you want to customize on the preview picture. The click automatically selects the item from the Item drop-down box for you. Either way, select an item that you want to change. For the purpose of demonstration, I suggest that you click or select Active Title Bar.

5. After you have selected an object that you want to change, use the Size, Font, and Color settings to customize your window, as shown in Figure 7-2. Keep in mind that the color settings here will apply only to the classic Windows interface. If you are running Aero Glass or the non-glass visual style, the color settings will not apply.

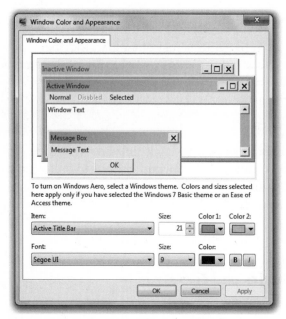

Figure 7-2: Customizing the sizes and fonts of the user interface

6. When you have finished customizing your window metrics, press OK to save your changes.

7. Click Save changes to activate your changes and close the Window Color and Appearance window.

You have now finished customizing your window metrics. Next you customize the system sounds.

Modifying System Sounds

Sounds can be assigned to many events in Windows such as logging on, logging off, minimizing a window, and maximizing a window. Themes can also include sound scheme settings, so I recommend customizing your system sounds for any custom theme.

Changing the event sounds is simple. Just follow these steps to launch and configure the sound properties:

1. Click the Start button, type **mmsys.cpl** in the box, and press Enter to launch the system Sound properties.

2. After the Sound properties loads, click the Sounds tab.

3. To adjust the sound clip for a specific event, click the event that you want to modify by navigating through the Program Events list, as shown in Figure 7-3.

4. When you have an event selected, the Sounds drop-down list becomes enabled, and you can select the sound clip that you want to use. You can select (None) from the top of the list if you do not want to use a sound for a specific program event. If you cannot find a sound that you like on the list, you can use the Browse button to pick a specific sound file on your computer to use.

5. Here you can also enable or disable the Windows startup sound by clearing the Play Windows Startup sound box.

6. When you have finished with your changes, just press OK to save your work.

Figure 7-3: Modifying the sound for the logon event

You have now finished customizing the sound events on your computer.

Customizing Mouse Cursors

The mouse cursors are yet another item saved in the theme file. Many different pointer schemes are included with Windows 7. Although not all of them are the nicest-looking cursors, they can really help out in some situations. In addition, Windows 7 includes special large mouse cursors so that the cursors will be easier on the eyes.

To get your cursors set perfectly for your theme file, follow these steps:

1. Click the Start button, type **main.cpl**, and press Enter to open Mouse Properties.

2. Click the Pointers tab.

3. You have two options to customize the cursors. The first is you can use the drop-down Scheme box to change all the pointers simultaneously to different styles, by selecting a different cursor scheme from the list, as shown in Figure 7-4. When you select the different schemes, all the cursors change automatically. Alternatively, if you do not like the cursor schemes, you can individually select a cursor from the Customize list by scrolling through the list and selecting the cursor you want to change. Then press the Browse button to change it.

4. When you have finished customizing your cursors, just press OK, and you are finished.

Now you are ready to move on to customizing the visual style that the theme will use.

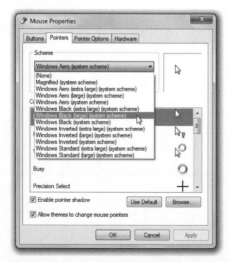

Figure 7-4: Changing the pointer scheme

Configuring Aero Glass Settings

If you have a computer that supports Aero Glass, you can also customize the color and transparency of the glass interface. These settings are also saved in your theme file, so it is a good idea to customize these settings, too. With these settings, you can change the color and adjust the transparency. Some users have found that the interface performs a lot better for them if they disable transparency completely, because it makes it easier to see and performs better on their hardware.

Just follow these steps to customize Aero Glass your way:

1. Right-click the desktop and select Personalize.
2. On the Personalization screen, click Window Color on the bottom of the screen.
3. Pick the color you want to use from the 16 on-screen options or click Show color mixer to set a custom color, as shown in Figure 7-5.
4. Adjust the glass transparency by adjusting the Color intensity slider.
5. When finished, click Save changes.

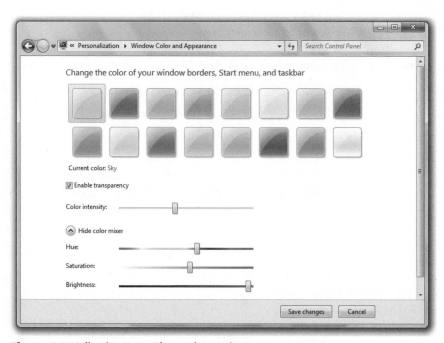

Figure 7-5: Adjusting Aero Glass color settings

Setting the Background Images

The title to this section is not a grammar mistake; new to Windows 7 is the ability to set multiple background images that are automatically rotated at a user set interval. This allows you to select any number of background images and they will automatically be changed with a nice fade effect. Enabling this feature is done on the normal change background screen. Follow these steps to change the background image on your computer and enable background slideshow:

1. Right-click the desktop and select Personalize.

2. Click Desktop Background on the bottom of the screen.

3. Next, click any image to set it as your background. If you want to set up multiple background images, simply hover over each image and check the box that appears. You can check as many boxes as you want as shown in Figure 7-6.

4. After all images are selected, configure the picture position and the change picture frequency settings. Click Save changes when finished.

Figure 7-6: Multiple background images

Saving Your Theme to a File

You have now customized all the aspects of themes and are ready to create your own theme file into a theme pack file that includes all the resources your theme uses:

1. Right-click the desktop and select Personalize.

2. On the Personalization screen you will see a My Themes section on the top with one called Unsaved Theme. Right-click that theme and select Save theme for sharing.

3. Type in a name and select a location to save your .themepack file and click Save.

You have now created a theme pack for your theme so that you can easily change back to it when you customize the user interface in the future. Additionally you can copy your theme pack to other computers or share it online. All the files used in your theme including background images are included in the .themepack file.

Automatic RSS Background Themes

Now that you created your own theme, I'm going to show you how to enable a secret feature by editing your newly created theme file. This will allow your theme to download and display backgrounds from an RSS feed on the Web automatically.

Activating this feature requires manually editing your theme file inside a theme pack you created in the last section. You also need an RSS feed that adheres to the RSS enclosures standard and includes images as enclosures in the feed. Some useful feeds that I like to use include the following:

- `http://www.webshots.com/rss?type=featuredPhotos`

- `http://feeds.feedburner.com/bingimages`

Compatible feeds can be identified by looking for the enclosure tag in the source of the feed for each <item>. For example, look for <enclosure url="http://www.site.com/image.jpg" type="image/jpeg" />. To learn more about the RSS enclosures standard check out the Wikipedia entry at `http://en.wikipedia.org/wiki/RSS_Enclosures`.

Now that you know of some sample feeds and how to identify other feeds you can get started:

1. First, you need to get to the .theme file packed inside your .themepack file you created earlier or from a file you downloaded online. Navigate to the directory where you saved your .themepack file and rename the file .cab. A theme pack file is nothing more than a specially Microsoft Cabinet file.

2. After you've renamed to a cab file, open the file with any compatible compression utility such as WinRAR (`www.rarlabs.com`) and extract the .theme file within.

3. After extracting the .theme file, right-click it and select Open With. Then expand the Other Programs section and open the file with Notepad.

4. Now you will be able to edit the theme file manually. Scroll through the file and look for the [Slideshow] section. If this section already exists, delete it.

5. Enter in the new [Slideshow] section, as shown next, at the bottom of the file in notepad.

```
[Slideshow]
Interval=600000
Shuffle=1
RssFeed=http://wingeek.com/ExampleFeed.aspx
```

The value of Interval is listed in milliseconds, so 600000 means the wallpaper will change every 10 minutes. Feel free to change this value. When shuffle equals 1, shuffle is enabled and 0 is disabled. Replace the value of RSS feed with the URL of a compatible RSS enclosure feed.

6. Save the changes you made to a new .theme file and close Notepad. Make sure you change the Save as type on the Save As dialog to All Files (*.*) before saving so the .txt extension is not appended to the filename.

7. Navigate to the new file you saved, right-click and select Open With and then Windows Shell Common DLL. This will load the file with the theme browser on the Personalization screen.

8. If your edits were successful you should get a message window called Apply theme asking you to Subscribe to RSS feed. Click Download Attachments to process all images on the feed as shown in Figure 7-7.

9. The images in the feed will be downloaded in a few minutes and applied as your background. The RSS background feed is now set up and should update once a day.

If several minutes pass after the interval you set and the background still does not change, chances are there is a problem with your RSS feed.

Customizing Aero Glass

First seen in Windows Vista, Aero Glass is relatively unchanged in Windows 7. A slightly different visual style is used but the core components work the same.

Powered by the Desktop Window Manager (DWM), the user interface is painted on 3D surfaces powered by Direct3D.

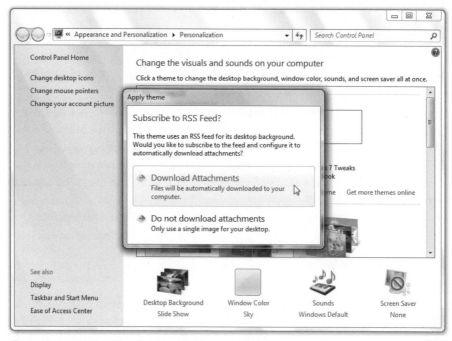

Figure 7-7: RSS feed background image download

In theory, because the DWM is powered by Direct3D, the same technology used in 3D computer games, Microsoft could allow you to fly through your windows just like a game. In fact, it is this ability that gave birth to the Flip 3D Alt+Tab replacement (Windows Key + Tab) that was a requirement in any Windows Vista demo.

Now that you know the brief history of the new user interface in Windows 7, I will show you how to start tweaking it.

Tweaking the Color of Aero Glass

In the preceding section about using themes, I showed you one way to change the color of Aero Glass on your computer. I am now going to show you another way to change the color of Aero Glass using the registry. This method has its own advantages and disadvantages. It allows you to create a registry file easily that you can then export to other computers, or you can take what you learn in this section to create a custom group policy (ADM template) that you can use in your domain environment to set the color of Aero Glass. The downside is that you have to deal with the raw hex color format (that is, in ARGB) to set the value of the registry setting. This can be rather difficult because you need to determine your color (which is usually easiest in a number format, and then you need to convert them to a specially formatted hex value that the DWM can read). This might sound too complex, but don't worry. I created an online converter that makes this easy.

Before you get started, I want to go over the basics of the color format and the components of it with which you will be working. As I said previously, the DWM color registry setting is stored in a hex ARGB format. ARGB stands for Alpha, Red, Green, and Blue. Each of these components has a separate value between 0 and 255, where 0 is off and 255 is completely solid. Red, Green, and Blue are easy to understand. All colors are made up of a mixture of these three basic colors. For example, one shade of orange is Red: 255, Green: 128, and Blue: 67. The Alpha component determines transparency (how well you can see through the color). The value of 0 equates to full transparency; 255 equates to no transparency.

Now that you know the basics of the setting value, let's get started:

1. Click the Start button, type **regedit**, and press Enter.

2. Navigate through `HKEY_CURRENT_USER\Software\Microsoft\Windows\DWM`.

3. Locate ColorizationColor, right click and select Modify.

4. You need to generate your new color value. Open your web browser and head over to `tweaks.com/39028`. There I have a useful number (decimal) for ColorizationColor value generator. Enter the Alpha value followed by Red, Green, and Blue numbers, as shown in Figure 7-8, to make your windows orange.

5. Copy and paste the generated ColorizationColor value from the web site into the open Registry Editor ColorizationColor value window and press OK.

6. Restart the DWM by typing **net stop uxsms** and **net start uxsms** at an administrative-level command prompt to see your changes. You can start an administrative-level command prompt by clicking on the Start Button, typing in **command prompt** and right-clicking on the shortcut and selecting Run as administrator.

Changing the Aero Glass Borders

Other than changing the color and transparency levels of Aero Glass, you can do one more significant thing to affect the look of Aero Glass: customize the window border. By default, the window border in Windows 7 is thicker than in previous versions of Windows. This can be nice or annoying depending on your personal preference. With the help of a simple tweak, you can easily customize the border width of your windows and by doing so, have a big impact on the look of Aero Glass. Take a look at Figure 7-9 for an example of how you can make major changes to your interface and what your windows can look like when you just change the border size.

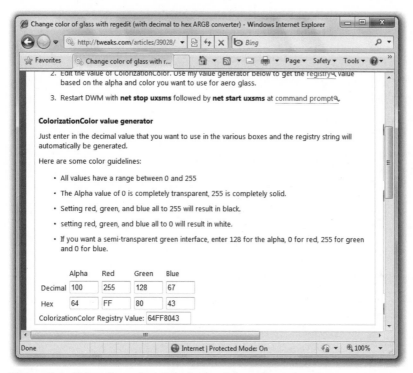

Figure 7-8: Using the online ColorizationColor value generator

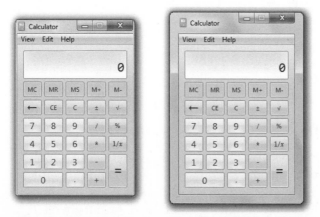

Figure 7-9: An example of a minimum border and fat border windows

The border setting can be tweaked by modifying a new window padding metric. Follow these steps to adjust this value to customize your window borders:

1. Right-click the desktop and select Personalize.

2. Click Window Color on the bottom of the window.

3. Select Advanced appearance settings.

4. On the Window Color and Appearance window, change the Item to Border Padding, as shown in Figure 7-10.

5. Adjust the Size value (default is 4) and press OK.

6. Click Save changes once more to see your changes.

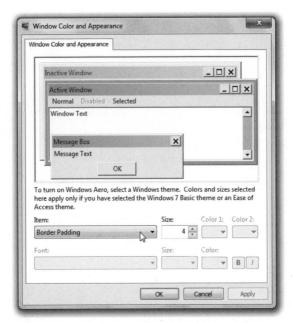

Figure 7-10: Changing the window border on the Window Color and Appearance screen

Disabling Animations

When demonstrating the Windows 7 user interface, I always get a lot of comments about the animations. Some love them, but others hate them and immediately ask how they can turn them off. This section is for all those users who find the minimize and maximize animations annoying and want to turn them off.

I personally like the animations, but I cannot help but notice how much faster my computer feels when they are turned off. There is not really much of a performance increase, but it just feels snappier because the instant I click Maximize or Minimize or even Close, the window instantly changes or is gone. I recommend giving this section a try even if you like the new animations; you might like the feel even better when they are disabled.

You can disable the animations a few different ways. In this section, I show how you can disable the animations using the registry. Follow these steps to get started:

1. Click on the Start Button and type in **Adjust the appearance and performance of Windows** and hit Enter.

2. Near the top of the list of features remove the check for Animate windows when minimizing and maximizing.

3. Click OK to save your change.

The change is applied immediately and you will instantly notice how much faster your computer feels.

Disabling Aero Glass

Are you one of the few users who prefer the non–Aero Glass look of Windows 7? Is the new user interface too much eye candy for you? This section walks you through turning off the new Aero Glass interface (in case you answered yes to any of those questions).

Before you proceed, you need to understand fully which features you will lose when you disable Aero Glass. Flip 3D will be replaced with the Windows XP–style tab box. Taskbar preview thumbnails will be gone, and some Windows applications such as Media Player are just not going to look as cool. If you are fine with losing these features and fine with the boring look of non–Aero Glass Windows applications, follow these steps to turn off Aero Glass on your computer:

1. Right-click the desktop and select Personalize.

2. Scroll to the bottom of the list of themes until you get to the Basic and High Contrast Themes section.

3. Select either Windows 7 Basic or Windows Classic.

4. Close the Personalization window.

Skinning Windows 7

Skinning Windows 7 is all about changing the look of the entire user interface with the help of third-party utilities and visual styles that allow you to make massive alterations to the look of Windows 7. By skinning Windows, it is possible to change the appearance completely and make it look like a different operating system, such as OS X, or something even more exotic. In the next sections, I show how you can use hacked visual styles as well as the leading skinning utility, WindowBlinds, to customize the look of your computer. This will help you take customization to the next level.

Using Hacked Visual Styles

Windows 7 uses an enhanced skinning engine based off the engine found in Windows XP to display the non-glass interface as well as the new glass DWM interface. In Windows XP, the visual style engine used bitmaps stored in a resource file. The visual style's resource file contains all visual elements such as images of buttons and window components as well as some configuration files. In Windows 7, the resource file has been modernized to include PNG images instead of bitmaps and is updated for the new interface design.

Creating visual styles for Windows 7 is accomplished the same way it is done for Windows XP and Vista. You start with an existing visual style, such as the default visual style that is included in Windows 7, and use a resource hacking tool to replace the images within the file. After you have replaced all the resources in the file with PNG replacements and created a new visual style file, you are almost ready to use the hacked visual style.

The last step before you can use any visual style that you downloaded or made yourself is patching the skinning engine files. The skinning engine in Windows 7 will only use visual styles that have a Microsoft digital signature on the file. Visual styles that you make yourself by editing the resources or other visual styles that you download from the Internet no longer have a valid Microsoft digital signature because the file content has changed. To use hacked visual styles in Windows 7 you need to patch the system files that impose this digital signature requirement on visual styles files.

Thankfully, there are a number of users that released utilities that patch the digital signature requirement. One that I'm going to show you is called UxStyle Core written by Rafael Rivera. This utility patches the digital signature requirement in memory so it does not modify any files on your computer.

Before you get started using UxStyle Core you need to download some Windows 7 visual styles to skin the interface. The following are some sites that I recommend to find compatible visual styles:

- `http://browse.deviantart.com/customization/skins/windows/visualstyle/`

- `http://tweaks.com/40051`

Make sure you only download visual styles created for Windows 7. Windows Vista and Windows XP visual styles are not compatible. After you have a few visual styles downloaded you are ready to configure your computer to us them:

Visit http://uxstyle.com and download the latest version of UxStyle Core.

2. After you have the utility installed it is best to reboot your computer and then check your list of services (run services.msc) for the Unsigned Themes and ensure it is started.

3. Next, you are ready to install a visual style that you downloaded earlier. Copy the .theme and corresponding files or folder to c:\Windows\Resources\ Themes.

4. Right-click your desktop and select Personalize.

5. Scroll down to the Installed Themes section and select the theme that you just copied to the Themes folder. After a few seconds your theme should be applied. If for some reason the theme reverts to the Windows 7 Basic or Windows Classic look, then something is wrong with the theme you downloaded or UxStyle is not working properly.

Now I'm going to show you another way to change the look without using hacked visual styles.

Changing the Look of Windows 7 Via WindowBlinds

Before visual styles were a part of Windows, only one way existed to change the way Windows looked: via the WindowBlinds program from Stardock (www.WindowBlinds.net). WindowBlinds is a classic Windows customization program. When it first came out, it transformed the boring gray interface of Windows into an attractive and colorful experience. Now that Windows 7 includes its own skinning engine, products that have their own skinning engines, such as WindowBlinds, seem less necessary. So, why am I even mentioning this application? Because the Microsoft engine will only run skins digitally signed from Microsoft unless you use a utility to get around the limitation. Additionally, the quality of visual styles available for WindowBlinds typically is better than the hacked visual styles available.

Using WindowBlinds is much easier than using hacked visual styles. Just follow these steps to get started using WindowBlinds on your PC:

1. Visit www.WindowBlinds.net and download a copy of WindowBlinds. Install it. Make sure that you reboot after you install WindowBlinds.

2. After a reboot, click the Start menu, type **windowblinds**, and press Enter to start WindowBlinds.

3. After the WindowBlinds Configuration screen has loaded, you will see a list of all skins installed on your computer at the bottom of the screen. Scroll the list horizontally and click a skin that you want to preview.

4. When you have the skin selected you want to use, it is also possible to customize the colors of the skin. Click Colours on the bottom of the screen and then adjust the color tint of the skin.

5. When you are ready to apply your customized skin, click Apply Changes on the top-left of the window and you will see your user interface transformed, as shown in Figure 7-11.

You can always change your skin back to the default Windows 7 look if you do not like any of the skins offered by WindowBlinds by selecting the Windows Aero skin from the horizontal list when you open WindowBlinds. If you want more skins, the next section is for you!

Figure 7-11: Example of a WindowBlinds theme

Adding More Skins for WindowBlinds

WindowBlinds has a strong skin base of thousands of skins that are easy to install. Thousands of WindowBlinds skins can be found at the Stardock operated site called WinCustomize. To get started, visit www.wincustomize.com/skins .aspx?libid=1 for a list of all skins available.

From the list of available skins, you can install a skin by clicking the Download link. It should automatically start to download. When the skin has finished downloading, WindowBlinds automatically loads it and prompts you by asking whether you want to apply it. After the skin has been installed, you can go back into the WindowBlinds Configuration screen to browse through the different versions and colors of the skin (assuming, of course, that the skin *has* multiple versions).

Summary

This chapter focused on the most important part of customizing your computer: the user interface. The visual interface is by far the part of the operating system that has the most impact when it is customized. Using the tools and techniques presented in this chapter, you can completely change the way Windows 7 looks.

The next chapter is all about customizing Windows Explorer, which is the program that you use to browse through all the files on your computer. I show you how you can customize the way it looks and works so that you can maximize its functionality to meet your needs.

CHAPTER 8

Fine-Tuning Windows Explorer

Windows Explorer is one of the most used components of Windows 7. Every time you go to Computer in the Start menu and browse through files on your computer, you are using Explorer. Using the icons on the desktop, right-clicking on files and folders, and copying and pasting files are all examples of using the features that Explorer provides.

Many of the features that Windows Explorer provides can be easily customized to make your Windows experiences even better. This chapter shows you how you can change many of the features and how to take advantage of some of the new, lesser-known features. It begins by showing you how you can customize the layout of the new Explorer interface. By the end of this chapter, you will have completely customized the Explorer features that enable you to browse through and create files on your computer.

Customizing Windows Layout

Explorer in Windows 7 includes various new panes, including Details, Preview, and Navigation that provide a wealth of new information that might change the way you use Windows Explorer. By default, all the new panels are turned on, which gives a cluttered feeling to the Explorer interface. Personally, I like to get rid of the panes that I don't use to speed up and streamline my Explorer windows. In addition to the new panels, Explorer includes many other new features, such as the Favorites section, Libraries and the ability to search subfolders. These next few sections show you how you can customize all of these.

Customizing Panes

The panes on the Explorer window are located on all sides of the window. Figure 8-1 shows a typical Explorer window with all panes visible.

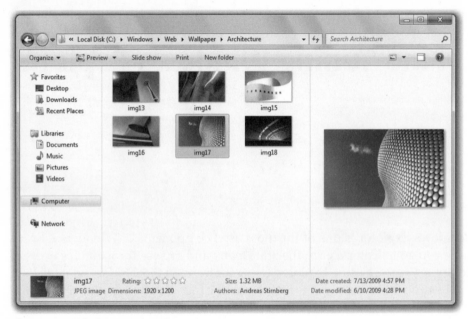

Figure 8-1: Windows Explorer's panes

As shown in Figure 8-1, the Navigation pane is on the left, Details is on the bottom, and Preview is on the right. Each pane offers a different array of features that can either help your Explorer experience or clutter it up. Dive into customizing each of the different panes, and hack up Explorer to make it work the way you want.

The Navigation Pane

The Navigation pane in Windows Explorer is divided into five key areas of information: Favorites, Libraries, Homegroup, Computer, and Network. You can think of the Favorite Links section as a sticky dock onto which you can drag any folder to create a shortcut for accessing it in the future. This allows you to access your common folder quickly and easily at the expense of file browsing space and making your Explorer window look cluttered.

Libraries can be thought of as a combined view of the contents of multiple folders that come pre-defined or are set up. Libraries will be discussed later.

The remaining sections, which are collapsed by default, offer a tree-driven interface that resembles the classic Windows Explorer that was in previous versions of Windows. Now that you know the basics, you can customize everything on the Navigation pane.

Adding and Removing Favorite Links

You can manage your Favorite Links section in two different ways. The easiest is simply to drag and drop folders and save searches onto the Favorites section to add them to the list. You can then remove items by right-clicking them from the list and selecting Remove. Alternatively, you can navigate to the Favorite Links folder that is located at `C:\Users\Username\Links`. There, you can easily copy and paste multiple folders or shortcuts at once to be added to the Favorite Links section.

I like to drag my hard drives into the Favorites section so I can quickly jump to them when needed.

Removing the Navigation Pane

If you want to have a super clean interface and have no use for the Favorite Links and Folders sections, you can easily remove the entire pane from view. Follow these steps to disable this view for your windows:

1. While a folder is open and showing the Navigation pane, click Organize on the toolbar.

2. Select Layout and then Navigation Pane. This will remove the entire left-side pane.

When you close the active window, the changes are saved to the registry.

The Details Pane

The Details pane, located at the bottom of the Explorer window, provides information on a file or folder when one is selected. Similar to the classic status bar in Explorer, the Details pane displays common information (such as the size of a file) but goes beyond that by also showing many other file settings. The actual contents of the Details pane depend on the type of file you have selected. For example, if you have selected a Word document, the Details pane will show the date modified, author, tags, size, title, comments, category, number of pages, status, content type, and offline availability. If you selected an image, it will show you a thumbnail preview as well as the date it was taken, tags, your star rating, dimensions, file size, title, author, and even the camera model.

The Details pane has proven to be a valuable source of information that can really help you tag and rate your personal documents, images, and music. Without the Details pane, setting all these values would be much more difficult.

Now that you know what the Details pane offers, you are ready to customize the look or remove it completely. You can customize the size of the Details pane simply by dragging the top border up or down. You can also right-click it and select Size and then Small, Medium, or Large. If you are not interested in using the Details pane at all, I suggest removing it completely to save screen real estate and create a cleaner Explorer interface. Just click the Organize button select Layout and then Select Details pane to remove the check and hide the pane.

If you choose to remove the Details pane, I recommend turning on the original status bar so that you have some indication of how many items you have selected and a quick and easy way to get file sizes. To do this, press Alt on the keyboard to bring up the classic menu bar, click View, and then select Status Bar.

The Preview Pane

The Preview window is the one pane that is turned off by default in most folders but can be very useful for browsing through an image collection or screening your MP3 files. When you are browsing through your music collection and select an MP3 file, the Preview pane shows a picture of the song's album and mini audio controls to play and sample the song. When you select an image file, a large thumbnail of the photo is displayed. Unfortunately, you can't customize much on this pane. You can adjust the width by clicking and dragging the left border left or right when the preview pane is turned on. Turn it on and off by clicking Organize, selecting layout, and then clicking Preview Pane.

Microsoft hopes that over time more companies write preview filters that work with Explorer so that you can see their file content previewed on the Preview pane.

Tweaking Search

One of the most useful new features in Windows 7 is the Search box that is in every Explorer window and many other applications. This Search box enables you to sort through your files like never before. Looking for all text files in a folder? Just type ***.txt** into the Search box and press Enter. Almost instantly you will begin to see a list of all text files in the current directory you are viewing.

Looking for all Word documents that refer to a specific company or person? Just go to your Documents folder and search for the name and press Enter. Windows Search can also look at the filenames, but it will also search the contents of your files. This is possible because Windows Search has built-in readers for many of the most popular file types.

As you can see, Windows Search is a comprehensive search solution compared to the prior search options in Windows. With the addition of this new search system comes the ability to customize searches even more than ever before. Various search settings are hidden deep in various windows and will help you customize the way searching works for you.

Adjusting Scope

Every time you perform a search, the results are based on the scope, the folders, and types of files in which the search software looks. Depending on the scope settings you have enabled, the results of your search can be drastically different. These next two settings will help you fine-tune what and how the search software searches, and then you will fine-tune the indexing service to index the files you want to be indexed for speedy searches.

Customizing What and How to Search

You can find all the "where to look" settings for Windows Search on the Folder and Search Options window in Windows Explorer. Follow these steps to customize where Windows Search looks:

1. Open Windows Explorer to a folder you want to modify the search settings for, click Organize, and select Folder and Search Options.

2. Click the Search tab, as shown in Figure 8-2.

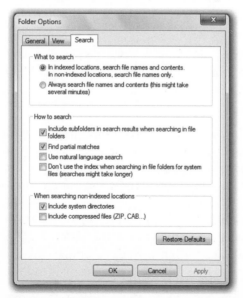

Figure 8-2: Windows Explorer search options

3. On the Search tab, you will see three separate sections. First, let's work with the What to search section. Here you can specify whether you would like the search software to use the indexing service's data or all data, on-the-fly. By default, Windows Search will search both filenames and contents of indexed files but just filenames of files not in the index. This works well for most users, but if you don't care about file contents or don't want to use the indexer at all, experiment with the other options.

4. Configure how searches are performed in the How to search section. Here you can choose from four different settings: the ability to search subfolders, report results with partial matches, turn on natural language searches, and disable searching from the index.

   The two settings here that you really want to pay attention to are the subfolder search and natural language search options. These features are usually the two that I tweak the most. First, to speed up searches, I uncheck searching subfolders. I also turn on the natural language search option so that I can perform easier searches. For example, if I want to find e-mails from a person, I normally have to type **Kind:email from:person** in the Search box. When I turn on natural language search, however, I can type **email from person** instead and get the same results.

5. The final section — When searching non-indexed locations — specifies what to do with compressed files and system folders that are not indexed or when index search is turned off. I leave these blank to speed up searches, but I strongly suggest that you do not turn on the compressed file option; it will cause your searches to take forever and make your hard drive go crazy with activity.

6. When you are finished tweaking the search options, press OK to save your changes. You might have to reboot for all settings to start working.

Customizing the Indexing Service

The indexing service runs in the background and reads and indexes your files when your computer is idle to speed up searches. This works by reading all the files and storing search keywords and other information in a single database that can be easily read instead of having to read all the file information again every time you perform a search.

In Windows 7, the scope of the indexing service is limited to the user folders by default. If you use search a lot, you might want to tweak the folders and types of files that are indexed. The following steps will help you customize which folders are indexed as well as the file types so that you can control what is indexed and what is not:

1. Click the Start button, type **Performance Information** in the Search box, and then press Enter.

2. After Performance Information and Tools loads, click Adjust Indexing Options on the left menu. When Indexing Options loads, you will see all the locations the indexing service is currently monitoring.

3. Now you should see the Indexing Options window. First, tweak where the indexer looks. Click Modify and then Show All Locations on the Indexed Locations window. Next, navigate through the list of your drives and folders, and simply check the boxes for the folders you want to be indexed. When you are finished, press OK and the indexer goes to work indexing the new locations.

4. Modify the file types that the indexer indexes. This can be done back on the Indexing Options window. This time, click the Advanced button and then click the File Types tab.

5. Scroll through the list of file extensions and select the file type that you would like to modify. Then, check the box and pick how the file should be indexed in the following section. If your file type is not listed, type the file extension in the box at the bottom of the window, as shown in Figure 8-3, and press Add, to add a new extension.

6. When you are finished, press OK and then Close to exit the indexing options.

Figure 8-3: Adding additional file extensions to be indexed

Because the indexing service runs only when the computer is idle, it may take up to a few hours before your new files, folders, and file types are added to the index and show up in the search results.

Modifying File Associations

Every time you click a file, Windows looks up in the registry the default program to open the file. Then, Windows loads that application and tells the application which file to open. This is something that you encounter almost all the time when you are using your computer. Often, when you install many programs on your computer, programs start to compete over which is going to be the default program to open a file.

One of the most common situations for this is when you install a bunch of similar applications. For example, I primarily use Windows Media Player for playing my music. When Apple releases a new version of iTunes, however, I usually install it to check out the new features. The next time that I try to play a CD or listen to an MP3, the music always opens in iTunes. My file association for my music has been stolen by iTunes. How do I take control of my file associations again? The following two sections will show you how you can customize the default launch application for any file type on your computer, as well as how your file types look.

Changing the Default Launch App

Windows Explorer uses information stored in the registry to find out what application is used to open a specific file type. This information is stored in the HKEY_CLASSES_ROOT section. With the Registry Editor, it is possible to browse to that key and the find the file type that you want to change and edit some keys. However, there is a better way to do this in Windows 7.

Windows 7's new Default Programs utility has the ability to change file association information easily without having to deal with the registry class ID junk. Just follow these steps to change the default launch app for any file type:

1. Click the Start button and select Default Programs.

2. When the Default Programs utility loads, select Associate a file type or protocol with a program.

3. Scroll through the list and select the file type you want to change as shown in Figure 8-4.

4. Click Change program.

5. The program to which you want to change it may be on the default Open With list. If not, just click Browse and select the program that you want to use to open the file.

6. Press OK and then Close.

Your changes to file launch apps are activated immediately after you click Close to save your changes. Now you will no longer have to worry about applications taking control over your files, because you know how easy it is to fix them.

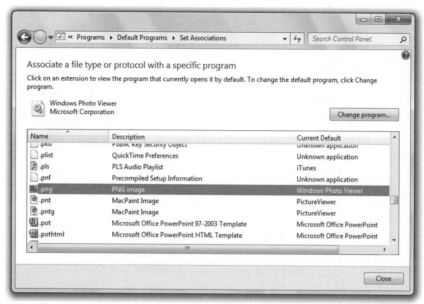

Figure 8-4: Changing file associations

Customizing the Context Menu

What is the context menu? It's the menu that pops up when you right-click anywhere on your computer. Over the years, these menus have become more and more useful. However, with the extra entries in the context menu, they can become cluttered with options and features that you just don't need. These next few sections show you how to get your menus back under control as well as how you can take advantage of the new features to make your own context menu entries.

I start off by removing items from the context menus and then move on to adding and customizing the components of the menus.

Removing Items from the Context Menu

Over time, your context menus can become cluttered with program entries from old programs that you may not use anymore. You might experience programs that take over all your context menus. Compression apps such as WinZip, WinRaR, or Picozip always end up adding program entries to all the context menus. I have Picozip installed on my computer and every time I right-click any file or folder, I see five entries from Picozip giving me different compression options. This can be a convenient feature, but if you don't compress and extract zip files very often, you might not need the added convenience. Instead, you could remove these entries from your context menu, which will give your system a cleaner interface as well as a small performance boost if you have a lot of extra entries in your context menu.

Removing these programs from your context menus can be a little tricky because they can be spread in different places in the registry. The only way to remove these types of entries is to edit the registry directly. Follow these steps:

1. Click the Start button, type **regedit** in the Search box, and then press Enter.

2. When the Registry Editor appears, expand the HKEY_CLASSES_ROOT folder. You will now see a list of every file type that is set up on your computer.

3. If the entry that you want to remove from the context menu appears in all context menus, such as the preceding WinZip example, you will have to expand the * folder. Otherwise, expand the folder with the file extension you want to modify.

4. After expanding the correct folder, expand the ShellEx and ContextMenuHandlers folders. Your registry path should be HKEY_CLASSES_ROOT*\ShellEx\ContextMenuHandlers.

5. Look through the list until you find the entry that you want to remove. Right-click the entry and select Delete. You will find that identifying some of the programs is easy. For example, WinRaR is labeled WinRaR, as shown in Figure 8-5. However, you may run into some items that are listed using their application/class ID or a vague name. If so, do a registry search of the class ID (Ctrl+F), which is formatted as {XXXXXXXX-XXXX-XXXX-XXXX-XXXXXXXXXXXX}, to find other references that will give you clues to what the ID belongs to. If that does not work, try doing a search on Google to see whether that turns up anything.

6. After you are finished removing all the entries from your context menus, just close Registry Editor and you are finished. Your changes will be in effect immediately.

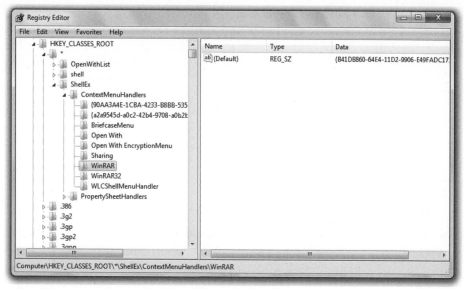

Figure 8-5: WinRaR's context menu entry in the registry

Modifying the Send To Menu

The Send To menu is one of the features of my context menus that I use the most. The ability to right-click any file and have a shortcut of it sent to the desktop is invaluable. How would you like to make it even more useful? It is very easy to add your own items to the Send To menu, such as folders to which you can send files. Do you have a folder in which you store all your music? How about a folder in which you store all your digital photos? Just follow these quick steps to add anything you want to your Send To context menu entry.

> **TIP** If you do not see any of the folders that are required in this section, you might have Hidden Files turned on. Because these folders are hidden by default, you will have to tell Windows to show all files. To do this, refer to the section on working with hidden files toward the end of this chapter.

1. Click the Start button and select Computer.
2. Click your Windows drive and browse through `Users\`*`Username`*`\AppData\ Roaming\Microsoft\Windows\SendTo`.
3. You will see all the files that appear in the Send To menu. If you want to add an entry to the menu, just copy a shortcut to this folder.

4. Perhaps you want to add your Digital Photos folder to your Send To menu. Navigate to your Digital Photos folder, right-click it, and then select Send To desktop. This will create a shortcut to the folder and save it on your desktop. Next, cut and paste the shortcut that was created from your desktop into the SendTo folder.

5. If you ever want to remove items from the Send To menu, just delete them from the SendTo folder.

It is that simple. You are now finished customizing your Send To menu.

Working with Libraries

Users often have similar data stored all over their computer and across multiple network shares. I have photos stored locally on my computer, some on one server and more on another server. Libraries in Windows 7 allow me to view all of my photos consolidated into just one folder where I can easily search and find the photo I am looking for. Although the actual photo files are still located in various folders on my computer and on two different network shares, I have one place to go to find all my photos.

Libraries can be thought of as a consolidated view of many folders. Best of all, these folders don't have to be on your local computer as mentioned earlier.

Windows 7 includes a number of Libraries set up by default for the user folders on your computer such as Documents, Pictures, Videos, and more. When you click on the documents Library you see a consolidated view of all the documents in your Documents folder and the All users folder on your computer. If you expand the Library folder you will see a list of all the folders that make up the library. Creating your own libraries is not only possible but also very easy to do.

Creating Your Own Libraries

Creating a library is very intuitive. Just follow these steps:

1. Click the Start button and then Computer.

2. On the Navigation pane you should see the available libraries listed right below Favorites. Right-click the Libraries heading and select New and then Library.

3. Type in the name of your new library and hit Enter.

4. Next, right-click the library you just created and select Properties.

5. Click Include a folder as shown in Figure 8-6 and select the folder to include. Repeat this step for all the folders you want to add to the library.

6. After you have all the folder locations added, you can change the default Save to folder by selecting a folder and then clicking Set save location. This will specify what folder will actually hold files if you copied and pasted files into your library.

7. Click OK and your library is ready for use.

Figure 8-6: Creating a library

If you want to delete a library, just right-click it and select Delete.

Customizing Your Folders

The folders of Windows 7 can be customized in ways that never were possible before. You can easily change the icon of the folder as well as the way the folder behaves after you open it. These next few sections will show you how you can take advantage of the great new folder features of 7.

Changing a Folder Icon and Picture

Changing the icon that is displayed for a folder is one of the easiest ways to customize the way a folder looks and make it stand out from the rest. This section shows you how to change the way your files and folders look as you browse through them by taking advantage of the high-resolution icons.

You change the folder icon and the folder picture within the folder proper-ties window. To see what you can do with these settings, create a new folder named Downloads on one of your hard drives. This folder can be used for all your downloads so that they do not clutter your desktop. Follow these steps to change the way this folder looks:

1. Right-click the new folder that you just created or right-click any folder that you want to customize, and select Properties.

2. Click the Customize tab to reveal all your customizing options.

3. First, customize the icon, because that is the most popular way to customize the look of the folder. To do that, click the Change Icon button on the bottom of the window.

4. Now you will be able to browse through the list of available system icons or you can specify your own by clicking the Browse button.

5. After you have selected the icon that you want to use, just click OK to return to the Customize screen. Then click Apply to see your changes.

6. Instead of changing the icon, you can show an image if you are using one of the larger icon views. This will display your image as if it were inside the folder — a cool-looking effect. To do that, just click the Choose File button on the Customize screen and specify an image to be displayed on the file.

7. After selecting the image, click OK to save your change. Then click Apply on the Customize screen to see your changes. Remember that you will see your new image only if you are using medium icons or larger. You can change to Thumbnail view by clicking the Views menu item.

When you are finished changing the way your folder looks, just click OK to save your changes and exit the folder properties window.

Changing the Template of a Folder

Windows 7 uses a few different pre-made templates, depending on the type of content inside a folder. For example, it has separate templates for general items, documents, pictures, videos, and music that show relevant file properties. Each template will automatically customize the folder view so that it looks best for the type of content that is in it.

You can customize the template that any folder uses so that you can take advantage of the cool new features in Windows 7's Explorer. This can be done by using the Customize tab in folder properties. Follow these steps to specify the template that should be used for a folder:

1. Navigate to the folder that you want to modify, right-click it, and select Properties.

2. Click the Customize tab.

3. Select the template that you want to use by expanding the drop-down box, as shown in Figure 8-7.

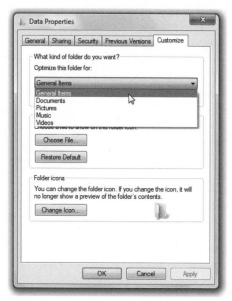

Figure 8-7: Changing the template of a folder

4. If you have a lot of folders within this folder with the same type of content, click the Also apply this template to all subfolders box so that your changes will be propagated to all subfolders as well.

You have now customized the template of the folder and are ready to customize the view.

Customizing the Folder View

Now that you have a specific template selected for your folder, you will have a more advanced feature list to work with so that you can display a lot of useful information about the files in your folder. First, you need to be aware of the views you can use in Windows 7:

- Extra Large Icons
- Large Icons
- Medium Icons
- Small Icons
- List

- Details
- Tiles
- Content

The icon size views are self explanatory, but the remaining views are different. List view fills the window with small icons and labels in multiple rows and columns. Details view arranges the folders and files in one long column with additional file properties. Tiles is similar to the List view but with larger icons as shown in Figure 8-8.

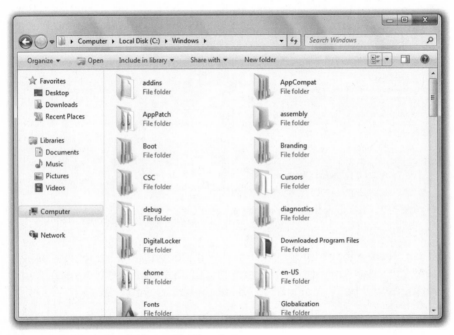

Figure 8-8: Displaying folders with Tiles view

Content view is new to Windows 7 and arranges the folders and files in one long column but with two rows for each file that display additional file and folder information, as shown in Figure 8-9.

Details view can be customized as no other view can be. All the columns that are displayed can be resized, removed, or rearranged, and more can be added. This can all be accomplished by using some of the lesser-known tricks of the interface. To start off, customize a folder that contains a bunch of MP3 files. By now, you should have already changed the template for this folder to one of the music templates so that you can use the advanced, music-specific features. If you have not already done that, go back to the last section to find out how. When you are ready, follow these steps to customize all the different parts of Details view:

1. Start off by resizing the columns. To do so, just place the mouse on the vertical line that is displayed between the columns and click and hold the left mouse button while you drag the mouse back and forth.

2. Add some of the new columns that display song information from the ID3 metadata tag embedded in the MP3 files. Right-click the column heading and select one of the many new options, such as Bitrate. You can even select More from the bottom of the pop-up menu to see a list of even more items that you can add, as shown in Figure 8-10. Repeat this step until you have added all the new columns that you want.

3. Most likely, there will be some columns that you just don't need. To remove these columns from Details view, just right-click the column heading and select the item again to uncheck it. This will instantly remove the column from the view.

4. The last part of customizing the view is to set the order of the columns in a way that you like the best. To change the order of a column, just grab the column header and drag it around by holding down the left mouse button and moving the mouse.

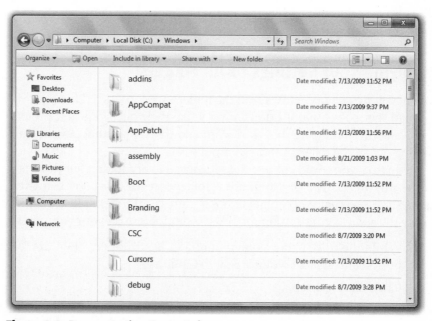

Figure 8-9: Demonstrating Content view

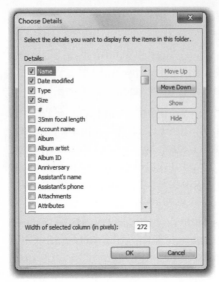

Figure 8-10: Adding new columns to Details view

If you want to customize the Details view of a folder that contains other multimedia files such as videos or photos, just repeat the previous steps and you will see additional column features with which you will be able to customize your Details view.

Applying Your Settings to All Folders

When you first use Windows 7, all the folders are configured the way Microsoft wanted them. Personally, I don't always like their decisions and prefer to customize them so they are the way I want and then apply that new default folder setting for all the folders on my computer.

To do this, you could change the settings of every folder, but there is a much easier way. Instead, just customize one folder on your computer using the previous sections so that you can get it looking great, and then follow these steps to apply the same configuration to all the other folders on your computer:

1. While the folder that you customized is still open, click the Organize button and select Folder & Search Options.

2. Click the View tab.

3. Click the Apply to Folders button and click Yes on the confirmation screen.

4. Click OK to close the Folder Options window and you are finished.

If for some reason you don't like what you did and want to restore all the folders to the original look, simply click the Reset All Folders button that was next to the Apply to Folders button to revert back to the Microsoft defaults.

Working with Hidden Files

Just like every other Windows version, Windows 7 likes to hide files. When you are interested in tweaking and customizing your computer, hidden files can become annoying because many of the system files with which you want to work are hidden. The following two sections will show you how to make Windows 7 display all hidden and system files as well as the super hidden files.

Showing Hidden Files

When tweaking your computer, you often need to edit different configuration files for different applications. This can cause a problem because those configuration files are often hidden. The only way to edit them would be if you knew the exact filename and typed it in the Browse box. Otherwise, you would be out of luck.

Telling Explorer to show hidden files and folders is the only solution to this problem. Making Explorer show hidden files is just a matter of getting to the right place. Follow these steps to show all hidden files:

1. Open a copy of Explorer by clicking the Start button and selecting Computer.

2. Click Organize and select Folder & Search Options.

3. When the window appears, click the View tab to see all the different file display options.

4. Under the Advanced settings section, scroll down the list until you see the entries for Hidden files and folders. Select Show hidden files, folders, and drives, as shown in Figure 8-11.

TIP While you are in the Folder Options Advanced settings list of features, I recommend clearing the Hide extensions for known file types box. This is always one of the first things I do right after installing Windows 7.

5. When you are finished, just click OK to save your changes and exit the configuration window.

You should now see all the files on your computer that are hidden. However, you may notice that some files are still not showing up. These are the system files. To show these files, continue to the next section.

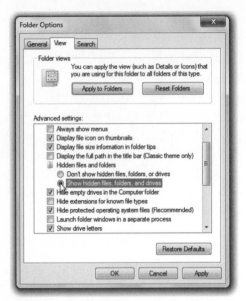

Figure 8-11: Revealing hidden files

Revealing the Super Hidden Files

Microsoft has added many features to Windows to protect the critical files of the operating system. The super hidden files feature allows Windows to protect itself even further by hiding some of its most critical files from users. If they can't get to it, they can't hurt it, right?

Revealing the super hidden system files is not very difficult. You can uncheck the box on the list on the View tab of Folder Options that says Hide protected system files, but where is the fun in that? Use the Registry Editor to turn this feature off:

1. Click the Start button, type **regedit** in the Search box, and then press Enter.

2. After the Registry Editor appears, navigate through `HKEY_CURRENT_USER\Software\Microsoft\Windows\CurrentVersion\Explorer\Advanced`.

3. Right-click SuperHidden and select Modify. If you are using the 64-bit version of Windows 7 right-click on ShowSuperHidden and select Modify.

4. Change the value to 1 and click OK to save your changes.

Now you will be able to see all the files on your computer, including the super hidden system files.

Summary

This chapter has shown you many different ways that you can customize how Explorer looks and works. You discovered how to change file associations as well as how certain file types look when viewed in Explorer. Then, you found out how to customize the context menu as well as how to clean it up. The last part of this chapter showed you how you can customize the different views of Windows 7 and control how and if hidden files are displayed.

The next chapter is all about customizing the next most frequently used program in Windows 7 — Internet Explorer 8. I will show you how you can customize the new features of the latest overhaul of Internet Explorer.

Personalizing Internet Explorer 8

Internet Explorer 8 is the latest version of Internet Explorer that has something for everyone. Improving the rendering engine was a primary goal in this release to help web developers make their pages render properly. The new "standards compliant" mode is on by default and is the result of a rewrite of the rendering engine that powers Internet Explorer. This is welcome news to the web developer community but IE8 also has something for ordinary consumers. Performance is another area that Microsoft dedicated a lot of resources to improve. JavaScript performance is becoming more important every day in the Web 2.0 world. Just about any interactive web site is JavaScript intensive and requires a good JavaScript engine. IE6 was just horrible at processing JavaScript quickly; IE7 was better, and IE8 is significantly better.

Aside from the performance improvements that benefit everyone, Microsoft also tweaked the interface, improved tabs and security, and introduced some new features called Accelerators and Page slices. In this chapter I show you how to customize these new features and many more so you can get the most out of IE8.

Customizing Search

First introduced in Internet Explorer 7, Microsoft improved the Search box in IE8 to provide a better search experience. This allows you to search almost any web site easily. I show you how you can customize the Search box to work with your favorite sites to search (instead of using what Microsoft wants you to search with). First, I cover the basics of this new feature, and then I show you how you can create custom search entries to search just about any web site on the Internet that has a Search box.

Adding Popular Search Engines

Before you get started customizing your search engines and developing custom entries, it is useful to go over the basics of adding and changing the default search engines that Internet Explorer uses. Doing so is easy. Just complete the following steps to find out how to add the major search engines through the Microsoft search site so that you have more choices aside from Microsoft's Live.com:

1. Open Internet Explorer if it is not already open.

2. Click the down arrow next to the Search box and select Find More Providers, as shown in Figure 9-1. Then click Search Providers on the side menu. Alternatively, you can browse to `http://www.ieaddons.com/en/searchproviders/`.

3. When you find a provider you want to add, just click the Add to Internet Explorer button.

4. When the Add Search Provider box is shown, make sure to check the Make this my default search provider box if you want to make it the default to replace Bing. Then click Add and you are finished.

Figure 9-1: Adding search engines to Internet Explorer 8

Our new search engine has now been configured. You can switch among active search engines by using the down arrow again, next to the Search box in Internet Explorer. If you already have your search engines set up and want to remove or change the default search engine, the next section is for you.

Managing Your Configured Search Engines

After you have all the search engines added to Internet Explorer, over time you might want to remove some or adjust the default search engine that IE uses. To do so, go to the advanced search settings found in Internet Options. Follow these steps to change the default search engine or remove a site:

1. Open Internet Explorer.

2. Click Tools and select Internet Options.

3. On the General tab under the Search section, click the Settings button.

4. You will now see a list of all the search engines that you have added to Internet Explorer. Select an entry from the list and click either the Remove or Set Default button to make changes to the search configuration.

Now that you understand the basics of search in Internet Explorer, you are ready to move on to the next section about creating custom search entries.

Adding Custom Search Entries

Don't like the search engines listed on the IE Add-ons site? This section shows you how to add any web site that has a Search box to be searched using the Internet Explorer Search box. You can do so in two ways. Web site owners can add special HTML to their pages that link to an Open Search XML file that allows users to add their site to be searched. Because few web sites actually support that feature, you can always add a site manually with a few tweaks. To add your own site, just follow these steps:

1. Open Internet Explorer and navigate to `http://www.ieaddons.com/en/` `createsearch.aspx`.

2. Open another tab or browser and go to the site for which you want to add a custom search entry. On that site, use the site's search function to search for TEST in all capital letters.

3. When the search result page is shown, copy the URL from the browser address window. Then switch back to the IE Add-ons page you opened earlier.

4. Paste the URL you copied in the previous step into the URL box on the IE Add-ons Create your own Search Provider page, as shown in Figure 9-2.

5. Type in a name for the Search Provider.

6. Click Install Search Provider.

7. Click Add on the Add Search Provider dialog.

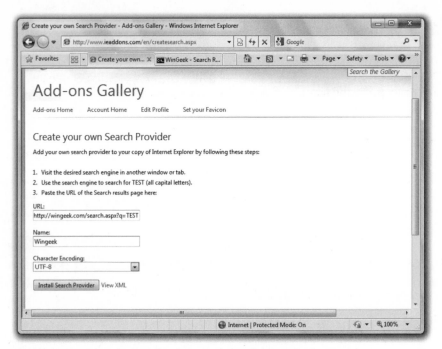

Figure 9-2: Pasting the URL for the search results page in the Search Provider Creator

If everything worked properly, you should now see the site you added as a new option in the Internet Explorer search provider list.

Creating Registry Files to Import Sites to Search

Another way to add sites to search in Internet Explorer is to write a registry file that can be imported into the registry. This allows you easily to add a site to search to multiple computers without your having to go through the manual step of using the IE Add-ons Search Provider Creator for each computer. The following example adds Tweaks.com to your search providers in Internet Explorer. Just follow these steps:

1. Click the Start button, type **notepad** in the Search box, and press Enter.

2. Type the following registry code into Notepad:

```
Windows Registry Editor Version 5.00
[HKEY_CURRENT_USER\Software\Microsoft\Internet Explorer\SearchScopes\Tweaks]
```

```
"DisplayName"="Tweaks.com"
"URL"="http://tweaks.com/search/?q={searchTerms}"
```

3. Click File, and then click Save As.

4. Change the Save as type to All Files (*.*).

5. Type **Tweaks.reg** as the filename and click Save.

You have now created a custom search registry file that you can import into any computer's registry by double-clicking the file. Keep in mind that this setting is a per-user registry setting, so every user on your computer who wants to use this must import it under that user's account.

Tweaking the Tabs

Tabbed browsing has been improved in Internet Explorer to make it easier to identify and group related tabs together. This section shows you how to get the most out of tabs in Internet Explorer. Specifically, I show you how to use keyboard shortcuts and multitab home pages and how to customize the tabs to fit your needs.

Tab Keyboard Shortcuts

Keyboard shortcuts allow you to get the most out of the new Internet Explorer tab interface by enabling you to do various lesser-known activities that can save time. These keyboard shortcuts require no setup; they are already active on your computer. Table 9-1 lists all the keyboard shortcuts that will help you take control of tabs, and explains how to start the Quick Tabs feature.

Table 9-1: Internet Explorer 8 Tab Keyboard Shortcuts

SHORTCUT KEYS	FUNCTION
Ctrl+T	Opens a new tab.
Ctrl+Click	Holding Ctrl while clicking on a link opens the link in a new tab but does not switch to the tab.
Ctrl+Shift+Click	Holding these keys while clicking a link will open the link in a new tab and immediately switch to and display web page on the new tab.
CTRL+Shift+Wheel Click	Holding these keys while clicking the mouse wheel over a link will open the link in a new tab behind the current tab.
Ctrl+W	Closes the current tab.
Ctrl+Alt+F4	Closes all background tabs.

Continued

Table 9-1: Internet Explorer 8 Tab Keyboard Shortcuts *(continued)*

SHORTCUT KEYS	FUNCTION
Ctrl+Tab	Moves to the next tab on right.
Ctrl+Shift+Tab	Moves to the next tab on left.
Ctrl+Q	Brings up Quick Tabs view, as shown in Figure 9-3.

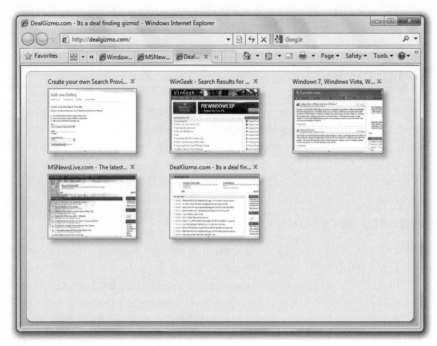

Figure 9-3: Quick Tabs view in Internet Explorer 8

Multitab Home Pages

From older versions of Internet Explorer, you are familiar with the concept of having a home page, a web site that is displayed when the web browser is loaded. In Windows 7, that classic browser feature has been mixed in with tabs. Now users can specify multiple web sites to come up by default when they load Internet Explorer and can display them in different tabs. Although this is not exactly a ground-breaking feature, it is a nice hidden feature that helps you customize your browser.

Using a multitab home page is easy when you know the secret. Just follow these steps to set up your own multitab home page:

1. Start Internet Explorer.

2. Click Tools, and then select Internet Options.

3. When Internet Options loads click on the General tab, you will see the Home page section at the top of the screen. To use multiple sites as your home pages, just enter each URL on a separate line, as shown in Figure 9-4. When you have finished, click OK to save your changes.

Click the Home button to instantly see your changes.

Figure 9-4: Setting multiple home pages for Internet Explorer in Internet Options

Customizing Tabs

Now that you have customized your home pages, you will fine-tune the tab settings to make them work the way you work. Back in Internet Options, you can change the way the tabs behave. You can alter the order in which new tabs open, specify how pop-ups are handled, and even customize what happens for various common actions. Follow these to get the Tabbed Browsing Settings, and refer to Table 9-2 for setting details and my recommendations:

1. Open Internet Explorer.

2. Click Tools, and then select Internet Options.

3. Locate the Tabs section on the General tab and click Settings. This loads the Tabbed Browsing Settings window, where you can toggle more than a dozen IE tab settings (refer to Table 9-2 for setting details).

4. Click OK to save your changes.

Table 9-2: Internet Explorer 8 Tab Settings

SETTING	FUNCTION
Enable Tabbed Browsing	Completely disables the tabbed browsing feature.
Warn me when closing multiple tabs	Displays a confirmation box when closing IE with multiple tabs open. I like to have this one disabled.
Always switch to new tabs when they are created	Changes focus to the last tab created.
Show previews for individual tabs in the taskbar	Displays each tab as its own thumbnail on the new Windows 7 taskbar.
Enable Quick Tabs	Allows the Quick Tabs feature shown in Figure 9-3 to operate. Keep this one enabled.
Enable Tab Groups	Responsible for colored tab groups.
Open only the first home page when Internet Explorer starts	Instead of opening all your multitab home pages, it just loads the first one listed.
When a new tab is opened, open one of these options	You can choose between a blank page, new tab page, or your home page.
Let Internet Explorer decide how pop-ups should open	Allows IE to make pop-up decisions. I recommend picking either of the following two options instead.
Always open pop-ups in a new window	Opens pop-ups in new browser windows.
Always open pop-ups in a new tab	Opens pop-ups in the same browser window but creates a new tab. This works well for most web sites, but I have found some pop-up windows that contain calendars do not properly close the tab when a date is selected.
Open links for other programs in a new window	This setting opens a link that you clicked in any Windows application, such as your mail client, in a new IE browser window.

Table 9-2: Internet Explorer 8 Tab Settings *(continued)*

SETTING	FUNCTION
Open links for other programs in the current window	This setting opens a link that you clicked in any Windows application in a new tab. I recommend enabling this one.
Open links for other programs in the current tab or window	This setting opens a link that you clicked in any Windows application in the currently active tab.

Fun with RSS

In recent years, RSS (Really Simple Syndication) has been taking over the Internet. It is not uncommon to see web sites offering various RSS feeds for their visitors that help them keep up-to-date with what is going on. With RSS, you can be notified when your favorite web site posts a new article or when there is breaking news from a major news outlet.

RSS is powered by a simple XML file hosted on web sites that follow the RSS standards. The RSS reader software interprets the XML file and displays it for your viewing. There are two different ways to view RSS feeds in Windows 7. Internet Explorer 8 includes a new RSS reader, and Windows Desktop Gadgets includes an RSS gadget that displays the latest headlines from an RSS feed right on your desktop.

Adding RSS feeds to Internet Explorer and your Desktop Gadget is a great way to customize your computer and make it work better for you. In this section, I show you how to subscribe to and configure RSS feeds in Internet Explorer and then view those feeds on your desktop with the Feed Headlines gadget. Then you fine-tune your RSS settings so that you always have the most up-to-date RSS content.

Subscribing to Feeds

Adding feeds, or *subscribing* as it is commonly known, is an easy task when you know the URL of the RSS feed you want to read. Identifying an RSS feed has become easier is recent years because many sites have adopted standard RSS image buttons. Others have simply provided RSS text links that point to their XML file rather than a button.

For this section, you need to find an RSS feed to use. Follow these steps to subscribe to an RSS feed in Internet Explorer 8:

1. Open Internet Explorer.

2. Browse to one of your favorite web sites, such as Tweaks.com, and click the RSS icon on the toolbar next to the Home icon.

3. This causes Internet Explorer to launch into RSS feed reader mode. On this screen, click the Subscribe to this feed link, as shown in Figure 9-5.

4. The Feed Subscription box will pop up on your screen. Type a name for the feed and click the Subscribe button.

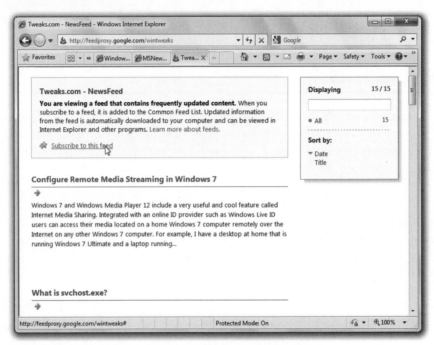

Figure 9-5: Subscribing to an RSS feed with Internet Explorer

You have now successfully subscribed to an RSS feed in Internet Explorer. Now that you have the feed set up in IE, you are ready to configure the RSS reader gadget that is part of the Desktop Gadgets.

Viewing Your IE-Subscribed RSS Feeds on Your Desktop

Windows Desktop Gadgets have a useful RSS reader gadget called Feed Headlines. This gadget uses your RSS feed data from Internet Explorer to display the latest headlines for one of your feeds right on your sidebar. After you have an RSS feed set up in IE, something you accomplished in the preceding section, you are ready to configure the RSS gadget to consume that feed and display it on your desktop.

When you are ready, follow these steps to configure the Feed Headlines gadget:

1. Right-click your desktop and select Gadgets.

2. Locate the Feed Headlines gadget and drag it to your Desktop.

3. The new gadget will load all your RSS feed already set up, including the default Microsoft feeds. You now need to change the gadget settings to use your RSS feed subscribed to in Internet Explorer. To do this, click the Tool icon while your cursor hovers over the gadget, as shown in Figure 9-6.

4. The options will now display. Change the drop-down box from All feeds to the feed you just subscribed to in Internet Explorer. Click OK.

The Feeds Headline gadget is now set up and configured to use your new IE-subscribed feed.

Figure 9-6: Opening a Feeds Headline gadget's options

Customizing Feed Settings

Now that you have your feeds set up in Internet Explorer, it is possible to fine-tune the feed settings (for instance, how often the source is checked for updates, a valuable setting because it determines how fresh your data is from the feed). You can modify feed settings by using Internet Explorer again, in much the same way that you subscribed to the feed. Get started by opening Internet Explorer:

1. After Internet Explorer has loaded, click the Favorites star button and then click the Feedstab.

2. Select the feed for which you want to modify the settings from the list of subscribed feeds.

3. After selecting a feed, you will notice that it is loaded in the browser RSS reader interface. You can access the feed settings by clicking View feed properties located at the bottom of the menu on the right.

4. When the Feed Properties window loads, I recommend that you go to the Update schedule section and select Use custom schedule.

5. Select a shorter update, such as 30 minutes, from the drop-down list.

6. When you have finished adjusting all the feed properties, including the archiving settings that specify how many articles of a feed to hold on to, click OK to save your changes.

Using Add-ons in Internet Explorer

Internet Explorer has a lot of new features, but is still behind in some of the features that other third-party web browsers offer. For one, Internet Explorer still does not have a spell checker built in to the application. Every time I post a message in a forum or to a web site, I usually have to write it in Microsoft Word and then copy and paste the text into Internet Explorer because I'm not the best speller. This can be a hassle; after all, I don't always want to have to complete this bulky process to ensure my spelling is correct. Instead, I can use an Internet Explorer add-on that adds spell-check capability within the web browser. In this case, I can forget about loading up Microsoft Word. I can just initiate a spell check in the browser and let the add-on check my spelling in all text fields.

This section is all about showing you some must-have add-ons for Internet Explorer, such as a spell check component just mentioned. First, I show you how to use the ieSpell add-on to save your web posting from misspelled words. Second, I show you how to use an add-on that remembers all your usernames and passwords and other registration information for you.

Using ieSpell

ieSpell is a great add-on for Internet Explorer that I have been using for years. This useful add-on is available free for personal use and for a small fee if used in a commercial environment. Installing ieSpell and using it in IE is easy. Just visit `www.iespell.com` and install it just like any other application.

After you have ieSpell installed, restart any open Internet Explorer instances you previously had open; ieSpell will be ready for action. When you need to use it, just right-click any text box on a web page and select Check Spelling from the context menu. That is all you need to do to initiate a spell check. Immediately after selecting Check Spelling, you will see a familiar spell-check interface that will help you ensure you have no spelling mistakes.

Using RoboForm

Another great add-on for Internet Explorer is called RoboForm. It is a great little utility that memorizes all your usernames and passwords and other registration information. RoboForm fills in the forms for you so that you don't have to type your personal information when you need to register for a web site or buy something online. This will save you time and help you remember all your accounts and passwords. Visit www.roboform.com to download and install the add-on.

After you have RoboForm installed, restart IE8, and the new toolbar appears. To get started using it, go to a web site that you normally sign in to and fill out the fields. When you click the Submit or Login button, you are given the option to save the logon information. The next time you visit that site, you will see a prompt on the toolbar that shows you the button to press so that the form fields are automatically filled in.

Advanced Internet Explorer 8 Features

While developers, performance, and security were the main focuses of Internet Explorer 8, there were two major new features for everyone. Accelerators are a new type of browser plug-in that accelerate your web browsing when you select and right-click text. Instead of copying and pasting text into a Search box or an address into a map site, you will have the option to jump directly to a search for the selected text or a map of the selected address. Web Slices are another major feature that allows you to see updates on a web page without actually going to a web page. Think of them as a special RSS feed that shows you a notification on the bookmarks bar when your content is updated and then allows you to interact with the content in a preview window without actually visiting the site.

In the next two sections I go into more details about how these new features work and how you can take advantage of them in Internet Explorer 8.

Using Accelerators

According to Microsoft, accelerators help you get everyday browsing tasks done without having to navigate manually to another web site. For example, you are looking for a place to go to dinner and found the web site of a good restaurant. You don't know where the restaurant is so you need to get directions. Typically you would copy and paste the address into a mapping web site to get directions. Accelerators in IE8 allow you to select the address, right-click, and see a map of the address in a small pop-up window as shown in Figure 9-7.

Figure 9-7: Using IE8 accelerators to map and address

The best part of accelerators is the plug-in platform. You can easily customize your browser to add or remove accelerators.

Adding Accelerators

The IE Add-ons Gallery has hundreds of accelerators available. To give you an example of the types of accelerators some of the most popular accelerators allow you to do the following:

- Map the selected address.
- Search Google, Yahoo!, or Bing for the selected term.
- Post the selected content to Facebook.
- E-mail the selected content.
- Search for a selected product on eBay.
- Translate the selected text.
- Get the weather for a selected address or ZIP code.

Adding an accelerator to your computer is similar to adding more search engines to your Search box in Internet Explorer 8. Just follow these steps:

1. Open up Internet Explorer and navigate to `http://www.ieaddons.com/en/accelerators/`.

2. Navigate through the available accelerators and click Add to Internet Explorer.

3. On the Add Accelerator screen, click Add.

After you have customized your accelerators you can remove and change the default by clicking Tools and then Manage Add-ons within Internet Explorer.

Using Web Slices

Web Slices is another new feature in Internet Explorer 8 that allows you to interact with a slice of a web page quickly from your Favorites bar in Internet Explorer. Instead of browsing to multiple web sites to find the latest headlines or sports scores or to monitor an auction throughout your day, Web Slices can be used instead and will even let you know when there is new information to view.

My favorite way to use Web Slice is to check the weather. When I'm browsing the Web I don't want to open a new tab and go to a weather site. With the Windows Live Weather Web Slice I can click a button on my Favorites bar and instantly see the weather in a small pop-up window as shown in Figure 9-8.

Figure 9-8: Checking the weather with a Web Slice

Web Slices come in many varieties. Some of the most popular slices help you watch an eBay auction or the latest news from a number of web sites.

After you have a Web Slice installed you can click the arrow on the right side of the bar to view the pop-up preview. If you want to go through to the web site, just click the button.

Adding a Web Slice

Adding a Web Slice to Internet Explorer 8 is very easy with the help of the IE Add-on Gallery:

1. Open Internet Explorer and browse to `http://www.ieaddons.com/en/webslices/`.

2. Navigate through the available Web Slices and click Add to Internet Explorer.

3. On the Add Web Slice screen click Add to Internet Explorer.

4. Click Add to Favorite Bar on the confirmation window. If no confirmation window is displayed you will be taken to another web page that contains or displays information about the Web Slice. A Web Slice can be idtified by the green button that appears when you hover over sections of a web page. When the button appears just click it and then click Add to Favorite Bar.

Just as with accelerators, you can remove Web Slices from the Add-on manager. Click Tools on the toolbar and then Manage Add-ons. Select Accelerators from the list and all your installed Accelerators will be displayed.

Summary

This chapter has been all about customizing one of the most used applications on your computer, the web browser. Internet Explorer has been greatly improved in Windows 7, and I hope you now understand how you can customize it to fit your specific needs. Earlier in this chapter, I showed you how to customize the search and tab features. Then I covered the new RSS features and how to make them work well with Windows Desktop Gadgets. This chapter comes to an end with some cool IE add-ons that will help you add more functionality, such as accelerators and Web Slices.

The next chapter is all about customizing everything related to media in Windows 7. I show you how to tweak Windows Media Player and how to build your own media center PC using the upgraded Media Center software included in the higher-end version of Windows 7.

Customizing Windows Media

The major media components in Windows 7 have been updated and enhanced to help you experience the very best your hardware can provide. Windows Media Player also received a major upgrade that improved performance and added dozens of cool features to help you browse your media collection. Windows Media Center has undergone a major upgrade, adding support for new technologies such as high-definition cable cards, IPTV, and an updated interface that looks amazing on your monitor or a high-definition TV.

This chapter shows you how to customize your experience by taking advantage of some of these new features and fine-tuning how they work. To get started, you are going to use some great new audio enhancements to tweak how all types of media sound on your computer.

Adjusting Your Audio Experience

The audio system has gone through a major upgrade in the kernel that is at the heart of Windows 7. There are countless new features, such as the ability to control the volume per application, as well as many others that are unnoticed by the end user and hidden away. This section talks about those lesser-known features and shows you how to take your audio experience to the next level. To do this, you are going to enable and tweak the new sound enhancements available on all newer high-definition audio cards.

The new audio enhancements are a collection of effects that allow you to do everything from boosting the bass to optimizing your surround sound using a microphone to get the perfect setup. These audio effects can be found on your output device properties. Follow these steps to get to the Enhancements settings tab:

1. Click the Start button and select Control Panel.

2. Click Hardware and Sound.

3. Click Sound.

4. The Sound properties screen will load. Select the Speakers playback device and press Properties.

5. After the Speakers Properties window loads, click the Enhancements tab. All the enhancement effects are now displayed, as shown in Figure 10-1.

6. Simply check the enhancement that you would like to enable. When selected, click the Settings button to fine-tune the operation.

Figure 10-1: Windows audio enhancements

As you can see, enabling and configuring the settings are easy to do, but before you start using these new enhancements, take a look at the next few sections describing the enhancements in detail.

Bass Boost

Bass Boost allows you to pump up the bass on your speakers. You can fine-tune the frequency and the level of the boost in dB, as shown in Figure 10-2. Experiment with what is best for your speakers, but I don't recommend setting it higher than 6 dB with most speakers. Otherwise, you might notice a loss of high notes in your sound.

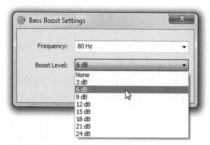

Figure 10-2: Using Bass Boost

Virtual Surround

Virtual Surround allows you to output surround audio over stereo outputs to a receiver that supports Dolby Pro Logic or another matrix decoder technology to convert the signal into an analog surround sound system. This feature is useful only if you have a receiver that does not have a digital input and are forced to use an analog stereo input. For everyone else, this feature will not help you. Microsoft really should have called this feature something else. It really got my hopes up that it would simulate surround sound using my two stereo speakers the way those old Winamp plug-ins did several years ago.

Room Correction

The placement of your speakers and the size of the room greatly affect the performance of listening to music and watching movies. The Room Correction enhancement automatically calibrates the volume and delay for each speaker for the best possible sound quality. This cool enhancement works by playing various test sounds on all your speakers and using your microphone to record the result. Next, analysis of the results is preformed and you are presented with optimal settings for each speaker. Simply OK the calculated settings and your sound is automatically optimized for all applications that run on your computer, including Media Center.

In my opinion, Room Correction is one of the best enhancements because it allows you to optimize your speaker system by just clicking a few buttons. I remember doing this with my surround sound receiver manually when I got a home theater system. This feature would have saved me a lot of time and the end result is better than a human ear could ever do.

Using Room Correction is very simple. While on the Enhancements tab, just check the option to enable it, press the Settings button, and follow these steps:

1. When the Room Calibration Wizard has loaded, click the Next button on the opening screen.

2. Select the microphone input you would like to use for the test. Make sure that you have a microphone plugged in to that input on your sound card. You can use any microphone for the calibration. If you have a studio-quality, omni-directional microphone, check This is a flat-rate, professional studio microphone. Click Next to proceed.

3. Position your microphone where you sit in your room. Make sure you elevate the microphone to roughly the height of your ears. For example, it is better to place your microphone on the armrest of a chair instead of the seat. Also make sure that your microphone is pointing straight up. When you are ready for the calibration test, press Next. It is best to leave the room when the test is running.

4. When the test is finished, press Next to view the results.

5. The results of the test for each channel will be displayed, as shown in Figure 10-3. When you are ready to apply the settings, press Finish.

Figure 10-3: Using Room Calibration

After the calibration wizard is completed, the Room Correction enhancement setup is finished and will be active immediately.

Loudness Equalization

There are many different sources of audio on your computer and among all these sources, the volume can vary drastically. Even within the sources, the volume can vary. For example, if you are watching a movie in Media Center, there will be times when you can barely hear people talking yet the background music in other scenes is very loud. The Loudness Equalization enhancement helps solve these problems by dynamically adjusting the volume on all the inputs so that they all sound constant.

The Loudness Equalization enhancement has only one setting that allows you to fine-tune the sample period. Click the Settings button to adjust it.

Headphone Virtualization

Available only on Headphone devices listed on the Playback tab, Headphone Virtualization allows you to simulate a surround sound system when using headphones. Say you are watching a DVD on your laptop on a trip; using this enhancement, you can enable special audio effects that simulate a five-speaker surround sound system using only two speakers. If you use headphones often, definitely give this enhancement a try.

Customizing Windows Media Player 12

Windows Media Player has been upgraded and greatly improved in Windows 7. The interface has been updated to include the new mini player known as Now Playing mode and a streamlined interface browses through your collection of music, movies, and videos with cover art. Similar to Windows Explorer, almost the entire user interface can be customized to your liking. The next few sections are going to show you how you can visually tweak Windows Media Player as well as customize the operation using some lesser-known features. I will start by showing you how to tweak the look.

Tweaking the UI

The user interface can be divided into two separate areas to tweak: how you navigate and how the information is displayed. Depending on your personal taste, Windows Media Player may be too busy for you, so you might want to cut down on the navigation options that are displayed to make a more slim and streamlined interface. The next two sections show you how to adjust the navigation and how the information is displayed.

Adjusting Navigation

Navigation in Windows Media Player 12 was updated to provide a cleaner and easier-to-use interface. The list on the left side can be fully customized to your liking. Any of the items can be removed and additional details displayed. Just follow these steps:

1. While in Windows Media Player 12, click Organize and then Customize navigation pane.

2. Scroll through the list and check each item you want to display. Remove the check to hide an item as shown in Figure 10-4.

3. To clean up the interface you can also hide the Music Services that show up on the bottom of the Navigation pane by removing the check next to Show Music Services.

4. Click OK to save your changes.

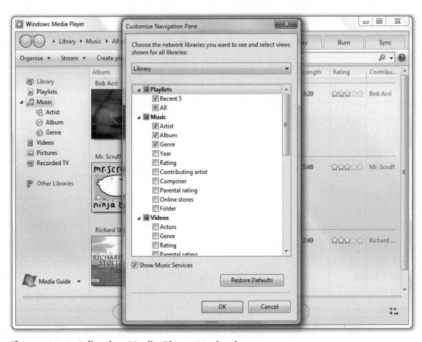

Figure 10-4: Adjusting Media Player Navigation

Adjusting Views

After you have your layout of the panels set up the way you want, you can also modify the way the information is displayed in the main pane that lists your media. By default, the Icon view is activated. This is a basic view that shows the album cover, title, and artist name. A Tile view is also available that adds the year and your star rating to the screen in addition to what is shown with the Icon view. The Details view provides the classic list view of the media.

You can modify the active view for the main panel by clicking on the View Options icon, as shown in Figure 10-5, and selecting the view.

Figure 10-5: Adjusting Media Player view options

Sharing Your Library

One of the lesser known but very useful features that I always enable when customizing Windows Media Player is the ability to share my music library with other computers in my home. I have a few different computers and laptops at home that I use for development for my web sites and other purposes. Instead of loading my personal music collection onto each computer, it is much easier to set it up on just one and then share that music library. Then, on any of my computers also running Windows Media Player, the library is automatically discovered and I can connect to it and easily listen to my music no matter what device I am on.

There are two different ways to share your music locally: through a Homegroup that also shares files other than media or through the Network and Sharing Center. Homegroups are great for beginner users, but I like to do it the old way that provides more control. I'm going to show you how to configure sharing with the Network and Sharing Center to show that you don't need to use a Homegroup to share your library.

Although this feature is easy to use, it is not as simple to set up as a Homegroup. Follow these steps to enable it on your computer:

1. Click the Start button and then click Control Panel.

2. Type in **Media Streaming Options** in the Control Panel Search box.

3. Then click Media streaming options listed under Network and Sharing Center.

4. Click the Turn on media streaming button.

5. Type in the name of your media library and select which devices on your local network you want to have access to your library as shown in Figure 10-6. By default Allow All devices will be selected so any new devices that come online after you configure the sharing will automatically have access.

6. Click OK and you are finished.

Figure 10-6: Configuring Media streaming options

Sharing Your Library over the Internet

New to Windows 7 is the ability to access your library at home over the Internet. Known as Internet Home Media Access, it is very helpful when you want to listen to a song or play a video clip from your home library when away from home. Using a Windows Live ID you can link Windows Media Player on your laptop to your Windows Media Player on your desktop at home. The process of setting everything up is rather complex:

1. Start up Windows Media Player if it is not already started. Then click Stream on the menu bar and Allow Internet access to home media.

2. Now you will need to link an online ID to your computer so you can configure authentication. Click Link an online ID to begin.

3. If this is the first time you are linking an online ID to your computer you will need first to download the provider plug-in. Click Add an online ID provider. The button will open your browser to a page that will show you all available provider plug-ins.

4. Windows 7 launched with only a Windows Live plug-in available. Microsoft says more providers will be available eventually. For now just click the Windows Live logo and download and install the plug-in.

5. After the online ID provider is installed it will be shown on the Link online IDs screen as shown in Figure 10-7. Click Link online ID next to the WindowsLiveID provider option.

Figure 10-7: WindowsLiveID provider

6. Next, enter in your Windows Live credentials and click Sign in.

7. Click OK on the Link online IDs screen.

8. Return to the Internet Home Media Access screen and click Allow Internet access to home media as shown in Figure 10-8.

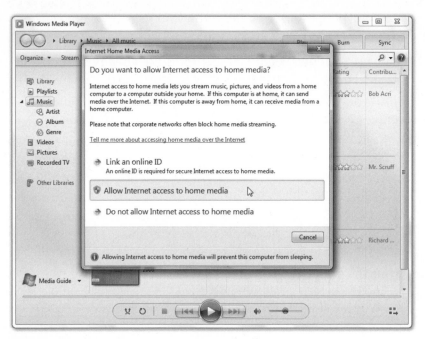

Figure 10-8: Allow Internet access to home media

9. Click OK on the final confirmation screen.

You have finished configuring your home computer to share its library. Now you need to set up your laptop to access your home library. The best way to configure a remote computer is to perform steps 1 through 9 on the remote computer. This will configure your online ID provider and also share your library on your remote computer so it can be accessed by your home computer.

If you ever want to disable Internet access to home media just click Stream on the menu bar and select Allow Internet access to home media. Then click Do not allow Internet access to home media.

Using Audio Effects

Windows Media Player has had a long history of supporting various third-party audio and video plug-in effects as well as a collection of built-in effects and features that are often hidden to the normal user. In this section, I show you how you can turn on a few of the best built-in effects that will help you customize and improve your Windows Media experience.

Accessing Hidden Effects

The simplified user interface of Windows Media Player has limited the access to some of the more powerful features such as audio effects. Accessing these effects is not as easy as it was in earlier versions, but it is not a huge annoyance, either, after I show you the tricks.

In Windows Media Player 12 the audio effects can only be found in the Now Playing mode. Click the icon in the lower right of the window to switch to Now Playing mode, as shown in Figure 10-9.

Figure 10-9: Switching to Now Playing mode in Windows Media Player

When in the mini player mode known as Now Playing mode, right-click the application and expand Enhancements. Then select the effect you want to use.

Using the various enhancements is very simple now that you have them displayed. Take a look at the few new sections for a quick overview of some of the more useful effects to use and customize.

Crossfading and Auto Volume Leveling

Ever wish that Windows Media Player would gradually fade out of one song and into the next as with other popular media players? Windows Media Player has had this feature for quite some time, but it was buried in a horrible UI so many people never even knew it was there. Using this feature allows you to set a custom period where the end of one song will fade in with the beginning on the new song, creating a smooth transition between songs without any dead air.

When Crossfading is selected, click the Turn on crossfading link and drag the slider toward the right to adjust the time the two songs will be faded together, to a maximum of 10 seconds.

Additionally you can turn on auto volume leveling that will make sure that the loudness of each song is relatively the same. This prevents having to adjust your volume manually between songs that were recorded at different volumes.

Graphic Equalizer

The graphic equalizer allows you to play around with the levels of different frequencies to help you make the song or video sound perfect on your specific speaker setup. Different types of music often require unique levels of values on the equalizer. Experiment with the different sliders or select one of the preset equalizer settings by clicking Custom.

Play Speed Settings

Play speed settings are more of a fun feature than a customization. Still, I figure it is worth mentioning because it can provide hours of fun for the right person or help you fast forward through a long file. When active, slide the slider to the right to speed up play or to the left to slow it down.

Quiet Mode

Think of this as auto volume leveling for just one song. It minimizes the differences between the loud and soft songs within a song.

SRS WOW Effects

The WOW effect provides a 3D sound effect that gives more depth to your audio. This effect also offers a TrueBass filter that increases bass.

Video Settings

Customize your standard video color setting here. You can modify Hue, Saturation, Contrast, and Brightness.

Dolby Digital Settings

These tweak the audio channel volumes depending on how and when you are listening to Dolby Digital encoded content such as a DVD with 5.1 surround sound. You can choose between Normal, Night, and Theater mode. Night mode reduces the audio range of all content but increases the center channel where dialog is typically found. This allows you to hear clearly what is going on without background music or noises overpowering voices. Theater mode increases the dynamic range of all content for a "full listening experience."

Customizing Media Center

Windows Media Center is included in Windows 7 Home Premium, Professional, and the Ultimate and Enterprise editions. New to Windows 7 is a refined interface and support for many new technologies such as Internet TV, where you can watch full-length TV shows for free. Over the years, Windows Media Center has matured into a valuable component of Windows providing users a high-quality and polished interface to explore all types of media from an interface that you can control with a remote control. Additionally, Media Center in Windows 7 includes support for Clear QAM channels (unprotected channels on digital cable) so you can pick up your local channels for free in HD from your cable provider (local channels on digital cable are typically unencrypted).

In this section, I show you how to customize and extend the functionality of your Media Center. I start by showing how to turn your PC that has Media Center but no TV tuner into a fully fledged DVR by adding a TV tuner. Then, I dive in to customizing the operation followed by cool Media Center add-ons that will enhance your experience.

Turning Your PC into a DVR

So, you have an edition of Windows 7 with Media Center but no TV tuner card installed? You are missing out on the main Media Center experience. With the help of this section and an inexpensive TV tuner card, I show you how to turn your PC into a fully functional DVR that will give any TiVo set top box big competition.

Before you can get started, there are some minimum system requirements that I must go over so that you will be able to watch TV on your computer. Your computer must have a video card with at least 128MB of RAM. To support the best appearance your video card must also support the Aero Glass effect.

The most important aspect of adding a tuner to your PC is picking one that is compatible with Windows 7 Media Center. Several tuner cards are on the market, but not all are compatible with Windows 7 Media Center. One way to find a tuner that Microsoft has certified compatible is to use the Windows Logo product search page located at `http://winqual.microsoft.com/HCL/Default .aspx?m=7` and search for compatible products. Just select either the 32-bit or

64-bit version of Windows you are running, set the Category to TV Tuner Cards and the Additional Qualifications box to MediaCenter, and click the Start button on the web page. You will be shown a list of all the cards Microsoft has certified.

As you can see, there are both internal PCI cards and external USB devices that can be added to your computer. The following are a few more models that are known to work well on Windows 7:

- **Internal PCI-E: WinTV-HVR-1250**
- **Internal PCI-E: WinTV-HVR-2250**
- **External USB: Diamond ATI TV Wonder HD 750 (TVW750USB)**

TIP I recommend the forum at www.TheGreenButton.com to find even more compatible TV tuners and tips to make them function properly if you have any compatibility problems.

Installing the TV tuner is also very easy, especially if you purchased an external USB tuner. Simply plug it in and install the drivers that came with the device. If you purchased an internal PCI or PCI-E card, just turn off your computer, unplug the power, open the case, and pop in the card in an open PCI or PCI-E slot. Make sure to install the drivers after you power your PC back on although in some cases Windows 7 will automatically install the drivers as it did with my PCI-E TV tuner card.

After installing your TV tuner card, you are ready to get started configuring it in Windows Media Center. Make sure you have your antenna or cable feed connected to the card. Follow these steps to get your Windows Media Center up and running:

1. Click the Start button, type **Media Center** in the Search box, and then press Enter.

2. If you are prompted with a setup wizard, just select the Express option. You are going to configure your card a different way. After you are on the main Media Center screen use the arrow keys to navigate down to the Tasks section. Then navigate to Settings and press Enter, as shown in Figure 10-10.

3. On the Setting screen, select TV and press Enter.

4. Select Set Up TV Signal and press Enter. At this point, you will get a Tuner Not Found error if your TV tuner hardware is not installed properly. If this happens, make sure that you have the latest drivers for Windows 7 installed.

5. Confirm your region by selecting Yes, use this region to configure TV services and click Next.

Figure 10-10: Configuring Windows 7 Media Center

6. Type in your ZIP code and click Next.

7. Click I agree on the Program Guide Terms of Service screen and then click Next.

8. If applicable, click I agree on the Microsoft PlayReady PC runtime EULA and then click Next. Microsoft PlayReady will be automatically downloaded and installed.

9. After the TV Signal detection has completed you will be presented with what Windows Media Center found. On my PC it said it detected Digital Cable (ClearQAM) and Analog Cable. If your results are correct click Yes, configure TV with these results. Otherwise click No, let me configure my TV signal manually and specify your setup. When ready click Next.

10. You will now be guided through setting up each of your sources where you pick the provider so Windows Media Center knows what program guide to provide you with. Click through the guide for each source and select your TV signal provider. When completed, click Next on the TV Signal Configuration confirmation screen.

11. Microsoft PlayReady updates will be downloaded along with the TV program guide. Then the TV channel scan will start automatically. This step will take several minutes. Once completed click Next on the results screen.

12. The TV signal should now be configured. Click Finish to exit and start using your new DVR.

Your Windows Media Center is now set up. You can begin to watch TV and set up shows to record in the guide. Now you are ready to further customize your Windows Media Center.

Creating Shortcuts for Windows Media Center

Windows already includes shortcuts to start Windows Media Center in the Start menu. Next, you'll create advanced shortcuts that will allow you to jump directly to different sections of Media Center. For example, how to make a shortcut that, when clicked, will open Windows Media Center and go directly to the TV Guide. It is also possible to go directly to other sections, such as Live TV, Recorded TV, Pictures, Music, and even Sports Scores as shown in Figure 10-11.

Figure 10-11: Sports scores in Windows Media Center

This is all possible with a special /homepage command-line argument that the Windows Media Center executable uses. First, right-click your desktop and select New and then Shortcut. Next, enter the location as shown in the following options, depending on what you want to happen. Press Next, name the shortcut, and you are finished.

Start Windows Media Center and Go Directly to TV Guide

```
%SystemRoot%\ehome\ehshell.exe /homepage:videoguide.xml
```

Start Windows Media Center and Go Directly to Live TV

```
%SystemRoot%\ehome\ehshell.exe /homepage:videofullscreen.xml
```

Start Windows Media Center and Go Directly to Recorded TV

```
%SystemRoot%\ehome\ehshell.exe /homepage:videorecordedprograms.xml
```

Start Windows Media Center and Go Directly to Music

```
%SystemRoot%\ehome\ehshell.exe /homepage:audio.home.xml
```

Start Windows Media Center and Go Directly to Photos

```
%SystemRoot%\ehome\ehshell.exe /homepage:photos.xml
```

Start Windows Media Center and Go Directly to Radio

```
%SystemRoot%\ehome\ehshell.exe /homepage:radio.xml
```

Start Windows Media Center and Go Directly to Movies

```
%SystemRoot%\ehome\ehshell.exe /homepage:movies.library
.browsepage.xml
```

Start Windows Media Center and Go Directly to Slideshow

```
%SystemRoot%\ehome\ehshell.exe /homepage:Slideshow.xml
```

Start Windows Media Center and Go Directly to Sports Scores

```
%SystemRoot%\ehome\ehshell.exe /homepage: SportsScoresPage.xml
```

Setting the Path Where Recorded Shows Are Stored

Inside Windows Media Center you can choose the drive in which you want to record shows; however, you cannot choose the exact folder. With the help of a simple registry hack, you can specify exactly where and on what drive recorded shows are stored. Follow these steps to customize where your shows are stored:

1. Click the Start button, type **regedit** in the Search box, and then press Enter.
2. Navigate through `HKEY_LOCAL_MACHINE\SOFTWARE\Microsoft\Windows\CurrentVersion\Media Center\Service\Recording`.
3. Right-click RecordPath and select Modify.
4. Enter in the full path followed by a backslash (\), as shown in Figure 10-12, and then press OK. Reboot for the settings to take effect.

The next time you record a show, the new location will be used.

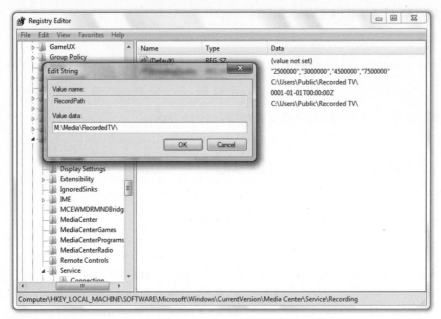

Figure 10-12: Modifying the location where recorded shows are stored

Configuring Media Center to Look for Recorded Shows on a Network Share

Personal network attached storage devices are becoming more and more common in the home environment. I recently purchased a 1TB NAS (Network Attached Storage) that I use to back up all my personal documents as well as store recorded TV shows. I have my Media Center recording shows all the time, so the hard drive on my desktop fills up very quickly. For the shows that I want to keep, I move the file from my record folder to a special folder on my NAS that I have configured Windows Media Center to watch and play files from. This is possible with a few setting changes within Media Center.

Follow these steps to configure Windows Media Center to watch for recorded shows in locations other than the main record folder:

1. Click on the Start Button, type in **Media Center**, and hit Enter to start up Media Center.

2. After it has started navigate to Tasks with arrow keys and then select Settings and hit Enter.

3. Click on Media Libraries.

4. Select the Recorded TV media library and click Next.

5. Select Add folders to the library and click Next.

6. Select Let me manually add a shared folder and click Next.

7. Type in the shared folder path such as \\Server123\SharedFolder and also a username and password that has access to the shared folder. Click Next when ready to connect to the share.

8. Click Yes, use these locations on the confirmation screen and then click Finish.

After you have added the new network share to your library you can click the green button in the top right of the Media Center window to return to the main menu. You are now able to watch recorded shows that are stored on another computer.

Using Third-Party Windows Media Center Add-ons

There are many very useful and cool third-party add-ons for Windows Media Center that really help you get even more out of it. As Windows Media Center is becoming increasingly popular, even more add-ons are being developed and released. The following is a list of some of the best add-ons available now for Windows 7 Media Center:

- **mcePhone for Skype (www.scendix.com/mcephone):** mcePhone is a great add-on for Windows Media Center that allows you to make and receive phone calls using your Skype account through Windows Media Center. This can be very useful and cool because you can use Skype through the Windows Media Center interface while sitting on your couch.

- **mceWeather (www.scendix.com/mceweather):** This is a useful add-on that allows you to get the latest weather forecasts and conditions for your area without leaving Windows Media Center.

- **Big Screen Headlines RSS Reader (www.mobilewares.net/mce/bshhtm.htm):** Are you a big RSS feed user? This add-on installs an RSS reader that allows you to read your favorite feed easily through Windows Media Center.

- **MCEBrowser (www.anpark.com/MCEBrowser_Screenshots.aspx):** Remember Microsoft's WebTV? Make your own WebTV and browse the Web on your television with this add-on and Windows Media Center.

Most of the Windows Media Center 2005 add-ons also seem to work well in Windows 7 Media Center. Visit www.benshouse.net/add-ons.php for even more Media Center add-ons that will work in Windows 7 Media Center.

Summary

This chapter covered almost every aspect of Windows Media. You started with tweaking your audio settings with the cool new features such as Virtual Surround sound and Room Correction. Then you moved on to customizing Windows Media Player 12 and taking advantage of its new features. Finally, I showed you how easy it is to add a TV tuner to your computer and turn it into a full-blown DVR that you can customize in many ways.

This is the last chapter of the second part of *Windows 7 Tweaks*. In the next part, I change the topic a bit — to increasing the performance of Windows 7. You begin by analyzing your system to get a good understanding of your computer hardware capabilities.

Increasing Your System's Performance

In This Part

Analyzing Your System

Have you ever wondered how fast your computer actually is? Sure, you may have an Intel 2.6 GHz dual core in your box, but the CPU is not the only factor in determining the speed of your computer. The true speed is defined by the combined speed of all your hardware, such as the read and write speed of your hard drive, front side bus speed, RAM speed, and even your graphics card GPU. Microsoft has attempted to provide users with a clearer picture of their computer's performance in Windows 7 with the Windows Experience Index benchmarking tool. This chapter helps you understand your Windows Experience Index as well as perform a more detailed analysis of the capabilities of your computer, and you learn how to make your computer faster.

Before you can jump into improving the speed of your computer, it is important to understand the limitations of your hardware and also to identify potential bottlenecks in your system. Using the tools discussed in this chapter, you will be able to run different tests that will help you decide which tweaks work best for your computer, in upcoming chapters.

Monitoring Your System Hardware

Monitoring the status of your system with various tools will help you understand what is going on behind the scenes, similar to the instrument panel of a car. If you are driving home and you notice that the temperature gauge is maxed out and the instrument panel is flashing with all sorts of warning icons, it is very easy to understand that your car is not performing at its best. Monitoring your system, for example, will reveal whether you are running low on memory, whether your CPU is overloaded, or whether your system has too many programs running at the same time. These are all useful and important things to know, and having that information available enables you to change settings to get optimal performance.

A variety of performance monitoring software is available. Get started by using the Reliability and Performance Monitor.

Using the Resource Monitor

Windows has a great diagnostic tool that's built right in, called the Resource Monitor. This cool utility can give you stats on just about every aspect of Windows. Similar to other system monitoring tools, its purpose is to help you diagnose problems and improve the performance of your computer.

To start the application, simply click the Start button, type **Resource Monitor** in the Search box, and then press Enter.

After the Resource Monitor loads, you will see the Overview tab that is filled with the most common system stats, as shown in Figure 11-1.

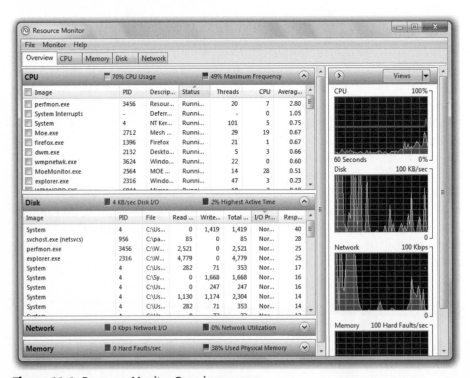

Figure 11-1: Resource Monitor Overview screen

By default, you are presented with a moving graph of the CPU, Disk, Network, and Memory usage. On the left you will find detailed breakout sections that can be expanded to show exactly how much each process is using the CPU, Network, and Memory as well as which processes and files are using the disk.

New to Windows 7 are dedicated tabs for CPU, Disk, Memory, and Network. Each dedicated tab has a wealth of information that is very useful.

Using the Detailed CPU Section

Here you will find a list of all the processes running on your machine, similar to the Processes tab of Task Manager, as shown in Figure 11-2.

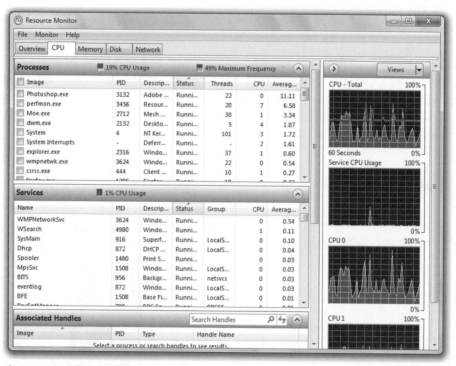

Figure 11-2: The detailed CPU section

On the top of the bar, you will find the current usage of your CPU as well as a maximum usage rate. The list of processes is below that, sorted by average CPU usage. Unlike the active process list in Task Manager, this list shows you only the average usage rate. This is very helpful when you're looking for an application that has an overall meaningful impact on your CPU usage. Additionally, you are shown the number of threads and CPU cycles the process is currently using.

Just below the processes you will find a list of all the services running on your computer and the corresponding CPU utilization.

When you select a process by checking the box next to the image name, the service list, handle list, and module list will display only services, handles, and modules a specific process is using. This is very helpful and is something I wish had been built into Windows for years.

The information you gain about your computer from the detailed CPU section will help you identify applications you run that have a big impact on the performance of your computer. If you have a process listed that has a very high average CPU time, try to identify what the process is by using the Description column or even a search engine if necessary. You might find that a simple application such as a desktop weather application that runs in the background is using a big portion of your CPU. With this information, you may decide to uninstall or disable the application to speed up your system. I'll talk more about that in the following chapters.

Using the Detailed Memory Section

The detailed Memory section shows you how much of the various types of memory each running process is using, as shown in Figure 11-3. The processes show the number of hard memory faults per second and the percentage of total physical memory that is in use. The memory overview is one of the most useful overviews in the Reliability and Performance Monitor.

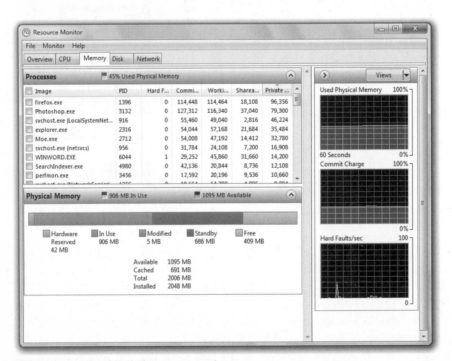

Figure 11-3: The detailed Memory section

Take a look at the number of hard memory faults and total percentage of physical memory that is in use. If you are getting any more than a few hard memory faults per second, you might need more memory for your computer. A memory fault occurs when something a program needs is not in memory and the memory manager has to get it and put it there. Usually it has to make room for the new data to be placed in memory by kicking some of the other processes' data out of physical memory and into the paging file on your hard drive. This can be a slow operation.

Also consider the amount of private memory a process is using. A process that is using a huge amount of private memory can steal your system resources from other processes, which results in more memory faults and a slow-down of your computer.

On the bottom of the Memory section you will find a useful chart that shows how your physical RAM is allocated. The chart includes hardware reserved, in use, modified, standby, and free.

Using the Detailed Disk Section

The detailed Disk section shows the read and write speed in bytes per minute of the various processes running, as shown in Figure 11-4. The list of open read and write per processes also shows the file that is in use. The Disk bar shows the total speed of all the disk operations as well as the percent of the time the disk is active.

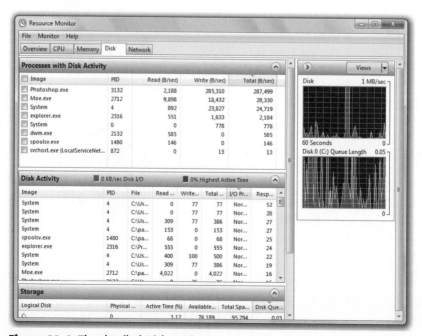

Figure 11-4: The detailed Disk section

These numbers enable you to see whether an application is hogging your disk and slowing down all the other processes on your computer because it is reading and writing so much data. This is especially useful when trying to identify what your hard drive is doing when you hear it going crazy and the hard drive read/write light seems as though it is constantly on.

Using the Detailed Network Section

The detailed Network section shows which processes on your system are using the network, as shown in Figure 11-5. The Network activity bar shows you the current network speed and the percent your network connections are utilized. Each open network connection is listed below with the name of the process using the connection. Additionally, you will find the network address the process has connected to as well as the amount of data sent and received in bytes per minute.

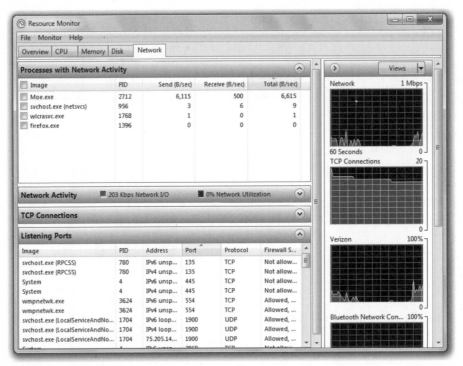

Figure 11-5: The detailed Network section

Have a slow Internet connection? Are the lights on your cable or DSL modem going crazy? These network usage stats will help you diagnose a process that is bogging down your network connection, such as a free peer-to-peer VoIP (Voice over IP) application. These applications can use your network connection even if you are not on a call. Other users' calls may be routed through your computer, resulting in your network connection slowing down. Using the information in the detailed Network overview, you can easily identify how much data is transferring both ways for every process on your computer.

NOTE With the detailed Network overview, it is easy to find out if your network connection has a high utilization rate by looking at the header bar. Keep in mind that the network card in your computer usually has a greater capacity and is capable of higher speeds than your Internet connection. If you have a 100MB network card in your computer and it is connected to a 10MB broadband Internet connection, then when your network card utilization is at 10 percent, your Internet connection is at 100 percent utilization.

Using Performance Monitor to Get More System Stats

Performance Monitor is one of the classic features of the Performance Diagnostic Console that has been around since Window NT and has been refined over the years to be a very comprehensive tool. In Windows 7, hundreds of different monitors are built-in that allow you to monitor just about every aspect of the operating system and your hardware. If you want, you can even view information about how fast your laptop's battery is charging or discharging. Similar to other system monitoring tools, the Performance Monitor is provided to help you detect problems and improve your system performance.

Just click the Start button, type in **perfmon.msc**, and hit Enter. When the Performance Monitor loads, select Performance Monitor listed under Monitoring tools. You should now see a graph of the Processor utilization percentage. This is a rather useless chart because you already have this information in the Resource Monitor or Task Manager. The real power of the Performance Monitor can be found in the performance counters.

TIP Performance Monitor gets the data for the counter from the system registry by default. A special flag for perfmon.msc allows you to change the data source to get the data directly from the Windows Management Interface instead. This is useful if you are getting some strange results and would like to get a second opinion on what is really going on. Simply click the Start button, type in **perfmon.msc /sysmon_wmi**, and hit Enter.

To add more performance counters, simply click the icon with the + symbol on it, or press Ctrl+I and the Add Counters window appears, as shown in Figure 11-6.

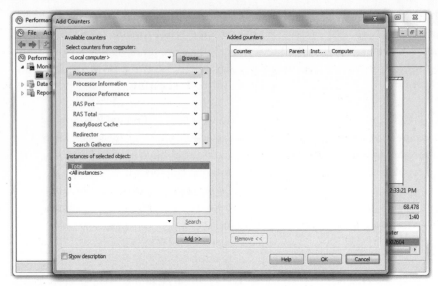

Figure 11-6: Adding a performance counter

When the Add Counters window appears, you will notice that the counters are organized in different component categories. Navigate through the list box and click the down arrow to see the individual counters available for the selected subject. Because some of the counter names are vague, you can turn on the bottom description pane to find out more details about a specific counter by checking the Show Description box in the lower-left corner of the window.

Let's say that you want to monitor remote desktop connections made to your computer. You can easily accomplish this with the right performance counter:

1. With the Add Counters window open, navigate through the list of subjects and expand Terminal Services.

2. You will find three counters: Active Sessions, Inactive Sessions, and Total Sessions. Select Active Sessions.

3. Depending on the counter, you may be required to select which instance of the object you want to track. If your computer has a multi-core CPU chip and you are using a CPU utilization counter, the Instances of selected object list box will display and allow you to choose what core of the CPU you want to track. For the selected Active Sessions counter, there are no instance options, so that box remains grayed out.

4. After you have the counter selected, click the Add button.

5. When a new counter has been added, you can always add more counters on the same screen. Select the Total Sessions counter and click Add again.

6. Click OK to close the Add Counters window and return to the Performance Monitor screen.

TIP When selecting performance counters, you can hold the Ctrl key and select multiple counters at once. Then click the Add button and all the selected counters are added instead of having to click each counter individually and then hitting Add. Additionally, if you want to add all the counters in a category, select the category name and click Add.

TIP When adding performance counters to the Performance Monitor, it is possible to add counters from a remote computer. If your computer is on a corporate domain and you have administrative rights, or if you have an administrative account on another home computer, you can easily monitor the performance remotely. When the Add Counters window is open, simply type the name of the computer in the Select counters from computer box. Alternatively, you can click the Browse button and select the computer if the remote computer's name is broadcast across your network. After entering the computer name, press Enter to connect. If you get an error, make sure that you have the correct permissions on your domain to use this feature and that your username and password for the account you are currently logged on to is the same on both computers, if this is in a home or non-domain environment.

You will now see the Terminal Services Active Sessions and Total Sessions counters listed on the graph, in addition to the CPU utilization performance counter. However, the line graph makes it hard to read these performance counters. The next section shows you how to customize the performance counter data display.

Viewing the Data

The Performance Monitor allows you to view the data in many different ways. The default screen is the line graph, as shown in Figure 11-7. This display method is adequate for a few performance counters, but when you have more than three or four, figuring out what line is for what counter starts to become a little confusing. Additionally, for certain counters such as Memory Cache Faults/sec and Cache Bytes Peak, the line graph doesn't make it easy to understand the data. Fortunately, Microsoft provides two other methods for viewing the data.

Another method of viewing the data is to use the Histogram display, as shown in Figure 11-8. To change to this display method, select Histogram bar on the View drop-down list that currently shows Line selected. This method of displaying the data is not much better than the default, but because it relies on one scale, the counters that report large numbers will dwarf counters that report small numbers. This limitation makes it almost impossible to read some of the performance counters.

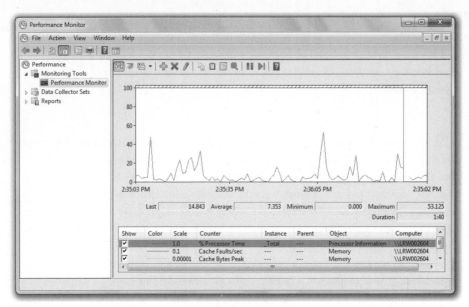

Figure 11-7: The default screen of Performance Monitor

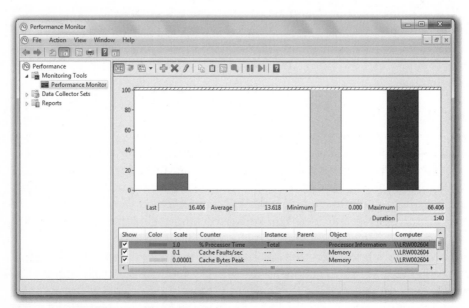

Figure 11-8: Performance Monitor's Histogram bar view

To make everyone happy, there is also a Report viewing method, which simply lists the counter numbers in text, as shown in Figure 11-9. You can activate this viewing method by choosing Select Report from the View drop-down list.

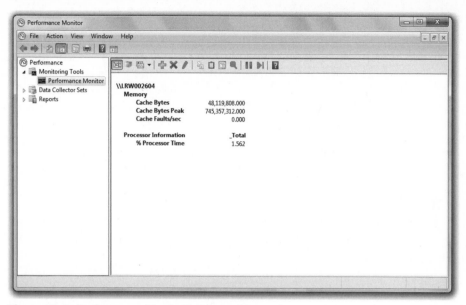

Figure 11-9: Performance Monitor's Report view

Setting the Update Interval

Now that you have all your performance counters set up and displaying data, you need to select the interval time of how often the data will be updated. How often you want the counters to be updated depends on your purpose for monitoring your hardware. For example, if you are trying to track how much data your computer is sending through your network adapter every day or hour, it is not necessary to have that counter update every second. You will just be wasting CPU cycles because you are making the computer constantly update that performance counter. However, if you are interested in current memory or CPU utilization, you will want a much faster update time.

To change the update interval, perform the following steps:

1. While in the Performance Monitor, right click on the graph and select Properties. Alternatively, you can press Ctrl+Q.

2. After the System Monitor Properties window loads, click the General tab.

3. Locate the Graph elements section and update the Sample Every text box. This number is in seconds.

4. Click OK to close the window and save your changes.

Now Performance Monitor will poll the data sources at your specified interval.

Analyzing and Detecting Problems

The Performance Monitor and the various performance counters make it possible to detect many problems and shed light on how to make your system run faster. You should familiarize yourself with a handful of tips that deal with specific performance counters listed next; these will prove to be invaluable in your analysis and decision-making. The following are some of the things to look out for when monitoring your system:

- **Physical Disk: Disk Read Bytes/sec and Disk Write Bytes/sec:** These two performance counters can tell you whether your physical disk is set up and functioning correctly. To determine this, consult the web site or the manual of the manufacturer of your hard drive. Look up the range of read/write speeds. If the readings that you are getting are far below what you should be getting, then your hard disk could be damaged or set up incorrectly. Run diagnostic software on the disk and make sure that it is set up properly in Device Manager with the correct transfer mode. Remember that most hard drives read at different speeds when they are reading from different parts of the disk. This is why there may be some discrepancies between your readings.

- **Paging File: % Usage and % Usage Peak:** These two performance counters can tell you how well your system is using the page file. If you set the size of the page file manually, these counters are very critical to deciding what size the page file should be. As a rule, if the page file % Usage is more than 95 percent or if the Usage Peak is near 100 percent, consider increasing the size of the page file if you have set the size manually.

- **Memory: Available MBytes and Paging File: % Usage:** These two performance counters help you decide whether you should put more RAM in your computer. If the number of your available megabytes is low and your paging file usage percentage is very high, then you should consider purchasing more RAM for your computer.

- **Processor: % Processor Time:** This performance counter monitors the activity and work your processor is doing. If your CPU is consistently working at or more than 50 percent, and you are not running any computation-intensive applications in the background, this would indicate that you should consider upgrading your CPU. The CPU is having a hard time keeping up with all your programs. You can also try closing open applications that are running in the background to make your computer more responsive and faster.

Saving Your Performance Counter Setup

After you have spent some time adding all the performance counters that you would like to use, it is possible to save this configuration so that every time you start the Performance Monitor and use Performance Monitor, your performance counters are automatically loaded.

To save the performance counters selected, do the following:

1. Right click on the graph and select Save Settings As.

2. Type a filename, specify a location, and click Save.

When you want to use your performance counters again, just navigate to the location where you saved the file and double-click it. If you changed your default Web browser make sure that it loads in Internet Explorer. The Performance Monitor tool will load as a Web page in Internet Explorer. Just click the green play button to begin monitoring.

Using the Reliability Monitor

As with the Performance Monitor, the Reliability Monitor is a system monitoring tool that is designed to help you diagnose problems and improve the performance of your computer. To start it just click the Start menu, type in **view reliability,** and hit Enter. The Reliability Monitor is especially geared to helping you solve various types of system failures that can lead to poor performance in all areas. It works by tracking all the software installs, uninstalls, application failures, hardware failures, Windows failures, and general miscellaneous failures to compile a System Stability Chart and System Stability Report, as shown in Figure 11-10.

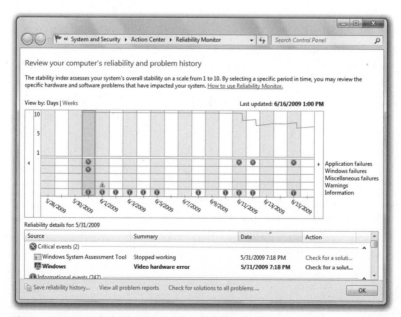

Figure 11-10: Reliability Monitor's reliability chart and report

Any of the icons on the System Stability Chart can be selected to move the scope of the System Stability Report to a specific time period. This is very useful because it allows you to see what happened the same day or just before some kind of failure occurred. Depending on this information, you will have a clue as to what may have been the cause of the failure.

Reading the System Stability Report

Every day your computer is given a System Stability Index rating based on the system activities of the day. The score is out of a possible 10 points. Depending on what has happened in the past, this score goes up or down. For example, if you have a Windows failure, your score goes down. As days pass, if you do not have any more failures, your score gradually goes back up again. However, if another failure occurs, it drops even more.

I recently had an issue with installing new video drivers for my laptop. I was trying to get the Aero Glass look in Windows 7 to work and was installing some drivers that were not exactly made for my laptop model. After I installed the new drivers, I had to reboot and was welcomed by the blue screen error. I rebooted again and the same thing happened. These system failures killed my System Stability Index. Before I had these problems I had a rating of 9.44; after my driver fiasco, I had an index of 4.711. As you can see, your reliability rating can drop very quickly if you have multiple major errors, such as a blue screen.

When you notice that your System Stability Index goes down, you are going to want to know why, so that you can fix the problem and get the performance of your system back in line. The System Stability Report is perfect for understanding exactly what happened.

With your mouse, select a time period on the System Stability Chart in which your score dropped significantly. Depending on presence of the information, warning, or error icons in the grid for the specific day, you will know what sections of the report you should expand to see the details of what happened. Figure 11-10 shows a red error icon in the Application Failures grid item on the selected day. This tells you to expand the Application Failures section of the report to see the details. After expanding the section, you will see which application failed and how it failed. Similarly, if this were a hardware failure, you would see the component type, device name, and why it failed. If it were a Windows or miscellaneous failure, you would see the failure type and details of what happened.

As you can see, reading the System Stability Report is a quick and easy way to see what exactly is going on. Next, you are going to use the new Event Viewer in Windows 7 to get even more detailed information about the state of the computer.

Using Event Viewer

Event Viewer in Windows 7 is a centralized source for reading all the system's various log files. When a component such as the Windows Firewall service has an error, notification, or a warning, it can be viewed in Event Viewer. When a third-party application causes your computer to crash, the details of the event can also be found in Event Viewer. Even when any user logs on to your computer, the details of the event can be found in Event Viewer. As you can see, Event Viewer is the ultimate source to find out what is happening and what has happened to your computer.

How can Event Viewer help with increasing the performance of your computer? Event Viewer enables you to identify hardware and software failures that you may not even know have been occurring. If you want to increase the performance of your computer, you need to fix any problems first. Skipping ahead without fixing the problems first is similar to tweaking your car engine for speed but not fixing the flat tires. Even if you increase the performance of other components of your computer, any errors or failures can offset any improvements in speed.

Using Event Viewer is very easy but requires an account with administrative privileges to run. To start Event Viewer, click the Start button, type **Eventvwr.msc** in the Search box, and then press Enter.

After Event Viewer shows up on-screen, you will see the Overview and Summary screen, as shown in Figure 11-11. The Summary of Administrative Events section provides an aggregated view of all your events. This groups them together from all your system logs and also gives you time-period stats on the different types of events. Expand the different event types, such as Critical, Error, and Warning, to see a more detailed aggregated view of all events that match that event type. You can also double-click the event types and events to view more details. Doing so will create a custom view for you automatically. I will get into those in more detail shortly. First, let's lay the groundwork for using Event Viewer.

Reading Logs and Events

The various system logs are organized in two grouping folders:

- **Windows Logs:** Windows Logs enable you to find events covering Windows core applications, security, setup, and the system.

- **Application and Services Logs:** You can find events such as hardware and specific software applications under Applications and Service Logs.

When you expand the top-level grouping folders and select a sub-event topic, you are presented with a list of all the events sorted by date by default. Simply select an event to view the details.

Reading the event log is very easy to do. After an event is selected, you will see details of the event in the bottom pane. The most important pieces of information for each event are the source, ID, and Description. If you do not see the description of the event on your screen, expand the Details pane up to review the description. Alternatively, you can double-click the event to bring up the Details pane in a new window.

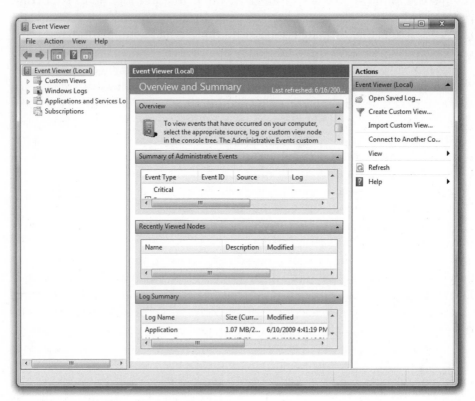

Figure 11-11: Windows 7's Event Viewer

If you have identified any events that signaled an error or warning, it is a good idea to research the event to find out whether it is important to fix. The most popular way to investigate an event is to do a search on either Google, Yahoo!, or Bing with the event ID. With the new version of Event Viewer in Windows 7, you can also click the More Information link on the General tab of an event. This will show you whether Microsoft has any information on the specific event.

Creating Custom Views

Using Event Viewer can be overwhelming because of the massive amount of data to which you have access. Custom Views is Microsoft's answer to data overload. Instead of looking through multiple log files, you can create a custom view in which you specify parameters for specific types of events. You can use the view to find all events that you specified no matter what log they are in. You first encountered a custom view on the Event Logs Summary screen. All the information in the Summary of administrative events section is populated by a custom view.

Creating your own custom view is easier than manually navigating through all the different log sources, and custom views are more flexible than the Event Logs Summary screen. Follow these steps to create your own custom view:

1. With Event Viewer open, right click on Custom Views and select Create Custom View.

2. The Create Custom View window loads, showing all the parameters of the view. You will see two tabs: Filter and XML. You will use the Filter tab because it automatically produces the XML for you.

3. Select the Time Period for your view. I like to use Last 7 Days for this option.

4. Check the boxes for the Event Levels you want to view, such as Critical, Error, and Warning.

5. Expand the Event Logs drop-down box and then select the log sources that you want to search in.

6. You have the option to set a specific object to view events for, such as a specific application or device. Alternatively, you can just leave this setting as <All Event Sources>.

7. To find all the events with a certain ID, enter in the Event ID. You can also exclude a specific event from the view by adding a minus sign in front of the ID (for example, –2030).

8. The last few settings are used less frequently. Here you can also specify the Task Category, Keywords for the event, and a specific computer user the event occurred with.

9. After finalizing the settings, click OK.

10. The Save Filter to Custom View screen will pop up. Type a Name and click OK.

After your new custom view has been generated, you can open it by expanding Custom Views and selecting it from the list.

Using Task Manager

The Windows Task Manager is a critical part of Windows that makes it possible for users to have full control over what their system is doing. Providing the ability to monitor individual programs and control any program or process, Task Manager is very useful. No special software must be installed to use Task Manager; just press Ctrl+Alt+Del and then click Start Task Manager. You can also press Ctrl+Shift+Esc or click the Start button, type **taskmgr** in the Search box, and then press Enter.

After Windows Task Manager has started, you will see a list of active applications running on your computer. Additionally, you will see tabs that list processes, CPU performance data, networking performance data, and active user data.

Monitoring Processes

Of all the applications on the computer that are running under your account, those that are hidden and those that are not can be found on the list on the Processes tab. On this list, you will be able to see how much memory each process is using as well as how much of the CPU each process is using. By clicking the column headings, you can sort the rows either numerically or alphabetically.

TIP By default, Task Manager shows you only the processes that were started under your account. When viewing the Processes tab, click the Show Processes from All Users button to view all processes. You will find that there are a lot of processes that run under the System account. Those are primarily system components.

There are many useful columns on the Processes tab:

- The Image Name column shows the name of the process.
- The User Name column shows who started the process.
- The CPU column shows what percentage of the CPU the process is using.
- The Memory - Private Working Set column shows how much memory a process is using.

If you find a process that is taking up a lot of your memory or eating up a big portion of your CPU, you might want to consider ending the process if it is not a critical one. Ending a process is very easy. Just select the row of the process you want to end, and click the End Process button.

Viewing Performance Data

The Performance tab, as shown in Figure 11-12, shows a lot of the same information that the Performance application shows. This tab is another place where you can view memory and CPU information, but in a far less detailed manner.

The Networking tab is a great way to monitor network performance. Each networking device on your computer has its own graph showing the percent that it is utilized. Although it does not keep track of bandwidth sent and received, it does show the speed that the hardware is working and if it is connected.

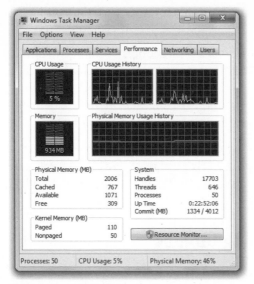

Figure 11-12: Windows Task Manager's performance information

Configuring Task Manager to Display CPU Utilization

When Windows Task Manager is started, a small histogram is displayed in the system tray that shows the CPU utilization. This little feature can be very useful if you always like to keep an eye on your CPU utilization but do not want Task Manager on top of all your windows. With a little bit of work, it is possible to start up the Windows Task Manager automatically on every start and run it minimized and hidden from the taskbar except for the system tray:

1. Click the Start button, navigate to All Programs, and locate the Startup listing.

2. Right-click Startup and select Open. A new window opens with the contents of your personal startup folder. Any shortcuts that you place in this folder will be automatically loaded when Windows starts.

3. When the Startup folder is opened, right-click in the open white space, select New, and then navigate to Shortcut.

4. When the new shortcut wizard loads, type **taskmgr.exe** in the text box asking for the location of the file, and then click Next.

5. Type a name for the shortcut and click Finish.

6. Now you are shown the startup folder again and a new icon for Task Manager. To start Task Manager minimized, right-click the new icon and select Properties.

7. Change the Run type where it says Normal Window to Minimized, and then click OK.

8. Now the shortcut is all set up. However, there is one last change to make, and you will need to open up Task Manager to make it. After Windows Task Manager is open, click the Options menu bar item and select Hide When Minimized so that when the program starts, only the CPU histogram will be shown and the program will not appear on the taskbar.

Your system is now configured to start the CPU meter on every boot in the system tray. Should you change your mind at a later time and no longer want the Task Manager CPU meter to show up, simply delete the shortcut from the Startup folder.

Other Performance Monitoring Utilities

In Chapter 6 I talked about how you can use Desktop Gadgets to add all sorts of cool gadgets to the side of your screen. There are several great performance monitoring gadgets that can be shown on your desktop and allow you to see performance information, such as drive space and CPU and memory usage. You can find these gadgets on Microsoft's Windows Live Gallery at `http://gallery.live.com` in the Tools and Utilities section.

Benchmarking Your System

The term *benchmarking* refers to testing your computer and assigning some sort of score to your computer's performance. The score can be an amount of time, such as the amount of time it takes your computer to solve a complex math problem. The score can also be a calculated point value that is determined by running a variety of tests, such as hard drive transfer speeds. The test can read and write files to your hard drive and then calculate a weighted score depending on how each test goes. The amount of time or calculated point value has very little value on its own; it is when the time or point value is compared to other results of the same test that it becomes valuable.

It is important to get an initial benchmark score for your computer so that you can compare your computer's initial performance to benchmark scores from tests that you may run at a later time. It would be nice to know how much of a difference some of the tweaks in this book actually helped your system. Or, if you upgraded the amount of RAM it would be helpful to see how it affected your system performance. By running an initial benchmark, you will have a score that you can compare all your benchmarks scores to after you make changes to your computer.

To benchmark your system, you need the help of a benchmarking application. A wide variety of different software programs can benchmark just about every part of your system. If you are interested in benchmarking the abilities of your 3D video card, for example, there is software for that. If you are interested in benchmarking your hard disk speeds, there is special software for that task as well. Next, I go over three popular benchmarking applications. I am going to start with the built-in Windows Experience Index.

Windows Experience Index

Microsoft included this feature in Windows 7 to make it easier for consumers to understand how powerful the combination of their hardware components actually is. The performance rating application generates an overall score based on the performance and features of your CPU, RAM, hard drive, and graphics card. For example, my computer has been given a score of 3.5 (see Figure 11-13). In addition to the overall score, you are also provided with individual component scores called the Sub Rating. These scores are useful to get a quick idea of the overall performance of your computer compared to other configurations.

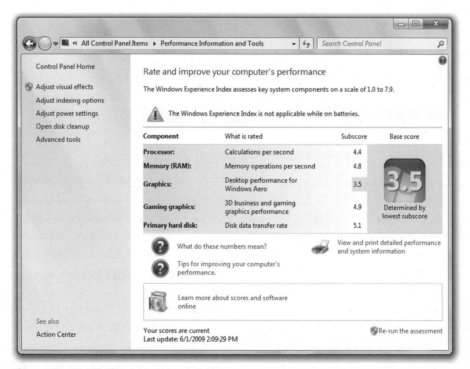

Figure 11-13: Windows Experience Index

The exact method of scoring different hardware components is unknown but is based on support of different levels of features and the performance of your hardware. For example, to get a score of 3.5, your hardware component must support feature x, y, and z, and perform between certain levels.

USING THE WINDOWS EXPERIENCE INDEX TO BUY COMPATIBLE SOFTWARE

In addition to providing a clearer picture of the performance of your hardware with Windows 7, the Windows Experience Index simplifies the process of identifying software that will work with your hardware. Remember the days of having to look at the system requirements on the side of a software box? To make it easier for less-technical computer users to select software that will work well with their hardware, there will be a Minimum performance rating on the box. Now even your parents can buy software and easily identify whether it will run well on their computer. It sure beats trying to explain why that new computer game that requires the latest video card will not work on the old budget PC you have at home. If it requires a Performance Rating of a 5 and your system is a 2, it's just not going to work well, if it even works at all.

Using and Understanding Your Windows Experience Index

As I mentioned earlier, the overall score of your computer is useful to determine how your hardware compares to other configurations. However, the main purpose of the rating is to determine how well Windows 7 will run on your specific configuration of hardware. The Sub Ratings are the most useful for the purpose of identifying possible bottlenecks and areas that you should investigate further. To get started, bring up the System window for your computer:

1. Click the Start button to display the Start Menu.

2. Right-click Computer and select Properties. This will load the new System information window.

3. Locate the System section and click the Windows Experience Index link next to the Ratings graphic, as shown in Figure 11-14, to open the Performance Information and Tools window.

4. If your computer does not yet have a rating assigned to it, click Re-run the assessment. This will start the rating tool and will take a few minutes while it generates scores based on performance tests and hardware specifications. It is best not to use your computer until the tests have completed to ensure accurate readings.

TIP If you ever change or upgrade the hardware in your computer, you should refresh your ratings after every change. The score will not refresh automatically.

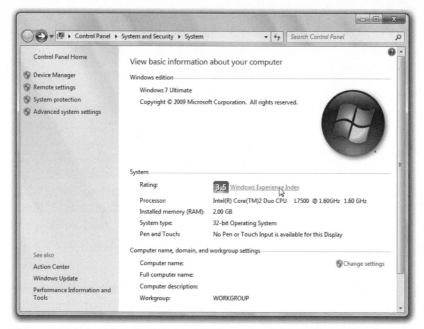

Figure 11-14: Loading the Windows Performance information and tools

Now that the Performance Information and Tools window is loaded and populated, you can analyze the results. I like to see whether any of the numbers may be holding back the overall score. For example, if all of my Sub Ratings are between 3 and 5, except for my RAM Sub Rating, which is a much lower 1.2, then it becomes very clear that I should concentrate on determining whether I should buy some better RAM. The lowest score in any Sub Rating determines the overall score for your computer.

Depending on your results, if you get a low score in the CPU, RAM, Hard Drive, or Graphics ratings, you should be able to determine what areas to focus on as you explore other more detailed monitoring tools in the next section.

Benchmarking with PCMark Vantage

PCMark Vantage Basic Edition, from Futuremark Corporation, is one of the most popular benchmarking programs for power users. PCMark Vantage has a cool online component that allows you to view your benchmark data and compare it to other users' computers. Additionally, the application generates an overall score that can be used to compare your system to other systems. The comprehensive score that is assigned to your system is the result of numerous test results testing various parts of your computer.

You can download a copy of PCMark Vantage from `www.futuremark.com/download/`.

The user interface of PCMark Vantage is very simple and easy to use. Simply click the Run PCMark button to start the tests. The free version includes only basic tests that simulate various computer usages to come up with your overall score. The basic system tests include the following:

- **PCMark Memories 1:** This test includes two simultaneous tasks that test CPU image manipulation and the performance of your HDD importing pictures into the Windows Photo Gallery.

- **PCMark Memories 2:** This test converts VC-1 HD video to a portable video player format WMV9 and uses two processor cores if available.

- **PCMark TV and Movies 1:** Two simultaneous tasks run that convert HD DVD video to VC-1 HD video while playing a HD video with SD commentary picture-in-picture.

- **PCMark TV and Movies 2:** The HDD is tested with Windows Media Center while playing HD DVD.

- **PCMark Gaming 1:** GPU gaming performance is tested by utilizing vertex shader operations provided by DirectX while data is loaded form the HDD and decompressed in memory.

- **PCMark Gaming 2:** The CPU is stressed testing artificial intelligence algorithms while the HDD is simultaneously tested.

- **PCMark Music 1:** Web page rendering is tested while an audio file is converted from MP3 to WMA and music is added to the Windows Media Player library all at the same time.

- **PCMark Music 2:** Pure CPU test that converts a WAV file to WMA format.

- **PCMark Communications 1:** AES data encryption is tested while data compression and Windows Mail is tested simultaneously.

- **PCMark Communications 2:** Three simultaneous tasks run including Web page rendering with multiple tabs in IE8, data encryption and HDD tests with Windows Defender.

- **PCMark Productivity 1:** Text editing is tested.

- **PCMark Productivity 2:** Contacts are searched, e-mail messages are searched by keyword, multiple web pages are rendered, and application loading is tested all at the same time.

After you click the Run PCMark button, the system tests will begin, as shown in Figure 11-15.

After the benchmark tests have been completed, you will be shown your system's overall score. To view the detailed scores of the different tests, you have to register on Futuremark's web site via the link on your results window. You can find out what hardware really performs and what hardware you should avoid. Overall, the PCMark Vantage web site adds a great amount of value to the application.

Figure 11-15: PCMark Vantage running the benchmark test

Summary

This chapter offered an introduction to the world of performance monitoring and benchmarking. Before you can make your computer faster, it is very helpful to know what your computer doesn't perform well with. This chapter showed you how to discover bottlenecks using applications such as the Resource Monitor, Performance Monitor, Event Viewer, Task Manager, Windows Experience Index, and PCMark Vantage. Use the information that you gained in this chapter in the upcoming chapters. For example, if you have a lot of applications that are using a ton of memory, pay close attention to recommended applications and services to disable in the upcoming chapters.

The next chapter starts to optimize the speed of your computer from the very beginning — the system boot.

CHAPTER 12

Speeding Up the System Boot

With the exception of Windows Vista, the boot speed has improved with every version of Windows. Developing Windows 7, Microsoft set a goal of reducing the boot time to 15 seconds. I would say that they got very close. If you have the latest hardware and a high speed solid state disk you can reduce the time to less than 15 seconds, but for the majority of users there is room for improvement.

This chapter shows you some tips and tweaks you can use to improve the boot performance further. It also shows you how to focus on reducing the workload put on your hardware and ways to improve the reading of data from your storage device.

Working with the BIOS

Every personal computer has a system *BIOS* (basic input/output system), which is what takes control of your computer the moment that you turn it on. The screen that you first see when you turn on your computer is called the *power on self-test screen*, better known as the *POST screen*. If you purchased your computer from one of the major computer manufacturers, this screen is often hidden by the manufacturer's logo. To get rid of this logo from the screen, just press the Esc button on your keyboard; you'll then see what is going on in the background. At this stage in the system boot, the BIOS is probing the hardware to test the system memory and other device connections. After the POST has completed, the BIOS proceeds to look for a device to boot from. When it finds your hard drive, it begins to load Windows.

The BIOS also acts as a main hardware component control panel, where low-level settings for all your hardware devices are made. The device boot order, port addresses, and feature settings such as plug and play are all found in the BIOS setup screens. For example, if you want to change the order of the drives that your computer checks to boot from, you want to modify the device boot order. I have to modify this setting almost every time that I install Windows because I want my computer to boot off the CD-ROM to launch the install DVD instead of booting off the operating system on my hard drive.

BIOSes on each and every PC may be made by different companies or accessed by a different method. Nevertheless, the most common way to access the setup screen is to press F1, F2, or the Delete key when the POST screen is displayed. Some computers even tell you which key to push to access the setup screen, as my notebook does. If your PC doesn't allow you to access the setup screen in this way, consult your computer documentation or contact your computer manufacturer for instructions.

NOTE While you are making changes in the system BIOS, make sure you do not accidentally change any other settings. If you accidentally change a value of a setting and do not know what to change it back to, just exit the BIOS setup screen as the on-screen directions indicate and select Do Not Save Changes. Then just reboot and re-enter the setup screen and continue hacking away at your system.

Changing the Boot Order of Your Drives

Most computers are set up so that when you first turn on your computer it checks to see whether you want to boot from drives other than your hard drive. The BIOS automatically checks to see whether you have a bootable CD in your CD drive. If your computer has a floppy drive, it checks to see whether you have a bootable disk in the floppy drive, too. Then, after it has checked all possible locations for a boot disk, the system defaults to your hard drive set in the BIOS and starts booting Windows.

What is the benefit of changing the boot order of your system devices? If you modify the order of the boot devices so that the hard disk with Windows installed will be searched first by the BIOS, the system does not have to waste time checking other devices for boot records. Just by changing the order of the devices, you can shave anywhere from one to several seconds off your boot time, depending on the speed of your hardware and number of drives your system has installed. The result is a faster startup with minimal negative consequences that I'll address later.

To change the boot order (or sequence, as some call it), you have to enter the system BIOS setup screen that was mentioned previously:

1. Press F1, F2, Delete, or the correct key for your specific system on the POST screen (or the screen that displays the computer manufacturer's logo) to enter the BIOS setup screen.

2. Look for where it says Boot, and enter the submenu.

3. Select Boot Sequence, and press Enter. Figure 12-1 shows an example of the Boot Sequence Setup screen.

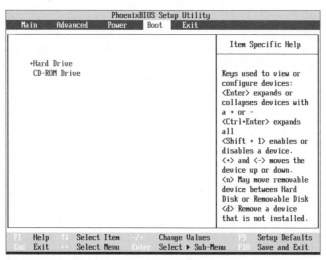

Figure 12-1: The Boot Sequence Setup screen

4. If your screen looks similar to Figure 12-1, you are in the right place. Navigate to where it states "first device" and cycle through the list to where it states "Hard Disk Drive" or "IDE0" (assuming that your hard drive is connected to IDE0). If your setup screen does not specifically state "first device" but rather just a list of all the devices, simply select the hard disk and move it to the top of the list. That can be done by using the Change Values keys (which for my BIOS, is made by Phoenix — the spacebar moves an item up and the minus symbol key moves an item down). The specific keys differ on almost every system, but the basic concepts are the same. You want to get your hard disk to the top of the list or listed as the first device from which to try to boot. If you do not know the keys for your BIOS, there are usually instructions located on either the bottom or right side of the screen where you will be able to find the correct keys for your system.

5. After you have made the changes, exit the system BIOS by pressing the Escape key, and make sure that you select to save your changes upon exit. After you reboot, the new settings will be in effect.

What are the consequences of changing the boot order? Changing the boot order will not hurt your system in any way if you do it correctly. If by accident you remove your hard drive from the list and save the BIOS settings, you will get an unpleasant surprise when your computer reboots and tells you that it cannot find any operating system. If you happen to get that message, don't worry; you did not just erase your operating system. Just reboot by pressing Ctrl+Alt+Delete at the same time and go back into the BIOS settings and make sure that you select your hard drive as a boot device. After you have done that, your system will be back to normal.

Another possible issue that you might encounter is just a matter of inconvenience. After you change the boot order of the system devices so that the hard drive is listed first, you can no longer use system restore CDs or floppy boot disks. If something has happened to your computer and you need to boot off of those drives to restore your system or run diagnostics, just go back to the system BIOS and lower or remove the hard disk from the first boot device and replace it with either a floppy or CD as needed.

Using Quick Boot Feature of the BIOS

All systems initialize in more or less the same way. During the POST mentioned earlier, the BIOS checks the hardware devices and counts the system memory. Out of all the different types of system memory, the random access memory, better known as RAM, takes the longest to be checked. Checking the RAM takes time, and on a machine that has large amounts of RAM, this calculation can take several seconds. For example, a machine that has 512MB of RAM may take up to three seconds just to check the memory. On top of the RAM counting, a few other tests need to be done because your computer wants to make sure that all the hardware in your computer is working properly.

The complete version of these tests is not needed every time you boot and can be turned off to save time. Most system BIOSs offer a feature called *Quick Boot*. This feature enables the user to turn off the full version of the test and sometimes enables you to run a shorter quick check test instead. Other BIOSes allow you to turn off the Memory Check only, which will still cut down on a lot of time.

To turn on the Quick Boot feature or to turn off the Memory Check, just do the following:

1. Enter the system BIOS again by pressing F1, F2, or the correct system setup Enter key on the POST screen for your system.

2. After you are in the BIOS setup, locate the text "Quick Boot" or "Memory Check," as shown in Figure 12-2. Navigate with the arrow keys until the option is highlighted.

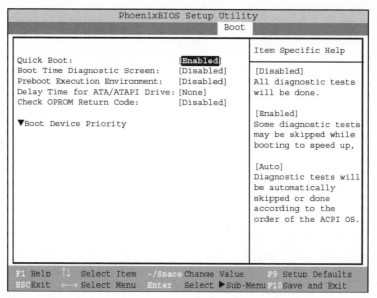

Figure 12-2: BIOS Setup screen displaying the Quick Boot feature

3. Use the Change Value keys to cycle through the options and select Enable for the Quick Boot feature or Disable if your system's BIOS has the Memory Check feature.

4. After you have made the change to the setting, exit the system BIOS by pressing the Escape key. Make sure you save the changes upon exit.

Use of the Quick Boot feature or the disabling of the Memory Check will not do any harm to your system. In fact, some computer manufactures even ship their computers with these settings already optimized for performance. The only downside to disabling the tests is in the rare situation in which your RAM self-destructs; the BIOS will not catch it, and you might receive errors from the operating system or your system could become unstable. If you notice that your system becomes unstable and crashes frequently or will not even boot, go back into the BIOS and re-enable the tests to find out whether your system's memory is causing the problems.

Modifying the Operating System Boot

You can use several different tricks to shave a few more seconds off the boot time. For example, you can reduce Timeout values and slim down the system to get rid of all the extra features and services that you do not use or need. Check out the following ways to do so.

Windows Boot Manager

If you have more than one operating system installed on your computer, you'll have to deal with the Windows Boot Manager installed by Windows 7. By default, the Windows Boot Manager gives you 30 seconds to select an operating system before it reverts to the default operating system. The only way not to wait 30 seconds is to select the operating system you want to use right away. If you use one operating system the majority of your time, you will definitely save time if you set that operating system as the default and lower the Timeout value to 1 or 2 seconds. That way, you will not have to select an operating system every time you turn on your system or wait 30 seconds before your computer actually starts to load the operating system.

> **TIP** Before you make any changes to the Windows Boot Manager (WBM), it is a good idea to back it up using the Boot Configuration Data Editor (bcdedit.exe) so that you can easily revert to an earlier version should you have any problems. At a command prompt run as the Administrator account, type **bcdedit /export "C:\Backup File"**. This will save the WBM to a file that you can use to import using the /import flag.

Lowering OS Timeout Values

As mentioned earlier, if you have multiple operating systems installed on your computer and the Windows Boot Manager is installed, the default selection timeout is often way too high. It is much better to set a lower timeout so that if you do not make a selection, it quickly reverts to the default OS, making your boot time much faster.

Changing the Timeout value is simple with the System Configuration utility. Follow the steps here to use the System Configuration utility to lower the OS Timeout value:

1. Click the Start button, type **msconfig** in the Search box, and press Enter.

2. When the System Configuration utility loads, click the Boot tab.

3. Locate the Timeout box and replace 30 with a much lower value, as shown in Figure 12-3. I recommend you use between 2 and 5. I use 2 because that gives me just the right amount of time to hit a key on my keyboard when the Windows Boot Manager is displayed on the screen.

4. After the value has been updated, click OK to exit.

Now that the Timeout value has been updated, the boot menu will no longer increase your system startup time. Even though this is a simple tip, it really helps a lot on systems that have multiple operating systems installed. Look at setting the default operating system on the Windows Boot Manager.

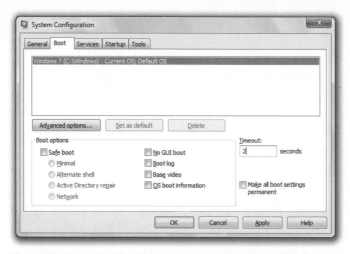

Figure 12-3: Setting the Boot menu Timeout value with the System Configuration utility

Setting the Default OS

In the preceding section, I set a new Timeout value that will cut down on the amount of time that is wasted before the operating system starts to load. That works great when your primary operating system is the default; but if it is not, you must remember to hit a key at the right moment every single boot. There is a much better way to handle the situation. Just make your primary operating system the default operating system in the Windows Boot Manager. This will allow you to benefit from the lower Timeout value and speed up the overall boot time.

Setting the default operating system can be configured with both the System Configuration utility or the command-line Boot Configuration Editor, bcdedit.exe. First, let's use the System Configuration utility:

1. Click on the Start button and type in **msconfig** and hit Enter.

2. Click on the Boot tab.

3. Select the operating system from the list you want to make the default and then click Set as default.

4. When finished click OK.

Using the System Configuration utility is the easiest way to set the default operating system but you can also set it with the bcdedit.exe utility. Follow the next steps to use the Boot Configuration Editor to set the default operating system:

1. Click the Start button and Type in Command Prompt.

2. Locate the Command Prompt shortcut at the top and right-click it to bring up the context menu.

3. Select Run as administrator from the context menu.

4. When the command prompt has loaded, you are ready to use the bcdedit .exe command. First, you need to get the ID of the operating system that you want to set as the default. To do this, type **bcdedit /enum all** in the open command prompt window. Scroll through the list of different entries and look for the one with the description matching "Windows 7".

5. After you have found the correct entry, note its identifier. That is used in the next step.

6. While still at the command prompt, run **bcdedit /default (entry identifier)**. For example, I ran bcdedit /default {b2721d73-1db4-4c62-bf78-c548a880142d}.

The default operating system on the Window Boot Manager is now set. The next time you reboot, your changes will be in use.

> **TIP** The Boot Configuration Editor is a powerful utility that you can also use to change many other settings of the Windows Boot Manager. Experiment with bcdedit.exe by running `bcdedit /?` from the command prompt. This will show you all the other available options and flags that you can use with the Boot Configuration Editor.

USING EASYBCD TO EDIT THE WINDOWS BOOT MANAGER

VistaBootPro is a cool and easy-to-use front end to the Boot Configuration Editor. Instead of using the command-line interface, you can use this free utility written by Mahmoud H. Al-Qudsi at NeoSmart Technologies. With EasyBCD, you can change the Timeout value, default selection, description, and even the boot order, as shown in Figure 12-4. Download a free copy of EasyBCD at `http://neosmart.net`.

Disabling the System Boot Screen

Windows 7 has a new high-resolution animated boot screen that looks much better than the previous Windows boot screens. The flag animation sure is a nice loading screen, but is it really worth an extra fraction of a second when your computer is loading? Disabling the boot screen can cut down on your boot time. Keep in mind that every fraction of a second counts.

This performance improvement works on a simple principle. It takes time for the computer to do anything. Taking away some work the hardware has to do, such as loading the boot screen, frees up time that it can spend loading your system files instead.

Figure 12-4: Using EasyBCD to edit the Windows Boot Manager

The process for disabling the system boot screen is similar to the process for modifying the default operating system timeout. For this change, you need to start up the System Configuration tool:

1. Click the Start menu, type **msconfig** in the Search box, and press Enter.

2. When the System Configuration tool loads, click the Boot tab.

3. Locate the No GUI boot check box and check it, as shown in Figure 12-5.

4. Click OK to close the System Configuration tool.

5. A small window will pop up and ask you whether you would like to reboot your computer now or reboot later. Make sure you have any open documents closed, and click Restart.

6. After your computer has restarted, the System Configuration tool may load automatically notifying you of the change. Check the box that says Don't show this message or start System Configuration when Windows starts and click OK.

After you close the System Configuration tool and reboot, the boot screen will be gone and you will have saved your computer from doing extra work while loading Windows 7 on your computer.

Figure 12-5: Disabling the boot screen with the System Configuration tool

Disabling Unneeded Hardware Devices

One of the most time-consuming portions of the boot is loading all the hardware drivers for your specific system setup. Every driver for each installed hardware device must be loaded and then initialized by the operating system while the system is starting up. Keep in mind that your computer has a lot of devices that you do not always use. When Windows has to load all the extra hardware on your computer, its performance is slowed down.

Although Windows 7 is more intelligent than previous versions on how it loads drivers and devices, loading those devices and initializing them still takes time. In previous versions of Windows, the system would load one hardware device driver and then load another device driver in a series. The problem with loading the hardware this way was that it could slow down the boot dramatically if one hardware device was taking a long time to initialize.

Windows 7 is similar to Windows Vista in the way it loads device drivers and initializes the devices. Instead of loading the hardware device drivers in a series, it now loads some of them in parallel. This allows the boot to be much faster. Although the hardware devices are loaded in parallel instead of in a series, the addition of more devices that the system has to load drivers for has the potential to, and most likely still will, slow down the boot.

Using Device Manager to Disable Hardware

Getting rid of extra hardware with Device Manager is an easy way to speed up your boot. Follow these steps to disable your extra hardware devices:

1. Click the Start menu, type **devmgmt.msc**, and press Enter.

2. After the Device Manager loads, you can browse through your devices that are connected and currently running or disabled by browsing through the device type sections. To disable a device, right-click the device name, and then select Disable.

3. To re-enable a device, right-click the device name and select Enable, as shown in Figure 12-6. This removes the check mark from the menu and re-enables the device.

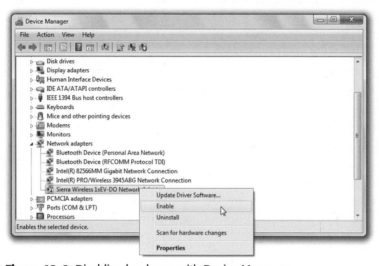

Figure 12-6: Disabling hardware with Device Manager

TIP To determine quickly the status of a device, check out the icon next to its name. All devices that are disabled have a down arrow over the icon. All devices that have a question mark or an explanation point on them are not set up correctly or are having problems. All devices with none of these additions to the icon are running — and doing so without any problems.

Which Hardware Devices Should I Disable?

Each user uses (or doesn't use) devices differently depending on the system setup. Nonetheless, some classes of devices are more commonly disabled than others. Knowing which ones will help you make your decision as to which devices you should disable. The following classes of devices are frequently disabled:

- **Network adapters:** Especially on notebook computers, there is often more than one network device. Disabling the network devices that you do not use will definitely save you some booting time.

- **FireWire:** If you have 1394 connections, otherwise known as FireWire, you might consider disabling them. Unless you are using your FireWire port to connect your digital video recorder to your computer, or have other external FireWire device, you have no need to have this device enabled.

- **Biometrics:** Some of the latest computer hardware includes biometric sensor equipment such as a fingerprint scanner. If you do not use these security features, you can save time by disabling theses devices, too.

- **Modems:** Do you have a broadband connection? If so, consider disabling your modem. If you rarely use it, why not disable it? If you ever need to use it again, just re-enable it.

- **TPM security chips:** Does your computer have a Trusted Platform Module (TPM)? These chips are typically used as a secure place to store an encryption key that would be used for something such as hard drive encryption. If you are not using any of these advanced security features of Windows 7, disable these devices, too.

- **Multimedia devices:** Your computer has lots of multimedia devices. Take a look at the "Sound, video, and game controllers" section in Device Manager. You will find a lot of device drivers that are loaded during your boot. Some are used by all users, but you will find a few that you do not use. For example, I do not use my game port or my MIDI device, so I disabled both of them.

- **PCMCIA cards:** If you are a laptop user, consider disabling your PCMCIA card controller located under "PCMCIA adapters." The PCMCIA (Personal Computer Memory Card International Association) slot is a special expansion slot that is rarely used today on laptops except for wireless and wired network cards and card reader attachments for compact flash and other solid-state memory cards. Most laptops now have built-in network adapters, and some even have built-in wireless adapters. If you do not use your PCMCIA adapter, it is yet another device you can safely disable.

CAUTION   Do not disable any hardware devices located under the Disk Drives, Computer, Display Adapters, IDE Disk Controllers, and the System sections (except for the system speaker). These hardware devices are critical to the operation of your system.

Removing Extra Fonts for Speed

Windows 7 has more than 130 different fonts and variations that it loads for use when the system boots up. Of these 130 plus fonts, only a handful are used on a regular basis. Every single font that Windows loads increases the amount of time the operating system takes to boot. If you are like me and have installed one of those font CDs that add hundreds of additional fonts to your system, you will notice that your computer does not boot up as fast as it once did. Simply put, systems with a lot of fonts will take more time to load because the system has to load and index each font. Thankfully, there is a very simple answer to this: just remove the fonts that you do not use from your font directory.

You can go about removing the unneeded fonts from your font directory in a number of different ways. The best way is to move the unused fonts to a separate folder on your system so that in the event that you ever want to use one of those extra fonts again, you just have to copy it back to the Fonts folder.

CAUTION When you remove fonts from your computer, you will no longer be able to use them in any software application, including Adobe Photoshop, Microsoft Word, and Excel.

Before you start removing fonts, take at look at Table 12-1. These fonts are commonly used, for reasons that the table explains. Be careful not to remove any fonts on which the system normally depends.

Table 12-1: Commonly Used Windows Fonts

FONT NAME	REASON
Segoe	The variations of this font can be found in elements of the Windows interface.
Calibri	Common font used in Office 2007 applications and documents.
Verdana	This font is often used on web pages and applications.
Arial	Another common web page font, and used in applications.
Trebuchet	Common application font and used in some web pages back in XP days. Some older applications may still require it.
Tahoma	Common Windows font that you may want to hold on to for application and web page compatibility.
Times New Roman	The default font for web pages and word processing applications such as Microsoft Word.
MS Sans Serif	Default font for Visual Studio applications that is now required for a lot of legacy and newer applications.

Now that you know which fonts you should not remove, you also need to be aware of one more thing before starting your adventure in the Fonts folder. Inside the Fonts folder are several fonts with similar names. The fonts are broken up not only by font name but also by the type style. For example, there is an

Arial Bold, Arial Bold Italic, Arial Italic, and so on. When sorting through the fonts to delete, you also can choose to delete only specific types of fonts.

Deleting fonts is fairly easy, but removing the fonts is a little trickier because the Fonts folder is not like a normal folder. To remove the fonts, you need to start off by creating a folder to put the old fonts in:

1. Click the Start button and select Computer. Navigate to the Local Disk (C:) or where you have installed Windows.

2. Navigate to the Windows folder and create a folder to store the fonts that you are going to remove from the Fonts folder. Right-click the whitespace that lists the folder and files, select New, and then select Folder. Call your folder **Fonts Backup** or some other name so that you can identify it as the place that your old fonts are.

3. After you have created the new folder, open it.

4. Without closing the new folder you just opened, click the Start button again and select Computer. Navigate to the Local Disk (C:) drive again and to the Windows folder, and then to the Fonts folder.

5. Now that you have both the Fonts folder open and your backup folder open, arrange the two windows on your screen so that they look like the two windows in Figure 12-7.

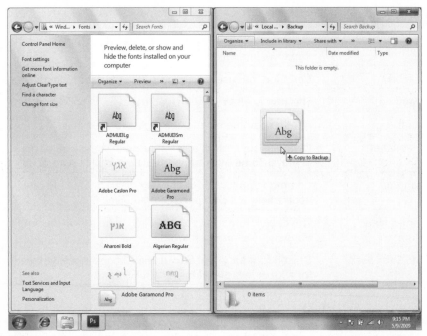

Figure 12-7: The Windows Fonts folder and a backup folder are arranged side by side on the screen

6. Now that the two font folders are side by side, drag the fonts you want to back up to your backup folder.

7. After you have backed up the fonts you want to delete, right-click the font files in the Fonts folder and select Delete.

In the event that you want to reinstall a font, all you have to do is drag the font file from the backup folder back to the Fonts folder. An Installation dialog box will flash just for a second as it adds the font back to the library. After you drag the file back to the Fonts folder, the file will still remain in the backup directory because it just copies it there. After you have confirmed that it was actually installed again, feel free to delete the font file from the backup folder.

Disabling Unneeded Services

A *service* is a software application that runs continuously in the background while your computer is on. The Windows operating system has numerous services that run in the background that provide basic functions to the system. Network connectivity, visual support, and external device connectivity such as printer services are all examples of the types of services that the Windows services provide. Each service that is running in the background takes up system resources, such as memory and CPU time. Also, during the booting of the operating system, the service has to be loaded. On most computers, there are nearly 20 services that are loaded upon startup. Of these 20 services, only a handful are system critical services; all the others can be disabled.

To disable a service, you first need to know more about what the services in Windows 7 do. Table 12-2 will help you understand what the most common services are, what they do, and whether they can be disabled. The services marked in bold are started by default in Windows 7.

Table 12-2: Common Windows Services in Use

NAME	USE
ActiveX Installer	Provides UAC validations for Internet-based ActiveX installs. This only runs when needed.
Application Experience	Provides a compatibility cache for older applications that caches requests when they are run. This service can be disabled, but I recommend leaving it started for application compatibility with the new architecture of Windows 7.
Application Identity	Verifies the identity of an application. Used by AppLocker.
Application Information	Allows you to run applications with all administrative rights. Keeps this service running.

Continued

Table 12-2: Common Windows Services in Use *(continued)*

NAME	USE
Application Layer Gateway	Provides support for additional protocols for the Internet Connection Sharing service. This service can be safely disabled.
Application Management	Used for software deployment and management through Group Policy. If you do not use Group Policy for software, you can safely disable this service.
Background Intelligent Transfer	Transfers data in the background when the connection is not in use. One use of this service is to download updates automatically in the background. This service is not system critical but can impair other services such as Windows Update if it is disabled. I would keep this service enabled.
Base Filtering Engine	Provides support for the firewall, IPsec, and filtering. I recommend keeping this service running.
BitLocker Drive Encryption Service	Provides critical support for BitLocker drive encryption. Only disable if you are not using BitLocker.
Block Level Backup Engine Service	Used by Windows Backup. Disabling would disable the backup and recovery operations of Windows Backup.
Bluetooth Support	Provides support for Bluetooth wireless devices. Disable this service if you do not use Bluetooth devices with your computer.
BranchCache	Provides a local cache of a remote file share in a branch office. Disable if you are a home user and have not configured BranchCache.
Certificate Propagation	Utilizes certificates from smart cards. Most users have no use for this service.
CNG Key Isolation	Isolates cryptographic operations to protect the cryptographic key. I recommend leaving this service as is because it runs only when needed.
COM+ Event System	Provides event notification to COM objects. Some applications depend on this service. I recommend experimenting with your applications to see whether you can disable it.
COM+ System Application	Used to configure and monitor COM object components. Leave as manual because it is started only when needed.
Computer Browser	Responsible for keeping the list of computers on your network and updating the list. If you have no need for this information, you can safely disable it if started.
Credential Manager	Provides secure storage and retrieval of passwords. This service only runs when needed and I would not disable it.

Table 12-2: Common Windows Services in Use *(continued)*

NAME	USE
Cryptographic Services	The main provider of all encryption and encryption operations for all types of applications. It manages private keys, certificates, and other encryption operations. I recommend leaving this service running.
DCOM Server Process Launcher	Starts DCOM processes. Several other system-critical services use this service to start, so I do not recommend disabling.
Desktop Windows Manager Session Manager	This service is behind the Windows 7 "glass" look and enhanced desktop features. If your hardware does not support the new "glass" look, I suggest disabling this service.
DHCP Client	Provides automatic network address configuration. If you set a static IP address, gateway, and DNS servers, disable this service.
Diagnostic Policy	Provides automatic problem monitoring and trouble-shooting of components. If this service is disabled, automatic diagnostics and searching for resolutions will be stopped. If you are an advanced user, you might be able to get away with disabling this service.
Diagnostic Service Host	Diagnostic Policy service helper service that is run only when necessary.
Diagnostic System Host	Diagnostic Policy service helper service that is run only when necessary.
Disk Defragmenter	The service behind the disk defragmenter. This service only runs when needed. Do not disable unless you have a SSD and want to ensure your drive won't be defragged.
Distributed Link Tracking Client	Used with NTFS file links across networks. If you have no need for this service, and not many do, you can safely disable it.
Distributed Transaction Coordinator	Provides support for managing transactions generated by applications. Some applications use this service, but it is not running unless it is in use.
DNS Client	Provides the computer the ability to resolve a DNS address such as www.Tweaks.com to an IP address as needed by web browsers and other Internet tools. Unless your computer is not connected to the Internet or any other type of network, you should keep this service enabled.
Encrypting File System (EFS)	Provides file system encryption support. If disabled, you will not be able to access any NTFS encrypted files.

Continued

Table 12-2: Common Windows Services in Use *(continued)*

NAME	USE
Extensible Authentication Protocol	Provides authentication support to the Wired AutoConfig and WLAN AutoConfig services. Unless you use all manual network configurations, leave this service enabled.
Fax	Provides support to send and receive faxes. No need for faxes? Disable this service.
Function Discovery Provider Host	Hosts other services that search the network for other devices such as the Media Center Extender service. If you have no need for these services, disable it.
Function Discovery Resource Publication	Allows this computer and devices connected to it to be published over the network so that other computers on your LAN can share them.
Group Policy Client	Responsible for applying local and domain-based group policy settings and restrictions. This service cannot be disabled in Windows 7.
Health Key and Certificate Management	Manages the keys used by Network Access Protection. Disable this if your network is not using any sort of authentication-based access.
HomeGroup Listener	Provides basic HomeGroup client services.
HomeGroup Provider	Provides basic HomeGroup server services.
Human Interface Device Access	Supports Human Interface Devices (HID) expanded functionality such as additional buttons on a keyboard, remote controls, and more.
IKE and AuthIP IPsec Keying Modules	Manages the keys used by IP Security (IPsec) network access. Disable this if your network is not using any sort of authentication-based network access.
Interactive Services Detection	Provides notification and access to interactive dialog boxes. Do not disable this service.
Internet Connection Sharing (ICS)	When started, this service allows you to share your Internet connection among other computers with Network Address Translation (NAT).
IP Helper	Provides IPv6 (Internet Protocol version 6) connectivity over an IPv4 network. Disable this service if you have no use for IPv6 network connections.
IPsec Policy Agent	Provides agent support for policy based IPSec policies and remote firewall management.
KtmRM for Distributed Transaction Coordinator	This is a helper service that aids in the communication between the Distributed Transaction Coordinator and the Kernel Transaction Manager.

Table 12-2: Common Windows Services in Use *(continued)*

NAME	USE
Link-Layer Topology Discover Mapper	Provides a generated network map of all computers and other connected devices.
Media Center Extender Service	Allows Media Center Extender hardware and software devices, such as an Xbox 360, to connect to your computer and share the Media Center features if installed. Disable this service if you have no use for this scenario.
Microsoft iSCSI Initiator	Manages connections to iSCSI-connected network devices.
Microsoft Software Shadow Copy Provider	Provides Shadow Copy file operations when needed by applications such as Explorer.
Multimedia Class Scheduler	Helps multimedia applications by prioritizing CPU loads of various system-wide processes and tasks.
Netlogon	Responsible for the connection between the domain controller and your computer if your computer is on a domain. Disable this service if your computer is not on a domain.
Network Access Protection Agent	Primary service for supporting the NAP (Network Access Protection) services.
Network Connections	Provides the user with the graphics interface to manage all network connections. If this service is disabled, Network & Sharing Center will not work. I recommend against disabling this service.
Network List Service	Manages a list of networks the computer has connected to and their individual settings and properties.
Network Location Awareness	Manages a list of networks the computer has connected to and their individual settings and properties.
Network Store Interface	Provides notification of network interface changes. This service is critical to network operation but can be disabled if you do not use a network.
Network TCP Port Sharing	Allows Windows to share TCP ports over the network. This service is disabled by default in Windows 7.
Offline Files	Provides file operations for the offline files feature of Windows Explorer. Feel free to disable this service if you do not use it.
Parental Controls	Provides parental rating controls on games, software, and other aspects of Windows 7. Disabling this will shut down any parental controls.

Continued

Table 12-2: Common Windows Services in Use *(continued)*

NAME	USE
Peer Name Resolution Protocol	Allows your computer to resolve names using peer-to-peer connections. This is required by applications such as Windows Collaboration.
Peer Networking Grouping	Provides peer-to-peer networking services. Depends on Peer Name Resolution Protocol Service.
Peer Networking Identity Manager	Provides peer-to-peer identification services for application and Windows peer-to-peer applications. This service also depends on the Peer Name Resolution Protocol.
Performance Counter DLL Host	Enables 64-bit processes to query performance counters from 32-bit DLLs.
Performance Logs & Alerts	Collects performance data for use in Windows Diagnostics and other troubleshooting utilities.
Plug and Play	Allows the computer to automatically detect and configure computer hardware. Several other services depend on this service to be running to operate.
PnP-X IP Bus Enumerator	Detects devices on the virtual network bus. It runs only when the service is needed.
PNRP Machine Name Publication	Broadcasts the computer name using the Peer Name Resolution Protocol.
Portable Device Enumerator	Provides support for portable storage devices, such as USB devices and MP3 players, to communicate with other Windows components such as Windows Media Player. You can safely disable this service if you do not use any such devices with WMP.
Power	Manages power policy and notification delivery. Do not disable.
Print Spooler	Allows you to save your print services to memory to allow for faster printing within your Windows applications. This service can be disabled but may impair printing in some situations.
Problem Reports and Solutions Control Panel Support	Provides support in Control Panel to view and delete problem reports generated by the Diagnostic services.
Program Compatibility Assistant Service	Aids in application compatibility. When this service is disabled, you can no longer run applications properly in Compatibility mode. This service is not system critical.
Protected Storage	Provides secure storage support to protect data.

Table 12-2: Common Windows Services in Use *(continued)*

NAME	USE
Quality Windows Audio Video Experience	Provides support for audio and video streaming over home networks with traffic prioritization. This service runs only when it is needed by an application.
Remote Access Auto Connection Manager	Automates the creation of connections when applications attempt to access remote computers.
Remote Access Connection Manager	Provides support for modem dial-up connections and VPN connections made through the Windows Networking features.
Remote Desktop Configuration	Provides all remote desktop services and session management activities.
Remote Desktop Services	Provides remote desktop services a way to connect to a remote computer and host incoming connections.
Remote Desktop Services UserMode Port Redirector	Provides the support for redirecting posts/drives/printers across RDP connections.
Remote Procedure Call (RPC)	Responsible for communication between COM components. It is not system critical but is used by dozens of other Windows services. I do not recommend disabling this one.
Remote Procedure Call (RPC) Locator	A helper service for the Remote Procedure Call service that manages connections and the lookup of components in its database.
Remote Registry	Provides remote access to your computer's registry when running. It is safe to disable this service.
Routing and Remote Access	Provides network traffic routing to incoming and outgoing traffic. This service is disabled by default.
RPC Endpoint Mapper	Resolves RPC interface identifiers to transport endpoints. If disabled any RPC services will fail. Do not disable.
Secondary Logon	Allows you to run applications using a different account. This is often used when it is necessary to start a program with an administrator account. I recommend leaving this service running.
Secure Socket Tunneling Protocol Service	Provides SSTP support to connect to remote computers over a VPN.
Security Accounts Manager	Acts as a database of account information that is used for authentication and validation. This is a system-critical service that should not be disabled.

Continued

Table 12-2: Common Windows Services in Use *(continued)*

NAME	USE
Security Center	Monitors of all your security applications such as antivirus and malware protection. This service is also responsible for notification messages that can drive advanced Windows users crazy. Feel free to disable this service but you will not receive warnings if protection software such as Antivirus utilities and your firewall is turned off.
Server	Allows you to share files, printers, and other devices over your network. This is not a system-critical service but is often useful in a home network environment and in the enterprise.
Shell Hardware Detection	Provides notification for AutoPlay hardware events.
Smart Card	Keeps track of smart cards that your computer has used.
Smart Card Removal Policy	Provides the ability to monitor your smart card and lock your computer when your smart card is removed.
SNMP Trap	Processes messages received by the Simple Network Management Protocol.
Software Protection	Provides support for digital licenses for software that are downloaded.
SPP Notification Service	Provides software licensing activation and notification.
SSDP Discovery	Looks on your network using the SSDP protocol to detect other compatible networked devices such as game consoles and extender devices. This service can be disabled but will affect Media Center Extenders in addition to other PnP network devices.
Superfetch	Provides caching of application information to speed up application loading. This service can be disabled, but its benefits outweigh the initial performance decrease of loading the service.
System Event Notification	Monitors system events and reports back to other COM components.
Tablet PC Input	Provides software support for Tablet PC's pen device and the use of ink in Windows applications. Disable this service if it is running and you do not have a Tablet PC.
Task Scheduler	Allows you to schedule processes to run at specified intervals. Windows 7 uses this service for all background maintenance, which will stop if this service is disabled. I do not recommend disabling this service.

Table 12-2: Common Windows Services in Use *(continued)*

NAME	USE
TCP/IP NetBIOS Helper	Provides NetBIOS protocol support over a TCP/IP connection. This is primarily used for machine name resolutions over a LAN.
Telephony	Provides support for applications to interact with the modem.
Themes	Provides support for visual styles that enable the non-classic Windows look. Disabling this service will result in the entire interface reverting to the classic Windows look.
Thread Ordering Server	Provides thread management and prioritization for Windows applications and components. Disabling this service may break applications and will also disable the Windows Audio service.
TPM Base Services	Provides access to the Trusted Platform Module used to store encryption keys and other important authentication information. It is run only when needed and is not available on computers that do not have a TPM chip.
UPnP Device Host	Provides the ability to host UPnP devices on your computer for use on your local network. This service is required for Windows Media Player library sharing.
User Profile Service	This is a system-critical service that loads your user profile when you sign on.
Virtual Disk	Responsible for managing your drives and file systems. Do not disable this service; it is required for many operating system requests. In addition, it does not run when it is not needed.
Volume Shadow Copy	Provides support for Shadow Copy hard drive data used by backup applications.
WebClient	Provides support for the WebDAV protocol for accessing remote servers over the Internet through Explorer. If you have no need for this protocol, this service can be safely disabled.
Windows Audio	Provides audio to Windows 7. I do not recommend disabling this unless you do not like audio. But who doesn't like audio?
Windows Audio Endpoint Builder	A helper service for Windows Audio that manages various audio-related hardware in your computer.
Windows Backup	Part of the backup application in Windows 7 that allows you to easily back up your documents and other important data.

Continued

Table 12-2: Common Windows Services in Use *(continued)*

NAME	USE
Windows Biometric Service	Provides applications the ability to capture, compare, manipulate, and store biometric data.
Windows CardSpace	Manages digital identities.
Windows Color System	Allows other applications to configure your monitor color settings in Windows 7.
Windows Connect Now - Config Registrar	Part of the Windows Connect Now feature that lets you automate the addition of other computers on your wireless network by saving the configuration of one machine to a USB flash drive and then using it to set up new PCs.
Windows Defender	The spyware protection application in Windows 7. If you have a different anti-spyware utility that you use, feel free to disable this service.
Windows Driver Foundation - User-mode Driver Framework	Supports drivers in User mode. Do not disable.
Windows Error Reporting	When things go bad, this service lets you check with Microsoft to see whether it has a solution for you and to notify Microsoft of what is happening to your computer. Don't feel like notifying Microsoft about your error messages? This service can be safely disabled.
Window Event Collector	Provides the ability to subscribe to remote event sources to monitor activity and store data.
Windows Event Log	This is the primary source of all local event management and collection. This service can be stopped but is used by a lot of the performance enhancements in Windows 7. Stopping it would result in a negative performance benefit.
Windows Firewall	Provides network security by blocking inbound and outbound network access based on the firewall rules applied. Unless you have a third-party firewall application that you use, do not disable this service; the benefits outweigh any performance decrease.
Windows Font Cache Service	Optimizes applications by caching commonly used font data.
Windows Image Acquisition (WIA)	Provides an interface used by applications to work with various types of scanners and cameras. This service is run only when needed.
Windows Installer	Allows applications packaged into MSI files to be installed and uninstalled from your computer. Do not disable this service unless you do not want any software to be installed, uninstalled, or modified.

Table 12-2: Common Windows Services in Use *(continued)*

NAME	USE
Windows Management Instrumentation	Provides an interface for scripts and other applications to control various components of Windows 7. Disabling this service will result in the Internet Connection Sharing, IP Helper, and Security Center services stopping, too. If you do not use these services, feel free to safely disable it.
Windows Media Center Receiver Service	Provides the Media Center application with TV and radio reception.
Windows Media Center Scheduler Service	Provides the Media Center application with notification of when to start and stop recording an application.
Windows Media Player Network Sharing	Provides the ability to share your music collection with other computers running Windows Media Player. This service requires the UPnP Device Host service to be running to function.
Windows Modules Installer	Allows Windows components and security updates to be installed and uninstalled.
Windows Presentation Foundation Font Cache	Similar to the .NET Optimization service in that it is designed to increase the performance of Windows Presentation Foundation applications.
Windows Remote Management (WS-Management)	Provides support for the WS-Management protocol to remotely manage your computer.
Windows Search	Provides the ability to index various files on your computer. This service can be disabled, but it will slow down any searches in your computer because the entire drive must be searched every time instead of just the index.
Windows Time	Responsible for syncing the time on your computer. It can be safely disabled.
Windows Update	Provides the ability to detect and download new updates for your copy of Windows 7. Disabling this service will stop both automatic updates and the ability to manually update Windows. Because security patches and automatic updates have been so critical to Windows in the past, I suggest keeping this service started.
WinHTTP Web Proxy Auto-Discovery	Provides both an API for applications to make HTTP connections and to auto-detect connection settings. This service is not system critical and can safely be disabled if you do not use the auto-detect connection feature in Internet Explorer and none of your applications use its' API.

Continued

Table 12-2: Common Windows Services in Use *(continued)*

NAME	USE
Wired AutoConfig	Manages your wired NIC connections, including support for 802.1X authentication. The Network and Sharing Center in Windows 7 may malfunction if this service is disabled.
WLAN AutoConfig	Manages your wireless network connections and settings. The Networking Center in Windows 7 may malfunction if this service is disabled.
WMI Performance Adapter	A helper service for the Windows Management Instrumentation service that runs only when requested.
Workstation	Provides support for creating network connections using the SMB network protocol (a.k.a. Lanman). Disabling this service disables Windows File Sharing.
WWAN AutoConfig	Manages mobile broadband such as GSM and CDM connections.

Disabling Services with the Services Utility

Now that you have an understanding of the dozens of services in Windows 7, you can start disabling the services that are not needed for your computer usage and that are slowing down your computer boot process. To do this, you will use the Services utility that enables you to start, stop, and configure Windows 7 services.

TIP Before you begin changing your service setup, set a system restore point — a configuration where you can easily restore your system. However, be careful when you restore from restore points. Any applications or files that were created after the system restore point will be deleted when reverting back to an earlier restore point.

The Services utility is included in all versions of Windows 7, but is hidden away. Disabling a service with the Services utility is easy. Just complete the following steps:

1. Click the Start button, type **services.msc** in the Search box, and press Enter. This will start the Services utility, as shown in Figure 12-8.

2. When the Services utility has loaded, you will see a list of all the services available on your computer and the ones that are started. Before you can disable a service from starting up, it is best to stop it first. Scroll through the list of services until you find the name of the one you want to disable. Right-click the service name and select Stop.

3. When the service is stopped, right-click the service again and select Properties. On the General tab, look for the Startup Type drop-down box. Click the arrow on the drop-down box and select Disabled.

4. Click OK. From now on, the system will not start the service during boot, which should speed up your system start.

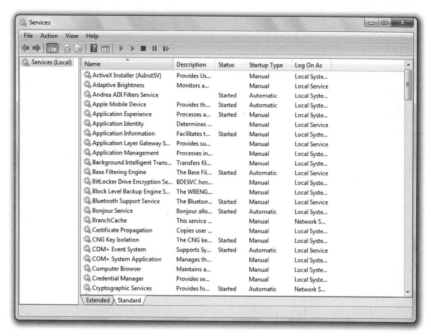

Figure 12-8: The Services utility

Bare-Bones Service Configuration

To get the maximum performance out of your system, you have the option of disabling all the services on your computer that are not critical to the system. This will take away a lot of the nice features and conveniences of Windows, but you would have a much faster machine. The following is a list of all services that started by default in Windows 7 and can be safely disabled:

- Application Experience
- Application Information
- Background Intelligent Transfer
- Base Filtering Engine
- Bluetooth Support

- Desktop Window Manager Session Manager
- DHCP Client
- Diagnostic Policy
- Diagnostic System Host
- Distributed Link Tracking Client
- EAPHost
- Function Discover Provider Host
- Group Policy Client
- IKE and AuthIP IPsec Keying Modules
- IP Helper (if you are not connected to an IPv6 network)
- Microsoft iSCSI Initiator Service
- Microsoft Software Shadow Copy Provider
- Multimedia Class
- Network Connections
- Network List
- Network Location Awareness
- Offline Files
- Policy Agent
- Portable Device Enumerator
- Program Compatibility Assistant
- Routing and Remote Access
- Security Center
- Server
- SSDP Discovery
- Superfetch
- Tablet PC Input (if you do not have a Tablet PC)
- TCP/IP NetBIOS Helper
- Terminal Services
- Themes
- WebClient
- Windows Audio
- Windows Audio Endpoint Builder
- Windows Defender

- Windows Error Reporting Service
- Windows Firewall
- Windows Management Instrumentation
- Windows Search
- Windows Time
- Windows Update
- WinHTTP Web Proxy Auto-Discovery
- Workstation

Recommended Service Configuration

The barebones system service setup is great for optimal performance, but you are eliminating a lot of the cool new features that make Windows 7 cool and new. Check out my list of recommended services to disable:

- Bluetooth Support
- DHCP Client (assign yourself a static IP address)
- Diagnostic Policy
- Diagnostic System Host
- Distributed Link Tracking Client
- EAPHost
- Function Discovery Provider Host
- Group Policy Client
- IKE and AuthIP IPsec Keying Modules
- IP Helper (if you are not on an IPv6 network)
- Microsoft iSCSI Initiator Service
- Offline Files
- Policy Agent
- Routing and Remote Access
- SSDP Discovery
- Tablet PC Input
- WebClient
- Windows Search
- WinHTTP Web Proxy Auto-Discovery

Disabling these least commonly used services provides a good balance between saving boot time while keeping the cool new Windows 7 features and application compatibility.

Optimizing the Location of the Boot Files

The speed at which your files are read depends on your physical hard drive access speed and where the files are located in your hard drive. To increase the speed of your boot, you want to have the files used to boot your computer in a location that will allow the fastest read speed possible.

Windows 7 does a good job of this from a fresh install, but over time as your hard drive fills up and you make changes to the configuration of Windows, some of your boot files can become scattered inside the hard drive, resulting in a slower possible read speed. In addition, adding new applications and new hardware can contribute to this even further. Over time, your original boot optimization fades away as your internal hard drive data makeup changes.

Using Windows 7 Disk Defragmenter

Starting with Windows XP and continuing in Windows 7, the Prefetcher service will automatically optimize the location of the boot files in your hard drive using Windows Disk Defragmenter. However, this occurs only after a certain number of boots and when it gets around to it (because it runs only when your computer is idle).

Microsoft has a talented team working on the Prefetcher service that even took into consideration your system boot changes. For example, you might install an updated device driver or add new hardware. To solve this problem, the systems will re-defragment the boot files every three days.

> **TIP** Windows keeps track of the last time that it optimized the boot file so that it can calculate how often it should run the boot defrag. If you are interesting in finding when the boot defrag was last run, open regedit, navigate to `HKEY_LOCAL_MACHINE\SOFTWARE\Microsoft\Windows NT\CurrentVersion\Prefetcher`, and then look for the key named `LastDiskLayoutTimeString`. The value is formatted as year/month/day – hour/minute/seconds.

An operating system that takes care of itself? Yes, Windows is getting smarter and smarter. However, there is still one problem: there is no possible way to initiate a boot defrag directly. The only way is to leave your computer on for a little while without using it at all. If you are impatient and do not want to wait, I have a solution for you.

As I mentioned earlier, the system will initiate the boot defrag only when the system is idle. Typing in a command that will start the boot is not possible.

However, you can tell your computer, even when it is not idle, to process the idle tasks. This will indirectly start the boot defrag. Because the boot defrag is most likely not the only idle task waiting to be run, other processes will be run, too, which can cause your computer to appear to be doing a lot of hard work — from a few minutes up to half an hour — as it completes all tasks. During this time, your computer should not be used for any intensive activities such as playing games. If you try to use your computer while the idle tasks are being processed, you will notice slow performance until the tasks are completed.

Perform the following steps to process all idle tasks:

1. Click the Start button, type **cmd** in the Search box, and press Enter.

2. When the command prompt opens, type **Rundll32.exe advapi32. dll,ProcessIdleTasks** and press Enter. Your computer will now work on the tasks.

Performing these steps will allow your system to defrag the boot files sooner; however, the boot defrag is done every three days. Processing the idle tasks more frequently will do nothing to help you boot because the boot defrag will not be on your idle tasks lists all the time.

Using Other Third-Party Boot Defrag Programs

The built-in boot defragmenter is pretty good. However, a number of third-party defrag utilities think they can do it better. To name a couple, Diskeeper, O&O Defrag, and PerfectDisk all offer boot defragmentation support. Third-party defrag utilities often use different defrag algorithms that they believe work best. For the next section, I show you how to use Diskeeper and PerfectDisk to run a boot defrag.

Boot-Time System Defrag with Diskeeper 2009

To defragment system files, and other files that are normally in use, the defragmentation must be run during the early stages of system boot. This will allow the defrag program to have full access to all files so that it can place them together on the disk. One program that allows this to be done is called Diskeeper, which was developed by Executive Software. A trial copy of Diskeeper 2009 can be found on Executive Software's web site (www.Diskeeper.com). If you have not already installed Diskeeper, do so now before proceeding any further. Any edition of Diskeeper 2009 will work fine. After you have it downloaded and installed, follow these steps:

1. Click the Start button, type **Diskeeper**, and press Enter.

2. When Diskeeper 2009 loads, click Action, expand Volume Properties, and select Boot-Time Defragmentation.

3. Boot-Time Defrag Properties will now load. Select the drive where your OS is installed, usually C:. You can also select multiple drives by holding down Ctrl and clicking them. This is useful if you may have applications that are stored on a drive different than where your OS is stored.

4. Under the Boot Time Defragmentation section, select Enable boot-time defragmentation to run on the selected volumes, as shown in Figure 12-9.

5. Check Defragment the Master File Table (MFT), too.

6. Press OK and reboot your computer.

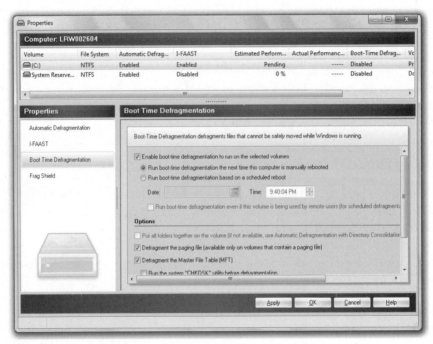

Figure 12-9: Using Diskeeper 2009 to run a boot-time defrag

When you reboot your computer, you will notice that instead of loading into Windows all the way, Diskeeper will run in a pre-Windows environment so that it can have full access to your disks before any system files load. Depending on the size of your hard drive, the defragmentation process can take hours. It is best to do a boot-time defrag overnight.

Boot-Time System Defrag with PerfectDisk 10

PerfectDisk by Raxco Software is another very popular third-party defrag utility. Similar to Diskeeper it allows you to run a defrag before Windows boots up so the utility has full access to all your system files. To get started, visit www.PerfectDisk.com and download the trial version of PerfectDisk 10 Pro. After you have it installed, follow these steps to perform a boot defrag:

1. Start up PerfectDisk by clicking the Start button, typing in PerfectDisk, and hitting Enter.

2. When loaded, select your C: drive and then click System Files, as shown in Figure 12-10.

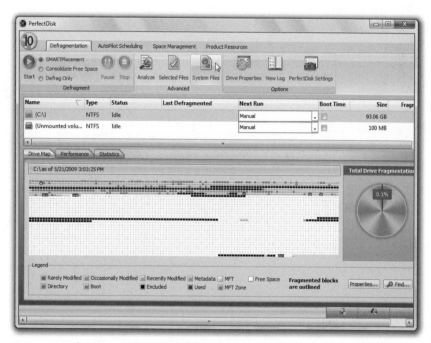

Figure 12-10: Using PerfectDisk to perform boot defrag

3. Click Yes on the "Offline defrag of your System Files could not run on drive C:\ because the drive is in use by another process. Do you want to force all open handles closed?" message box.

4. Click Yes on the "System files on the drive C:\ can only be defragmented at boot time. Would you like to defragment these files during the next reboot of your system?" message box.

5. You will now have the option to reboot your system. Click Yes followed by Reboot Now on the following screen.

After your computer restarts it will launch the PerfectDisk defrag utility in a pre-window environment and defrag your system boot files. When completed it will reboot again and return to the normal Windows environment.

Summary

This chapter showed you many ways to reduce the amount of time it takes your computer to boot. First, you worked on changing some of the BIOS settings that would optimize your computer for maximum boot speed. Then, you learned how to remove your boot screen to shave off some more time. After that, you disabled other parts of Windows, such as hardware, fonts, and services that you may never use, but which all take up time when your computer starts up. To wrap up this chapter, you optimized the placement of the files used when your computer boots using the Prefetcher service and a third-party disk defragment tool.

This chapter showed you how to speed up the first half of your computer's startup. The next chapter picks up on the second half — the system logon. I show you some cool tips on how you can speed it up, too.

CHAPTER 13

Making Your Computer Log On Faster

Ever wonder why it takes your computer so long to start up after you log on? After all, the system already loaded the majority of the operating system components. Does your computer take longer to load after you sign on than it used to take when you first brought it home? These are all questions to which you will find answers in this chapter. You can make your system load faster by using a number of cool tweaks and hacks. The last chapter touched on how to make the system boot faster. This chapter concentrates on how to make the system load faster after the operating system has loaded and you are presented with the welcome sign-on screen.

After you turn on your computer, it goes through the boot-up process, which loads the main system components and drivers. Eventually, when those are finished loading, the Windows shell is started and you are presented with the sign-on screen. After the welcome screen is displayed and you sign on, the system begins to load your user profile settings and the rest of the Windows shell. When that is finished loading, the system runs the applications that are in the startup folder as well as other sneaky registry startup programs. After these applications are finished loading, your mouse will no longer display the hourglass and you are set to do whatever you want with your computer.

This chapter begins by examining ways to speed up the logon process. Then it discusses how to get rid of all those extra applications that run at startup that further slow down your computer. When you use the tips you will learn in this chapter, your system will have a much faster loading time.

Speeding Up the Logon

As I just mentioned, a lot occurs when you log on to your computer. Windows has to validate your password, load your profile settings, apply the settings, and then launch any additional applications that are registered to start automatically. Those are a lot of areas to fine-tune to allow for a faster logon. To get started, take a look at automatic logon.

Enabling Automatic Logon

If you are the primary user of your computer and you do not have any other users, or if everyone in your household uses the same username, you are the perfect candidate for enabling automatic logon. Automatic logon is a great technique that will save you time that is often wasted when your computer is waiting for you to type your password. Even if you do not have a password assigned to your account, you are still required by the logon welcome screen to click your name to sign in. Having to do these tasks yourself is unnecessary and a waste of time if you are a candidate for automatic logon.

CAUTION Automatic logon can be a great feature but it can also create a security problem for your computer. If you use your computer for business, if you have data you prefer to keep safe from others, or both, I strongly recommend that you do not enable this feature. If you happen to step out of your office or if your laptop is stolen, you have left the door to your computer wide open. By enabling automatic logon, you are trading convenience for physical access security. However, you are not changing your network security, so your data is still safe from network attackers. The risk of someone remotely connecting to your computer is the same as if you did not have automatic logon enabled.

Enabling automatic logon is a quick and easy registry hack. Follow these steps to speed up your sign-on with automatic logon:

1. Click the Start button, type **regedit** in the Search box, and then press Enter.

2. After Registry Editor has started, navigate through `HKEY_LOCAL_MACHINE\SOFTWARE\Microsoft\Windows NT\CurrentVersion\Winlogon`.

3. Locate the AutoAdminLogon entry. If the key does not exist, create it by right-clicking the Winlogon folder and then select New, String Value.

4. Right-click the AutoAdminLogon entry and select Modify. Set the Value to 1, as shown in Figure 13-1. Then press OK to save the new value.

Figure 13-1: Setting AutoAdminLogon
to 1 to activate automatic logon

5. Locate the DefaultUserName entry or create a string value if it does not exist.

6. Right-click DefaultUserName and select Modify. Set the value to the username that you primarily use to sign in to Windows. Press OK.

7. Locate the DefaultPassword entry or create a string value if it does not exist.

8. Right-click the DefaultPassword entry and set the Value to your password.

9. Close Registry Editor and restart your computer.

After you reboot your computer, Windows 7 should automatically sign on to your account. You will notice that your computer will now get to the desktop much quicker than before. If you ever want to disable automatic logon, go back into Registry Editor and set the AutoAdminLogon entry to 0. Its also a good idea to delete the DefaultPassword string value so your password is not stored in plain text in the registry.

Adjust the Startup Programs

After you sign on, the system loads your profile, finishes loading the Explorer shell, and then begins to load the startup programs. If you have ever purchased a computer, either online or from a retail store, then I am sure that you have noticed all the annoying software programs that automatically load right after you sign on. Some computer manufacturers go so far overboard with startup applications that Windows has to hide them automatically from appearing in the system tray so that your taskbar has enough space to show open windows. If you are like me and have built your own computer, you do not have to deal with all the preloaded junk that comes from the big computer manufacturers. Nevertheless, you are still vulnerable to auto-start programs that get installed by many of the popular applications you use. Over time, as you install more applications, the automatic startup applications can get out of control and definitely slow down your logon.

Popular applications such as Adobe Photoshop, AOL Instant Messenger, iTunes, Windows Live Messenger, and many more install auto-start components. Consider all the extra auto-start components these applications add on top of the auto-start applications already installed on your computer, such as antivirus and anti-spyware applications. Your logon can easily become slowed to a crawl by dozens of applications that load after you sign on. This section helps you see what programs are starting automatically and then will show you some great tricks to stop them all from starting up.

Identifying and Disabling Auto-Start Applications

The first step in stopping the auto-start applications is to identify exactly what is starting up and whether it is needed. You can use two different utilities to find this information. The first is the System Configuration utility that comes with Windows 7. System Configuration enables you to easily see which applications start on logon. Another great utility is called Autoruns by Microsoft Sysinternals. Autoruns is a more comprehensive utility that allows you to see all applications that run on logon as well as other types of auto-starts such as browser or shell plug-ins.

First, I cover using Windows 7's System Configuration to identify and disable unneeded auto-start applications. Then I dive in to using Microsoft Sysinternal's Autoruns to disable auto-start applications as well as other auto-start components.

Using System Configuration to Identify and Disable Unneeded Startup Applications

The System Configuration utility included in Windows 7 is very easy to use. First, you need to get a list of all the applications and components that automatically start up when you sign in. Follow these steps to discover the applications that automatically start up on your system:

1. Click the Start button, type **msconfig** in the Search box, and then press Enter.

2. After the System Configuration utility has loaded, click the Startup tab, as shown in Figure 13-2.

3. Now that the list of the active startup programs is visible, you need to research what programs should be removed.

4. Because almost every computer has different programs starting up after logon, it is best to search the Web with the executable file name to find out if the application can be safely removed from startup. One useful site to visit is a database of common startup programs called AnswersThatWork,

located at www.answersthatwork.com/Tasklist_pages/tasklist.htm. At that site, you will find a recommendation for each of the programs listed. If you cannot find one of your programs listed, just do a quick search on Google and most likely you will find several web sites showing what the program does and what removing it will do.

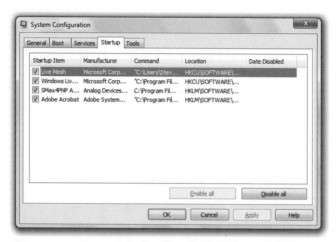

Figure 13-2: The System Configuration utility's Startup tab

It's easy to remove the automatic startup applications with the System Configuration tool. When you have the System Configuration tool open, follow these steps:

1. Locate the item you would like to disable from starting up and clear the box to the left of it.

2. When you are finished unchecking all the applications that you no longer want to auto-start, press OK to save your changes.

3. You are asked if you would like to Restart now or Exit without Restarting. I recommend that you restart now instead of waiting.

4. After you restart, you are reminded by the System Configuration tool that you have just made some changes to your startup. Check the box that says Don't show this message or start System Configuration when Windows starts.

After removing some of the automatic startup applications, you will notice that you can sign on much faster. If you have any problems after disabling a startup application component, you can always enable it again by checking its box in the System Configuration tool.

Using Autoruns to Identify and Disable Auto-Start Components

Autoruns by Microsoft Sysinternals is a more comprehensive tool to identify and disable unneeded auto-start applications, components, and plug-ins. Similar to the System Configuration tool, Autoruns operates in the same way but also shows the auto-start components of other items such as browsers and the system shell.

Autoruns is also easy to use. To get started, you need to download a free copy of the Autoruns software from `http://technet.microsoft.com/en-us/sysinternals/bb963902.aspx` or `http://live.sysinternals.com/autoruns.exe`. After you have Autoruns downloaded and extracted to a folder, follow these steps to get started:

1. Go to the directory where you have extracted Autoruns and run autoruns.exe.

2. When Autoruns has started, click the Logon tab, as shown in Figure 13-3.

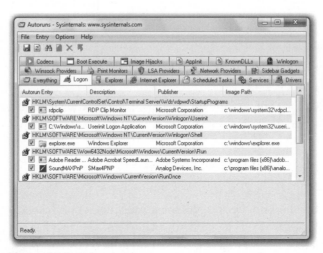

Figure 13-3: Using Autoruns

3. You will see all the automatic start applications, similar to the System Configuration tool. Identifying an unneeded service is even easier in Autoruns because of the right-click search feature. Right-click any entry and select Search Online. This automatically opens your web browser and searches Google for the process name. Simply selecting the entry will also provide more information about what it is.

4. Disabling a process is also similar to the System Configuration tool. Just clear the box to the left of the process name and it will no longer start after a reboot.

The power of the Autoruns software lies in the ability to control other automatic starting components such as browser add-ons and Explorer shell plug-ins. Check out the following list of additional, useful tabs available in Autoruns:

- **Logon:** Everything that runs when you log on.

- **Explorer:** This tab helps you get your shell extensions under control as well as see all the applications that tap into Windows Explorer with DLL files.

- **Internet Explorer:** This tab lets you find applications that hook themselves into IE.

- **Boot Execute:** This tab enables you to find applications that have integrated themselves into the system boot.

- **Print Monitors:** Use this tab to get rid of extra print monitors for features that you don't use.

- **Drivers:** This tab provides another way to disable drivers for your hardware devices.

- **Winlogon:** This tab lets you find all the applications that run on your logon screen.

- **Sidebar Gadgets:** Although these are called Desktop Gadgets in Windows 7, you can still use this tab to disable gadgets you don't want loading when you log in.

When you uncheck any options, simply restart your computer for the change to take effect.

Controlling Auto-Start Applications That Keep Coming Back

You may experience some applications that you have previously disabled automatically starting up again. Software developers often use various techniques to check that their application is registered to auto-start when you log on. If it is no longer set to auto-start, it will automatically set it up again to do so. The software developers may be trying to make sure you use their application by making it difficult to disable auto-start. In other cases, applications are just trying to make sure that other programs are not disabling their program or taking over their turf.

Competing software applications can often conflict and compete with each other for use on your computer. This occurred when I installed several media players on my PC. After installing the programs Winamp, iTunes, RealPlayer, and Windows Media Player, I noticed that they would fight for my music file associations (that is, which application would open the file). Every time I would run RealPlayer, it would change all my music files over to be played in their player by default. The same thing happened when I would try to play my music files in other players. From this experience, I found that it was not uncommon for an application to install a program to be run at system startup that would check and take over (or preserve, as the developers call it) itself from other applications.

Getting rid of these applications from your startup is much trickier than unchecking a box in the System Configuration utility or Autoruns. It involves digging into the preferences of each application and changing several options. In the paragraphs that follow, I show you how to disable two of the most popular and most difficult applications from starting up automatically. Additionally, the methods used can be applied to disable other sneaky applications from starting up.

Getting a Handle on RealPlayer

Real Networks, the developers of RealPlayer, could have made it a little easier for users to disable some of the extra program features. RealPlayer is a good application, but it comes bundled with so much extra junk that knowing how to disable all the extra features becomes a necessity.

TIP RealPlayer does not come preinstalled with Windows 7. If you did not download and install this application yourself, and it cannot be found on the Start menu, then you do not need to worry about taming RealPlayer.

One of the features of RealPlayer that is most annoying is the Message Center application that is automatically set up and starts when you log on. When you least expect it, no matter what you are doing on your computer and after you have run the RealPlayer program, you get a little pop-up message (see Figure 13-4) that alerts you to some random information or advertisement.

Figure 13-4: RealPlayer Message Center alert

You can do two things to get RealPlayer under control. First, you need to stop the scheduler from starting up every time you start Windows. You will recognize this application in the System Configuration utility as realsched.exe. No matter how many times you uncheck this item in the System Configuration utility or Autoruns, it will keep coming back. The only way to stop it is inside the RealPlayer application. Follow these steps to stop it for good:

1. Start the RealPlayer application by clicking the Start menu, type in RealPlayer, and hit Enter.

2. After RealPlayer has loaded, click the Tools menu bar item and then select Preferences. This loads the program preferences.

3. Expand Automatic Services and then select AutoUpdates.

4. Clear the Automatically download and install important updates box, as shown in Figure 13-5.

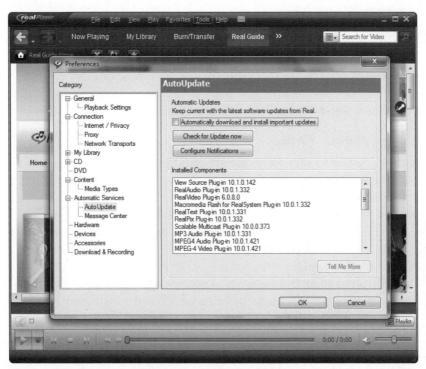

Figure 13-5: Disabling RealPlayer's automatic updates

5. To make sure that you will never again see a message from the so-called Message Center, select the Message Center entry listed under Automatic Services.

6. Click the Select Message Topics button on the right side of the window.

7. When the Message Center window is displayed, uncheck all items on the screen. Navigate through the categories of messages and uncheck those as well. When you are finished, press the Save Changes button.

8. Close the Message Center window so the Preferences window can be viewed again.

9. After you are back to the Preferences window, press the Configure Message Center button.

10. Clear all the boxes on the screen.

11. Press OK to close the Configure Message Center window.

12. A warning window displays informing you that you are disabling the Message Center. Click Yes to proceed.

13. Close the Message Center window again so that you can view the Preferences window.

14. Press OK to save your changes and close the Preferences window.

That's it. RealPlayer is now under your full control and will not start up automatically and will not send you advertisements. As you can see, it is more difficult than just unchecking one box in the System Configuration utility, but it is not that much more complex after you know what boxes to clear.

Disabling Windows 7 Action Center Alerts

Windows 7 Action Center alerts are not only an annoying feature for advanced users, but they also slow down your logon time because they have to start automatically when you log on. Disabling this feature by clearing a box is simply not an option using the System Configuration utility or even Autoruns. Action Center alerts are deeply embedded into Windows 7 and can be turned off only from within the Windows Action Center application, similar to what you had to do with RealPlayer.

If you are unfamiliar with security alerts, these are the little boxes that pop up from your system tray that inform you that you are missing antivirus or other types of computer protection. If you are an advanced user, you do not need to be reminded all the time that your security settings may be insecure.

In Windows 7, Microsoft made it easy to disable security alerts from starting automatically. Just follow these steps:

1. Click the Start button, type **Action Center** in the Search box, and then press Enter.

2. After Action Center loads, click Change Action Center settings.

3. Then, remove the check next to all the messages you don't need to see, as shown in Figure 13-6.

4. Click OK, close Action Center, and you are finished.

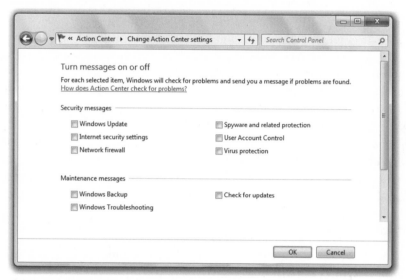

Figure 13-6: Disabling security alerts in Action Center

TIP Interested in more security-related tweaks and tips? Check out Part IV of this book to learn how to fine-tune Windows security and your Internet settings, and how to protect your privacy.

As you can see, stopping sneaky programs from starting automatically requires you to go into the program's options/preferences/settings. After you are inside a program's settings, you have to uncheck any options of features that start up automatically. Most programs such as Windows Security Center alerts are easy to disable from starting up automatically from within the preferences. However, other programs, such as RealPlayer, require a little more work as you have to disable automatic updates and several Message Center features.

The best way to stop other sneaky programs that keep starting up automatically after you try to remove them using the System Configuration utility is to dig through the program's settings. Look in the program's help file for information about how to disable automatic startup if you are stuck. If you cannot find any information, try searching the Web for information, or post a request for help on one of the various computer support web sites, such as Tweaks.com's forum at `Tweaks.com/forum`.

Customizing Auto-Start Programs for Other Users

Each user account on your computer can have different auto-start applications associated with it. Certain programs may start up for one user but not for another. All these settings are stored in the system registry. With the help of the Registry Editor utility, you can manually change these entries.

First, I go over where Windows 7 stores the auto-start information in the registry. Windows stores auto-start information in two places for every user. It stores which programs will start for a specific user under the user's registry hive/location. It also stores a list of programs that will start automatically in the local machine hive. Registry entries in the local machine hive will start up for all users of the computer. Removing these entries will remove it for all users of the computer.

Now that you know the two different types of startup items, user-specific and all user entries, you can begin hacking the registry to change the startup programs. First, you will find out how to modify the startup programs for all users, and then you will learn how to modify the startup programs for individual users.

To modify the startup programs for all users, follow these steps:

1. If you have not already done so, start Registry Editor by clicking the Start button, typing **regedit** in the Search box, and pressing Enter.

2. After Registry Editor has loaded, expand and navigate through HKEY_LOCAL_MACHINE\SOFTWARE\Microsoft\Windows\CurrentVersion\Run. You will see a list of all the auto-start applications in the local machine context, as shown in Figure 13-7.

3. If you want to remove a startup program, just right-click the name and select Delete. Alternatively, if you want to add a new entry, right-click the white space and select New and then String value. Right-click your new entry and select Modify so that you can edit it and set the value to the path of the executable you want to run.

That is it. You now know how to add and remove programs that will start up for all users on the computer. The steps for modifying the startup programs for individual users are very similar. The only difference is you have to go to a different place in the registry.

Instead of navigating in the registry under HKEY_Local_Machine, you have two options. You can log on to an individual's account and then go to HKEY_CURRENT_USER followed by the same navigation path used earlier. Alternatively, you can go to HKEY_USERS, expand the account SID (Security Identifier) key, and then follow the path used earlier.

TIP When navigating through HKEY_USERS it can be hard to identify what SID belongs a specific account. I wrote a handy utility available for free at http://Wingeek.com/Software called SID Resolver that will translate the account SID to the actual account name.

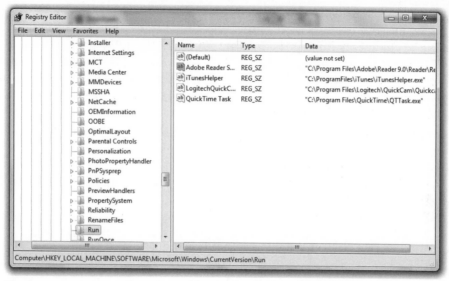

Figure 13-7: Registry Editor showing auto-start programs for all users

Either method will result in the same outcome. However, if you don't have access to a user's account, you can still modify his or her auto-start applications by going to HKEY_USERS.

Other Time-Saving Tips

The preceding paragraphs covered the largest contributors to a slow logon, but there still are a few other tips that can save you additional time. These tips, individually, do not save a lot of time, but when they are applied in combination, they can really add up. Furthermore, if you are running Windows 7 on older hardware, these tips will help you significantly decrease your logon time even further.

Assigning Alternative IP Addresses

Over the years Microsoft has experimented by changing when the network devices are initiated to make sure that the boot is not held up by a slow DHCP server. Windows XP made big advances in this area and Windows 7 has an entirely new TCP/IP stack that is optimized for performance. However, assigning an alternative IP address to your network cards is something that can only help because it saves your computer from an outgoing network request to the DHCP server to get an IP address. No matter where Microsoft moves the network initiation in the boot, it cannot eliminate the need to get an IP address.

To review, every time you turn on your computer, it has to set up the IP configuration for your network card. Often, this setup can result in your computer pausing for moments during the loading process. The delay occurs because the PC is waiting for the DHCP (dynamic host configuration protocol) server to assign the computer an IP address and provide other network information. On most healthy networks this is not an issue, but in some cases DHCP servers can respond slowly causing the startup delay.

One easy solution to this problem is to assign alternative information to your network card. This information is only temporary to allow your computer to continue the loading process. Hopefully after you log into your computer the slow DHCP server will have finally responded and provided the real network information. Follow these steps to specify an alternative IP configuration for your computer:

1. Click the Start button and select Computer.

2. When Explorer loads, type **network connections** in the address bar, as shown in Figure 13-8.

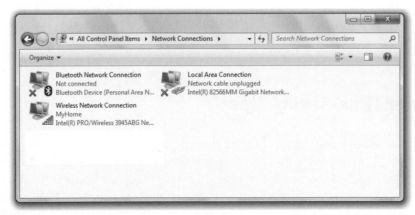

Figure 13-8: Accessing network connections using any Explorer window

3. Now that you are in the Network Connections window, you will see a list of network adapters on your computer. Right-click your wired network card adapter and select Properties.

4. Click the Internet Protocol Version 4 (TCP/IPv4) to select it. Then click the Properties button.

5. After the Internet Protocol Version 4 (TCP/IP) Properties window is displayed, click the Alternative Configuration tab. This is where you will enter your alternate network information.

6. Click the User Configured radio button to allow the text boxes to be edited.

7. Type an IP address for your computer that will be used as a default in the event that your computer cannot get a DHCP address. I recommend using 192.168.1.*X*. Replace *X* with any unique number for each computer between 2 and 254.

8. Type **255.255.255.0** as your Subnet Mask.

9. Your Default Gateway should be set to 192.168.1.1 because that is a valid gateway address. As I mentioned earlier, the exact numbers do not matter. You just want to have the computer assign some value instead of spending time searching when it will not find a DHCP server.

10. Enter what your DNS servers should be. You can get this from your ISP, but this information really isn't that essential because this configuration will almost never be used to connect to the Internet. It is just a default fallback in the rare case that you are having networking trouble. Feel free to leave these fields and the WINS fields blank.

11. Click OK and then click OK for the network properties screen.

Your network adapter is now optimized for the fastest possible logon time in all scenarios. For more network-related tweaks, check out Chapter 13.

Turning Off the Logon Sound

The music that Windows 7 plays every time the logon screen displays and then again when you log on is something that you can do without. Hearing the tunes was really cool back when most people didn't have sound cards in their computers. Nowadays everyone has a sound card and the cool new Windows 7 logon sound is starting to get old. Less is more, and when your computer has to load a 500KB media file to play, it slows things down. I recommend that you disable the logon sound. To do so, follow these steps:

1. Click the Start button and then Control Panel.

2. Click Hardware & Sound followed by Change System Sounds listed under Sound.

3. Locate the Program Events box, scroll through the list and select Windows Logon. Remove the assigned sound by setting it to (None) with the Sounds drop down list.

4. Below the Program Events list, remove the check next to Play Windows Startup sound as shown in Figure 13-9.

5. Click OK and you are finished.

Now that was not too bad. Plus, you just shaved another second off your loading time. If you want to save even more time in Windows, you can experiment with turning off all sounds by changing the Sound Scheme on the Audio Devices and Sound Themes screen to No Sounds from Windows Default.

Figure 13-9: Audio Devices and Sound Themes screen

Summary

Throughout this chapter, you found out how to remove unnecessary steps from your logon to cut the fat from the system load and make your computer load faster. You have learned how to remove auto-start programs as well as how to master the tricky programs that are hard to disable. This chapter also covered other ways to get that loading time down.

The next stop on our performance makeover is speeding up Windows Explorer. I will go over a few cool ways to speed up the most popular program in Windows: the shell.

CHAPTER 14

Speeding Up Windows Explorer

Now that you have optimized the boot startup and your logon, let's speed up the most used application in Windows 7: Explorer. Windows Explorer is responsible for almost the entire GUI with which you normally interact in Windows 7. The Start menu, taskbar, and file exploring windows are all part of the Explorer shell. As you can see, Explorer is a very expansive application that is a major part of the operating system.

This chapter shows you how you can use some cool hacks to increase the performance of Explorer. First, you improve the speed of browsing and accessing files on your computer. Then you adjust the visual effects of Windows 7 so that it performs better on your computer hardware — finishing off with tweaking Windows Search for optimal performance.

Speeding Up File Browsing and Access

Browsing through lists of files and reading and writing files are the most basic operations that your computer performs. All the other operations that your computer performs build off these common tasks. If you are launching an application or playing a game, no matter what you are doing, it all breaks down to the simple process of reading a file from a device at some point. Windows Explorer is no exception. The speed of Windows Explorer is greatly influenced by the performance of these basic operations. Therefore, the performance of Windows

Explorer, as well as all other applications, can be improved by optimizing these basic operations.

How can you speed up these basic operations? All these basic operations have to do with interactions with your file system. Using various tweaks to the file system settings and using performance utilities, you can improve the performance of your file system resulting in an increase in performance of the basic file operations.

Before you go any further, be aware that the following speed tips for the file system will work only for the NTFS file system. If you do not know what file system your computer is using, you can go to Computer in the Start menu, right-click your hard drive, and select Properties. This will bring up the Local Disk (C:) Properties window, which will tell you the type of file system your hard drive is running. If your hard drive is running FAT32, these tips will not work for you.

In my opinion, NTFS is the best file system for Windows 7. It has many advanced security features and also performs better on many machines. If you are still running FAT32, or for some odd reason your computer came prein-stalled with FAT32, consider converting your hard disk to NTFS.

QUICK TIP

Converting your drive to NTFS is a snap. Click the Start button, type Command Prompt in the Search box, and then press Enter. Then, right-click the Command Prompt shortcut that shows up at the top of the Start menu and select Run as Administrator. Command Prompt will now load with administrator access that is needed to run the convert tool. Next, at the prompt, type **convert c: /fs:ntfs** and press Enter to start. If you want to convert a different drive letter, just replace the C: with the drive letter that you want. For example, if you want to convert your D: drive, then you will have to type **convert d: /fs:ntfs**. The actual conversion process will take a little while, especially on large drives. Keep in mind that after you convert to NTFS, you cannot convert back to FAT32.

Now that the requirements are cleared up, you are ready to get started.

Disabling Legacy Filename Creation

Legacy filename creation is a feature of the NTFS file system that is included in Windows for backward compatibility with older applications. During the years, the file system in Windows has changed dramatically. One of the first things that changed was the limitations of the old MS-DOS 8.3 file naming standard. The old MS-DOS file system limited filenames to a maximum length of eight characters plus a three-character extension. As Windows became more advanced, this needed to be changed to allow for greater flexibility. Eventually these limitations were expanded with the release of Windows 95, which bumped up the maximum filename limit to 255 characters. However, there was a hidden price to pay that affects Windows 7, too.

Microsoft has always believed that backward compatibility contributes to the success of Windows because it enables users to upgrade to a new version while allowing their older applications to continue to work. However, that mentality often results in performance reductions caused by code that had to be tweaked to allow for new functionality while preserving existing functionality. The legacy filename creation is a perfect example of this scenario. For Windows 7 to support older Windows applications, the NTFS has to support both the old MS-DOS file naming standard as well as the new updated standard that allows for longer filenames. How do they do it? It's rather simple. When a file is created, the file system creates two names for it: one name in the MS-DOS 8.3 standard and another in the latest filename standard.

Creating two filenames for every file is not the kind of buy-one-get-one-free situation that is good. Creating the second filename takes more time and slows down the performance of the file system. Although this legacy feature has good intentions, it causes the performance of file creation to decrease by 200 percent. Disabling this legacy feature will help you get that lost performance back.

Disabling legacy filename creation will kill any application you have that needs the 8.3 filename standard. If you try to run an application that requires 8.3 filenames, you will get various error messages. Even though this technology is more than 15 years old, there are some major software developers — mentioned in the following paragraphs — that still write code that requires the ancient 8.3 standard. Unfortunately, in the software world, some companies don't bother fixing things if they are not broken simply to increase the performance of the user's computer. For the most part, they do not have to worry about it because Microsoft supports the lazy programmers by leaving these old, inefficient features in the operating system.

Even though some applications will fail when this feature is disabled, I highly recommend trying to disable this on your computer. In the worst-case scenario, you would have to turn the feature back on again. However, you will discover that almost all your programs will work just fine. For those that don't, try to download a new version from the company's web site, or perhaps use this as an excuse to buy a version of the product from this century.

One type of program that has the most problems when the 8.3 standard is disabled is the installer application that many software developers use to get their programs up and running on your computer. For some reason, a few installers are still programmed using the old 16-bit technology that depends on the short filename compatibility feature to function.

Users frequently run into this error with Symantec's AntiVirus software. According to Symantec, users may receive a `1639. Invalid command line` `argument` error when they install certain versions of Symantec's software. For users of Symantec software who want to disable the old support for greater performance, the company recommends that they enable the 8.3-standard filename compatibility support when the software is being installed and then disable it after the software is installed. The software should then work fine.

That basic Symantec approach can be applied to any situations that you may run into where applications are being installed and errors received. Just enable the 8.3-standard filename compatibility support during the install, and then disable it again after the install is complete.

Now that you are aware of the possible problems that can be caused by disabling the legacy filename standard, and also know what to do if you experience any, you are ready to disable the feature. Follow these steps:

1. Click the Start button, type **Command Prompt** in the Search box, and then press Enter.

2. Command Prompt appears at the top of the list in your Start menu. Right-click the shortcut and select Run as Administrator, as shown in Figure 14-1.

3. After Command Prompt has loaded in the Administrator context, you can access the NTFS configuration utility. At the prompt, type **fsutil behavior set disable8dot3 1**, as shown in Figure 14-2 and press Enter.

4. Close Command Prompt and restart your computer to activate the change.

Enabling the legacy filename feature is also very easy. Just repeat the preceding instructions but run **fsutil behavior set disable8dot3 0** instead, and then restart.

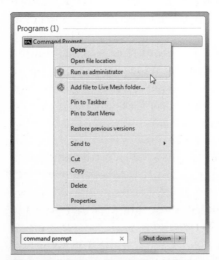

Figure 14-1: Running Command Prompt as administrator

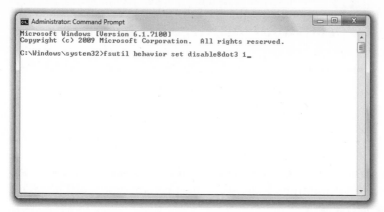

Figure 14-2: Disabling legacy filename creation with the file system utility

Disabling the File Access Timestamp

Every time you or an application accesses a file on your computer, the file system records the date and time the file was accessed and stores the timestamp in two locations. Simply accessing a file requires the system to write to the master file table (MFT) and the directory the file is located in, which results in two writes for every file read. Windows Explorer is one of the most read intensive applications on your computer. Nothing requires more reads to your file system than browsing through your files. In Windows 7, Explorer has a number of new file previews that require even more file reads. All these file reads add up to extra timestamp writes, resulting in slower performance.

The Microsoft NTFS file system engineers were smart enough to realize that all this timestamp logging can get out of control very quickly, resulting in an even greater performance slowdown. Applications usually open only a small chunk of a file at a time and then repeat the small chunk reads until the entire file is open. This can generate hundreds and maybe even thousands of file reads, depending on the file size and application. As you can imagine, many file reads in a short amount of time can put a lot of extra work on the file system. To handle this problem, Microsoft designed NTFS to update only the last access timestamp about every hour, which breaks down to just one, two-step timestamp update for each file per hour. This solves the preceding problem but it still has to do two writes for every file; it just limits the need to update the same file over and over again.

Disabling the file access timestamp is a great way to speed up Windows Explorer, but it is not without side effects. Often backup applications utilize the file access timestamp to determine which files to back up when performing a sequential backup operation (a backup operation that copies only the files that have newer timestamps since the last backup date). Check with your backup application's web site to find out if it will be affected. If it is, consider doing full backups instead of sequential backups. Full backups are not affected by the lack of a last access timestamp.

The process for disabling the file access timestamp is very similar to disabling MS-DOS filename support. Just follow these steps:

1. Click the Start button, type **Command Prompt** in the Search box.

2. Command Prompt appears at the top of the list in your Start menu. Right-click the shortcut and select Run as Administrator.

3. After Command Prompt has loaded in the Administrator context, you can access the NTFS configuration utility. At the prompt, type **fsutil behavior set disablelastaccess 1**.

4. Close Command Prompt and restart your computer for the change to take effect.

If you run into any problems with this change to your backup application or any other applications, you can easily undo the tweak. Just type **fsutil behavior set disablelastaccess 0** at the Command Prompt instead.

Adjusting NTFS Memory Allocation

The NTFS file system likes to cache files that are open in physical memory for the fastest possible access to the raw data. This is accomplished by first reading the data from the hard drive and transferring it to physical memory. Depending on the amount of RAM in your computer, portions of the open files may be paged to disk in the paging file because the entire file cannot fit in the available physical memory. This results in slower overall performance because for an application to read the entire file, existing data in the physical memory cache has to be paged back to the hard disk to make room and then other unread portions have to be pulled back from the hard drive into physical memory. This carefully orchestrated memory swap requires a lot of CPU, memory, and hard drive processing time. Whenever memory paging occurs, it slows down the overall performance of your computer.

If you use your computer for anything that requires fast reads of hundreds of files, such as indexing your MP3 collection, you might notice that it takes your computer a while to read these files. This is because the file system has only a certain amount of physical and paging file space allocated to it, which results in increased paging activity. Depending on the amount of physical memory in your computer, you might be able to get away with increasing the memory allocated to the NTFS file system on your computer. This will increase the performance of high disk read operations.

Before you get started, you need to analyze the available physical system pool memory on your hardware. Increasing the NTFS memory allocation on a machine without enough of the right type of free memory will result in a decrease in overall system performance because other system components have to use less memory, which can increase paging.

Follow these steps to determine whether you can increase the memory allocation:

1. Click the Start button, type **perfmon** in the Search box, and then press Enter.

2. When the Performance Monitor loads, click Performance Monitor under Monitoring Tools.

3. Click the chart and press Ctrl+I to add performance counters.

4. Navigate to the Memory section and expand it.

5. Locate and select Cache Bytes Peak and press Add.

6. Locate and select System Cache Resident Bytes and press Add.

7. Press OK when both counters are added.

8. Switch to the Report View by pressing Ctrl+G until you see the performance counters listed, as shown in Figure 14-3.

9. Note the values of all three counters on a sheet of paper so that you can refer to them even after a reboot.

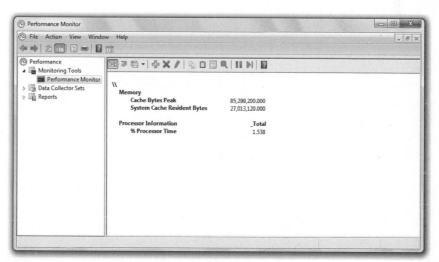

Figure 14-3: System pool memory performance counters

Now you need to analyze the counters you just gathered. Cache Bytes Peak shows the maximum amount of physical system pool non-page memory in use since your computer was last rebooted. This number is very important because the memory manager in Windows 7 limits you to 256MB (268,435,456 bytes) of physical system pool non-page memory regardless of the amount of RAM in your computer. If your Cache Bytes Peak value is within 20MB of the 256MB limitation, this is a big red flag not to attempt this hack. In that scenario, you might slow down your computer even more by implementing this hack.

Next, let's take a look at your total System Cache Resident Bytes. This is the current size of the file system cache in physical system pool non-page memory. When you implement this hack, the value can increase by up to 50 percent. Take 50 percent of the System Cache Resident Bytes value and add it to the Cache Bytes Peak value. Make sure that it is less than the 256MB limit.

If your results of the two previous tests are on the borderline for passing, you should still implement this hack. It is easy to undo this setting and it will not harm any of your hardware or have a permanent effect on the performance of your computer.

Follow these steps to increase the memory available to the file system:

1. Click the Start button, type **Command Prompt** in the Search box.

2. Command Prompt appears at the top of the list in your Start menu. Right-click the shortcut and select Run as Administrator.

3. After Command Prompt has loaded in the Administrator context, you can access the NTFS configuration utility. At the prompt, type **fsutil behavior set memoryusage 2**.

4. Close Command Prompt and restart your computer to activate the change.

After your computer has restarted and you have loaded your usual applications, check to make sure that your Cache Bytes Peak value in Perfmon is still less than 256MB. Also find the difference between your new System Cache Resident Bytes value and the value before the change. Add that to the old Cache Bytes Peak value you wrote down earlier to ensure that the sum is also less than 256MB. If it is greater, you might be stealing memory from other system components, resulting in an overall slowdown in performance.

If you notice any decrease in performance or have bad results from the preceding test, undoing the change is very simple. Just type **fsutil behavior set memoryusage 1** at the prompt instead and reboot.

Speeding Up the User Interface

Windows 7 is all about the Aero Glass visual experience. Unfortunately, the visual features that contribute to the experience can put a heavy load on your hardware. Unless you have a newer PC with a recent graphics card and a fast CPU, you may see a slowdown in performance caused by the visual effects and features. This is noticed most when you are navigating between windows and closing them. These effects can sometimes give the impression that your computer is slower than it actually is because the animation is not running as fast as it was designed to run.

In Windows 7, you can fine-tune the settings of the entire user interface for maximum performance. You don't want to disable all the settings, however; instead, find a good balance between a good-looking interface and what you are willing to compromise for speed. The following paragraphs show you how to do this.

Fine-Tuning Performance Options

As I mentioned earlier, Windows 7 is all about the new experience that the visual effects create for the user. These new visual effects require more computing power from your hardware than ever before, resulting in slower performance on older hardware.

I do not have the latest graphics card or a fast multi-core CPU — although my hardware does meet the minimum requirements for the new Aero interface — so the new visual effects run. Unfortunately, they do not always run very well and even appear to slow down my system at times. Often the animation effects appear rough and when I drag windows around there appears to be a slight lag. The poor performance occurs because the value ATI video card that I have can barely keep up with the work it has to do. The new visual interface is provided by the Desktop Windows Manager (DWM). This new composition engine uses your 3D accelerated graphics card with DirectX 9 or DirectX 10 to draw the entire desktop on 3D surfaces. Because my video card is at the bare minimum requirements, I need to fine-tune the visual effects of the Aero interface so that it runs better on my system.

Adjusting Animations

The visual effects of Windows 7 can be adjusted very easily, allowing you to fine-tune the performance of Windows Explorer to work well with your hardware configuration. This can be done using the Windows Performance Options settings. Click the Start button, type **SystemPropertiesPerformance** (no spaces between words) in the Search box, and then press Enter. This starts Performance Options, as shown in Figure 14-4.

When Performance Options is started, you will notice three preset options and one custom option:

- **Let Windows choose what's best for my computer:** Windows uses your Windows Experience Index to pick the settings it thinks will result in the best balance of appearance and performance for you.
- **Adjust for best appearance:** Turns all settings on.

- **Adjust for best performance:** Turns all settings off.
- **Custom:** Allows you to select manually the individual settings to use.

Figure 14-4: Windows 7 Performance Options

Select the Custom option so that you have total control over which settings to enable and disable. Now that you have the Custom option selected, you can pick the individual settings that work best for your hardware. Take a look at the following list of visual effect settings:

- **Animate controls and elements inside windows:** This setting will animate controls inside windows although it does not affect most applications.

- **Animate windows when minimizing and maximizing:** This effect will animate the window when it is minimized to the taskbar, as shown in Figure 14-5. It is a cool-looking effect, but it is graphics intensive and can slow down the performance of the GUI. I recommend disabling this effect to gain some extra speed.

Figure 14-5: Windows 7 animated minimizing/maximizing folders

■ **Enable desktop composition:** This setting is one way to turn off the DWM (desktop window manager) composition engine that is responsible for the Aero Glass interface. Disabling this will cause your computer to revert to the non-glass GUI that is similar to the Windows XP visual style engine. Although disabling this feature will give you a big performance increase, it kills the 7 look; therefore, I recommend keeping this setting checked.

■ **Enable transparent glass:** One of the most graphics intensive operations of the Aero Glass interface is the transparent glass. This requires various calculations to be run that blur the background behind the glass to complete the transparent effect. Disabling this will give you a performance increase on less powerful graphics cards. Glass still looks good even if transparency is disabled, as shown in Figure 14-6.

Figure 14-6: Non-transparent Aero Glass

■ **Fade or slide menus into view:** This effect allows the menus that pop up throughout the system to fade in. You will experience this when you navigate through a menu bar or when you right-click something. This effect does not affect the performance of the system except for when the effect is called on. Some users who have older computers and slower video cards can experience better performance by disabling this effect.

■ **Fade or slide ToolTips into view:** This effect will allow the ToolTips in various parts of the system to slowly fade in when either an event occurs or you hold your mouse over the object. This effect doesn't affect performance of the system of most users, but once again, those with older systems should disable this effect for better performance.

■ **Fade out menu items after clicking:** This effect will fade the submenus in the Start menu out after you click an item within the menu if you are using the Classic Start menu. Unless you are using the Classic Windows 2000–style interface, this setting will not affect you. This effect, just as the other fade effects, is slower on older systems and should be disabled for best performance.

- **Save taskbar thumbnail previews:** This setting will allow the system to cache thumbnail previews so you always have a thumbnail to display when hovering over an opened application on the taskbar.

- **Show shadows under mouse pointer:** This effect allows the mouse to have the 3D effect. I have not found this feature to affect performance.

- **Show shadows under windows:** Allows you to toggle if you want to enable or disable shadows. Disabling the shadows creates a very different look for the interface.

- **Show thumbnails instead of icons:** This feature allows you to view thumbnails of your images instead of the associated file icon. Unless you have problems with a slow hard drive on your computer and a low amount of RAM, or have directories with thousands of pictures in them at once, I feel this feature provides more value and is worth the performance decrease. However, if you don't like thumbnail views of your images, disable this to gain speed while browsing your image files.

- **Show translucent selection rectangle:** When this effect is enabled, you will see a nice-looking blue border with a semi-transparent blue interior when you drag the mouse to select items instead of the old dotted line box as we have all seen in older versions of Windows. Figure 14-7 shows the two different types of selection rectangles. On older machines, I have seen this effect work very slowly and often interfere with the mouse's selection of items because it seems to use up a lot of the CPU. On the average computer, this effect presents no problems at all. If you have a slow machine, then disable this effect; otherwise keep it enabled and enjoy the nicer look.

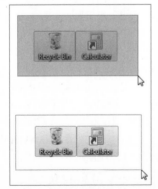

Figure 14-7: Selection rectangle comparison. A translucent selection rectangle appears on top .

- **Show window contents while dragging:** If you are using the Aero Glass interface and experience a lag when moving windows around, disabling this option will help because you will see a box outline instead of the entire window image when moving it. If you have to deal with a tiny lag, then keep this effect enabled because it definitely looks nice when it is enabled.

- **Slide open combo boxes:** This effect has no noticeable effect on performance.

- **Smooth edges of screen fonts:** This feature seems to depend more on your video card and monitor than your system. Use of any type of font smoothing will require it to do more work. On older machines, I would disable this effect. Also, if you have a cathode ray tube type (CRT) monitor, you will not benefit all that much by having this enabled. The font smoothing effects, especially ClearType, work best on flat panel LCD monitors.

- **Smooth-scroll list boxes:** This has no effect on performance based on my tests. You would have to be crazy to disable this effect because it is just so cool.

- **Use drop shadows for icon labels on the desktop:** Unless you do not like the look of this feature, I do not recommend disabling it. The performance benefit of disabling it is insignificant.

- **Use visual styles on windows and buttons:** Disabling this effect is one way to make your computer look like it is from ten years ago. If you don't like the Aero Glass look and also do not like the non-glass visual style, disabling this will give you the Classic Windows 2000 look. You will see a huge performance increase, but your GUI will also look really old, so the choice is up to you.

Now that you know what all the settings do, just uncheck any of the options that you would like to disable and press OK to save your selections. Your computer will then pause for up to 15 seconds while it adjusts all the settings.

If you ever change your mind and want an effect back, just go back to the Performance Options tool and recheck any options you disabled.

Disabling Aero Glass for Faster Performance

Now that you know how to fine-tune the settings of Aero Glass on your computer so that it performs better, you may still want to make Windows Explorer even faster. Disabling the Aero Glass composition engine will allow you to have a much faster user interface experience on slower hardware. However, you will lose most of the cool visual effects, such as the windows transitions and the cool new Flip 3D window switcher, as shown in Figure 14-8.

Disabling Aero Glass will turn off the Desktop Windows Manager and Windows will use a visual style engine similar to what was in Windows XP. The older visual style engine works great on slower hardware that ran XP well. However, the look of the user interface is a little different, as shown in Figure 14-9.

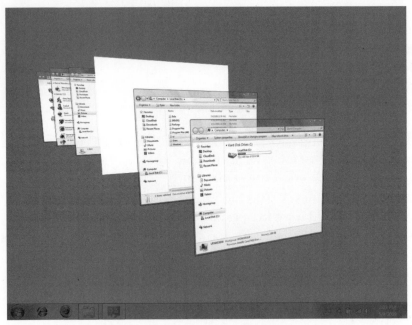

Figure 14-8: Windows 7's Flip 3D Alt+Tab replacement

Figure 14-9: Windows 7's non-glass look

If you are willing to compromise the Aero Glass look for a big increase in performance, follow these steps to disable Aero Glass:

1. Right-click the desktop and select Personalize from the menu.

2. Scroll down to the Basic and High Contrast Themes.

3. Click the first theme in the section. It is called Windows 7 basic. In a few seconds the basic theme will be applied.

4. Close the Personalization window.

Windows Classic Look for Maximum Performance

If you are a performance freak and need the best possible performance out of Windows 7 at any expense, then you are still in luck. Windows 7 still has the old Windows 2000 classic look built into the operating system. Enabling the old classic look will take you back in time and make your Windows 7 PC feel like Windows 2000 with most of the benefits of Windows 7, as shown in Figure 14-10. Reverting back to the classic look will also free RAM and extra work for your CPU, resulting in the best possible user interface experience.

Figure 14-10: Windows 7 in Classic mode

If you are willing to sacrifice all of Windows 7's great looks for performance, step into the time machine:

1. Right-click the desktop and select Personalize from the menu.

2. Scroll down to the Basic and High Contrast Themes section.

3. Click the second theme in the section called Windows Classic. In a few seconds the basic theme will be applied.

4. Close the Personalization window.

Welcome back to 1999. Make sure you are ready for Y2K.

Adjusting Explorer's Search

The ability to search files and folders is available throughout the user interface in Windows 7. Almost every window has a search box that allows you to find documents, images, applications, and other files almost instantly. Accelerated by the Windows indexing service, Windows Search can quickly search through a file index that is continuously updated by the indexing service running in the background. For a search in Windows to be successful, there needs to be a good balance between the amount of time it takes to get results and the overall system performance decrease caused by the background indexing service.

There are some cool tricks that you can use to increase the success of a search while also increasing overall system performance by reducing the amount of work the indexing service has to do. First, I will show you how to adjust the scope of where Explorer searches for an item when browsing through folders. Then you will look at adjusting some settings on the indexing service as well as how to use Windows Search without an index. All these hacks will help you increase the performance of Windows Explorer and your overall system performance.

Adjusting Search Scope

Typically when you use a search box when browsing through folders you are looking for a specific file. In Windows, you can configure if you want it to search the content of the files or just the filename. By limiting what it is searching through, you can increase the speed of your results.

Adjusting the scope of a search is very easy to do. If you want, you can even have different search scopes for different folders. This allows you to have it both ways. For example, if you are browsing files in the c:\Windows directory and you want to search for a specific file, you can configure Windows Search to look only in the C:\Windows folder. It is also possible to configure the scope of a search placed in a different folder, such as your home folder, to search all information available. Follow these steps to adjust the search scope for any folder:

1. Click the Start menu and select Computer.

2. Navigate to a folder for which you would like to change the search scope. Press the Alt key to bring up the Classic menu bar.

3. Click Tools on the menu bar and select Folder Options.

4. When Folder Options loads, click the Search tab.

5. Under What to search, select In indexed locations, search file names and contents. In non-indexed locations, search file names only.

6. If you would like to increase the performance even more at the cost of losing additional functionality, uncheck Include subfolders in search results when searching in file folders. located under How to search.

7. After you have made your changes, click OK to save them.

Your updated search scope is now activated.

Adjusting Windows Indexing Service

The search scope is just one part of the search feature in Windows. The real brains behind allowing you to search quickly through the various types of files on your computers are in the indexing service. This service runs in the background and monitors only folders and file types it was directed to monitor. The content of any files located in folders the indexing service monitors are read by the service and indexed. That indexing data is then stored in a centralized database.

The indexing service allows you to search through the Start menu search box and find all files, documents, and images that match the search term in both the filename and within the document. If the file indexed is a popular file format, most likely there is a reader for it within the indexing service. In theory, you could search for the word "the" and find all documents and e-mails on your computer that contain that word. This is all controlled by the settings for the indexing service.

You can adjust the settings that the indexing service uses to index only the types of files and locations you care about, which will reduce the amount of work the indexing service has to do. This will increase the overall performance of your computer, causing it to have more free resources because they are not wasted indexing files you don't care about. Adjusting these settings is easy when you know where to do it. Just follow these steps to get started:

1. Click the Start button, type **Indexing Options** in the Search box, and then press Enter.

2. When Indexing Options loads, you will see all the locations the indexing service is currently monitoring, as shown in Figure 14-11.

Figure 14-11: Indexing Options for Windows Search

3. Click Modify followed by Show all locations. This is where you can fine-tune exactly where the indexing service looks. You can even navigate between locations while on the Modify screen by using the summary list at the bottom of the window.

4. Navigate through the list of drives and folders and uncheck any locations you do not want the indexing service to monitor. When finished, click OK.

5. When you are back on the Indexing Options window you can adjust the file types that the indexing service reads by clicking the Advanced button and then the File Types tab.

6. Scroll through the list and uncheck any file types that you do not want the indexing service to keep track of. By default, hundreds of files are checked. Reducing the number of files that the indexer has to monitor will greatly improve performance. Click OK when you are finished.

7. Now is a good time to rebuild the index. Click the Advanced button again on the Indexing Options window.

8. Then click Rebuild on the Index Settings tab.

You are now finished adjusting the Windows Indexing service for maximum performance while preserving the ability for fast searches in Windows Explorer.

Using Windows Search without an Index

As I mentioned earlier, the indexing service plays a key role in accelerating searches within Windows 7. Although this service provides a lot of value by allowing you to search thousands of files quickly, it is not a requirement of Windows Search. It is possible to disable the indexing service completely; however, searches with Windows Search will require much more time to complete and can cause your hard drive to do a lot of work while Windows Search iterates through folders and files instead of just accessing a search index.

Disabling the indexing service will save your computer extra memory and CPU time required to run the application in the background. Depending on how often you use the Windows Search feature, you can decide whether it is worth sacrificing fast searches for a little extra performance from Windows Explorer. Follow these steps if you decide to disable the indexing service:

1. Click the Start button, type **services.msc** in the Search box, and then press Enter. This loads the Services utility.

2. After Services has loaded, scroll through the list and locate the Windows Search service. This is the indexing service. Right-click this service and select Stop.

3. When the service is stopped, make sure that it does not start again. Right-click the service again and select Properties.

4. Locate the Startup type drop-down box. Change the Startup type from Automatic to Disabled.

5. Press OK to close the window.

You have now successfully disabled the indexing service that is used by Windows Search. Although your searches are now slower, you have freed up processing power that can be used instead by other processes such as Windows Explorer.

Summary

You have now finished optimizing Windows Explorer. The things that you have done in this chapter may seem to make only minor changes to the performance of your computer, but these hacks will have a big impact on the performance of Windows Explorer as well as other applications on your system. Tweaking the file system settings, fine-tuning the visual settings, and adjusting Windows Search are all valuable skills to have when you want your computer to run at top performance.

You are now ready to optimize the core Windows components. In the next chapter, you learn tricks to add more RAM to your computer and fine-tune the paging file, and other hacks that will take your computer's performance to the next level.

CHAPTER 15

Optimizing Core
Windows Components

The core Windows components can be thought of as the steel structure of a skyscraper. This basic structure of the building provides support for all the other components. Windows 7 has various layers of components that support each other and at the lowest level interacts directly with the hardware. This chapter helps you tweak the core components of Windows to increase the overall performance of your computer. Instead of a steel beam structure, Windows 7's core components are short-term memory (RAM, a.k.a. volatile memory), long-term storage (your hard drive, a.k.a. non-volatile memory), and the CPU. All the programs that run on Windows, including Windows itself, eventually break down to these three core components.

To get started, you are going to tweak your system's short-term memory using some techniques and features of Windows 7 to increase the speed of memory operations. Then you will tweak another critical component, the paging system, and finally speed up your hard drive and adjust how your CPU works.

Windows Loves RAM

Microsoft made a lot of improvements in Windows 7 to reduce the memory utilization compared to the notorious memory hog Windows Vista. This has helped significantly, especially on Netbooks, but Windows still performs the best when the computer has sufficient memory. I already covered trimming the fat from Windows 7 by disabling components and services that you do not need to use. This helps, but on some computers it is just not enough.

According to Microsoft the minimum amount of RAM required to run the basic version of Windows 7 is 1GB. I'm not sure how that is determined exactly, but I feel sorry for you if you are running Windows 7 on just 1GB. That is plenty for the core operating system and one or two running applications, but if you are doing anything more I highly suggest more physical RAM. Before I continue, let's cover the basics of RAM.

RAM is the fastest type of memory on your computer outside the CPU cache. No matter how you use your computer, RAM is always in constant use. Your computer uses RAM as a high-speed temporary storage location to store data and applications with which the CPU is currently working. Every time you launch an application, Windows has to load it from your hard drive into RAM so that the CPU can execute the code. Depending on the available memory, Windows may have to kick some other data currently in memory out. That is called paging, which is covered in greater detail later in this chapter. Paging is a slow process because it saves current memory back to the slow hard disk. It is best to avoid paging as much as possible so that as little time as possible is lost trying to make room so your applications or data can fit in memory. When you consider all the memory that Windows 7 uses on top of your normal applications, you will see why it is so important to have the right amount of high-speed memory available.

Adding RAM to Your Computer

Sometimes your only option to add even more speed to your computer is to give it more of what it likes most — RAM. If you have a low amount of RAM on your computer — say you are right at the bare minimum requirements according to Microsoft to run Windows 7 and you have already tried all the performance enhancements in this book — I recommend upgrading your RAM as a final move. I have never seen any hardware upgrade increase the speed of a computer greater than upgrading the RAM. Upgrading the amount of RAM you have on your computer is an easy and low-cost method to jump-start the speed of your computer. Unsure whether you have the skills to do it yourself? No problem — just follow the recommendations that follow for help with buying and installing your new RAM.

Buying RAM for Your Hardware

Picking out RAM can be very confusing because there are so many different types of it. The following are two main points that will take the complexity out of buying RAM:

■ **Type of RAM your hardware requires:** You can usually go to the web site of your computer manufacturer, type in your model number, and find the exact type of memory that will work with your hardware. Alternatively, you can visit the manufacturer of your motherboard. I recommend writing down the type of memory your manufacturer states you need and buying the memory from a different company. Use a price comparison web site to find the best deal on the type of RAM you need. Often buying direct from the major computer manufacturers are more expensive. After you know what kind you need, you can get it from pretty much anywhere and usually much cheaper if you buy it online.

■ **Number of open RAM expansion slots:** To add additional memory to your computer, you need to consider the number of open RAM expansion slots you have on your motherboard. Most computers have either two or four slots and, depending on your manufacturer or whether you built it yourself, you may be using up all the slots. If your slots are all in use, don't worry — you can still upgrade your RAM given you are not already at the max your machine supports. Pieces of RAM usually come in combinations of 256MB, 515MB, 1GB, 2GB, or 4GB of memory per stick. Say you have two RAM slots and they are both currently filled with 256MB RAM chips; you can still buy two 515MB chips to replace them, which doubles the amount of RAM you have. Ideally if you have a lot of slots free it is a good idea to buy DDR memory in pairs so you can take advantage of the dual channel architecture. You will notice two different colored DIMM slots on your motherboard if you system supports dual channel.

Installing Your New RAM

After you have ordered or picked up your new RAM, it is really easy to install it yourself. Keep in mind that opening your case may void your warranty. Having fun yet? Follow these steps to pop in your new memory:

1. Unplug all the cables on the back of your computer, including the power cable.

2. Use a Phillips screwdriver or push the case release button to remove your case.

3. When you have access to your motherboard, locate the memory expansion slots, as shown in Figure 15-1. Attach your anti-static wristband at this time. Don't have one? No big deal. Just touch any part of the metal case frame with your hand to discharge yourself.

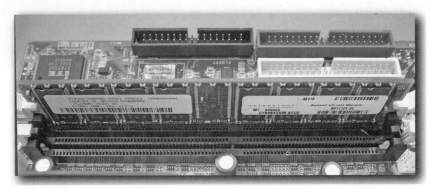

Figure 15-1: RAM expansion slots

4. Removing any existing pieces of RAM is very simple. Push the plastic or metal clips away from the sides of the stick of RAM. This will usually cause the RAM to pop out.

5. Putting a new stick of RAM in is just as easy. While the plastic clips are open (pushed away from the sides of the slot), align the chip the correct way so it fits in the slot properly and gently push down. As the stick of RAM goes down, it will cause the plastic clips on the sides to snap in place.

Put your case back on and hook up your cables and you are now finished. If you have any errors when your reboot on your BIOS screen or if your computer does not recognize the new RAM you put in, make sure you got the right kind of memory and that it is seated properly in the slot.

Using a USB Storage Device to Add Memory

Although upgrading the amount of RAM you have in your computer is a good last resort if you are having performance issues, Windows 7 includes a cool trick to assist the amount of RAM you currently have. As I mentioned earlier, any time your computer has to kick applications and data out of RAM — because there is not enough room — it slows down your computer because it has to store that data on the slow hard drive. In Windows 7, a new feature called Windows ReadyBoost allows you to use faster solid state memory devices, such as a USB memory device, to store this data instead of your slow hard drive. This provides an instant boost to system performance without even opening your case.

How does it work? The concept is simple. Solid state flash USB 2.0–based storage devices have a faster read and write speed than most hard drives on the market. Windows ReadyBoost, with the assistance of Windows SuperFetch (another caching technology), works with a memory management system to redirect cached data to the high-speed device. At any time, you can remove the device if you need to use it for another purpose. To protect the data that is cached on your removable USB device, Windows encrypts it so that if the device is removed, your data is safe.

Setting up Windows 7 to use your USB drive to increase performance is very easy. To get started, you will need a 256MB or larger USB 2.0 flash drive. Then follow these steps:

1. Plug your USB drive into one of your available USB ports.

2. After your computer recognizes the new device and it shows up in Computer, make sure that you have at least 235MB of free space on the drive. Right-click the drive and select Properties, as shown in Figure 15-2.

Figure 15-2: Opening Properties for your USB drive

3. When the Properties window is shown, click the ReadyBoost tab.

4. Select Use this device and adjust the slider to set the amount of space to use for ReadyBoost, as shown in Figure 15-3.

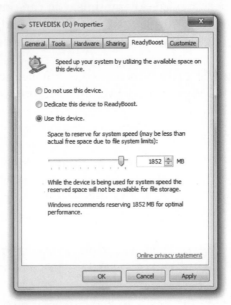

Figure 15-3: Using Windows ReadyBoost to increase performance

5. Click OK when you are ready and Windows ReadyBoost is now set up on your computer.

After you set up Windows ReadyBoost on one of your USB devices, it can be removed at any time. You can disable it by selecting Don't use this device on the ReadyBoost tab you worked with earlier. Also, after you set up Windows ReadyBoost on your USB device, it cannot be used for Windows ReadyBoost on another Windows 7 computer without first having Windows ReadyBoost disabled on the computer it was set up with.

Tweaking the Paging File

The Windows paging file, also known as the swap file or virtual memory, is very important to the operation of Windows. As I mentioned earlier, the operating system uses the paging file as a place to store data that was once in physical memory but was kicked out because Windows needed the space for other purposes.

The method that Windows uses to decide what programs will stay in physical RAM is very complex and impossible to alter. However, there are several tweaks that will help you optimize your computer's use of the paging file. It is possible to prevent certain system files from being pushed into the paging as well as completely disabling the paging file to prevent the entire system from using it.

This next section guides you through the steps of optimizing the paging file for your computer.

Disabling the Paging File

If you have a large amount of RAM in your box, you have the ability to stop the operating system from pushing any data out into the paging file. This will cause faster memory management and memory access than is physically possible for your RAM. Reading and writing directly to the RAM is always significantly faster than having to use the paging file. Reading and writing to the paging file requires multiple steps and that takes time. First the data has to be copied out of physical RAM to the hard drive, and then the new data must be loaded from the hard drive into RAM and then executed. The hard drive is a big bottleneck in this situation.

If you have 4GB of RAM or more in your computer, you can consider disabling the paging file. If you have less than 4GB of RAM, do not even consider disabling the paging file or you will be running into problems.

What can happen if you disable your paging file? If you have enough RAM, nothing, but if you do not have enough RAM, applications may refuse to load or even crash. For example, if you run Photoshop and are working on a large image, you will run into "out of memory" errors and the application will crash, causing you to lose all your work. This is a pretty extreme example, but it *can* happen to you if you don't have enough RAM and disable your paging file.

Basically, stick to the 4GB minimum and you will have no problems in most cases, but be aware that if you ever choose to run some memory-intensive applications, such as rendering a two-hour movie, or if you just like to run dozens of programs at once, you can run out of memory easily.

So, now that you know the concerns, you are ready to follow these steps to disable the paging file:

1. Click the Start button, right-click Computer, and select Properties.

2. When System has loaded, click Advanced system settings, as shown in Figure 15-4.

3. Under the Performance section, click Settings.

4. Click the Advanced tab and then click Change under Virtual Memory.

5. This will load the Virtual Memory screen. Uncheck the box that says Automatically manage paging file size for all drives.

6. For each drive listed in the box that has a paging file configured on it, select the No paging file option and press Set, as shown in Figure 15-5.

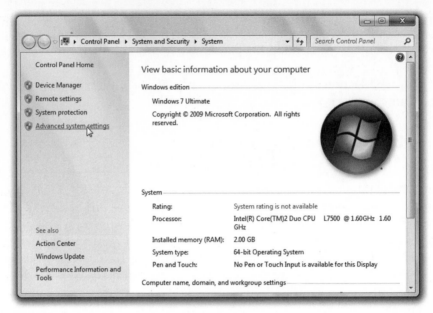

Figure 15-4: Selecting Advanced system settings

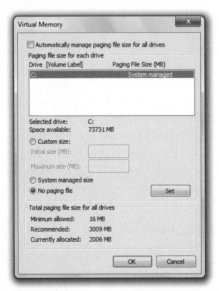

Figure 15-5: Using No paging file in Windows 7

7. After you have gone through the list and verified that you no longer have any paging files configured on your drives, click OK to exit.

Your paging file will now be disabled after a reboot. Feel free to delete the pagefile.sys file from your hard drive after your reboot to gain a chunk of space back. You will have to disable Hide protected operating system files on the View tab of Folder Options to see the pagefile.sys file.

If you do not have enough RAM to disable the paging file completely, follow the directions in the next section to adjust the size of the paging file for best performance.

Adjusting the Size of the Paging File

The size of the paging file can be set automatically by the system or it can be set by the user. In some situations, having the paging file managed by the system is a good idea, but in others, it is better to manage the paging file yourself.

The biggest argument for setting the paging file size and limit manually is to eliminate growing of the page file when it is set by the system. When the system is managing the size of the paging file, it will monitor the size of the file and will then automatically make it larger when it is needed. This causes two problems. First, it will cause a noticeable delay for all applications running on your computer because the computer has to expand the paging file, and this is a hard disk–intensive operation. Second, allowing the system to grow and shrink the paging file causes fragmentation errors.

For the sake of having enough speed, your page file should not have any file fragments. In the next section about defragmenting you will learn exactly how to fix this. Before the defragmentation can be successful, however, the page file needs to have a constant size. If the page file will be growing frequently, the defrag utility cannot put the file in a place on the hard disk so that it will never get fragmented. Only when the page file is set to a constant size can the defrag utility ensure it will never become fragmented again.

Setting the paging file to a constant size has some disadvantages. For example, the lost disk space taken up by the paging file can be as high as several gigabytes. Additionally, when you set the maximum paging file size manually, you are setting a limit that your computer can never go above. Should you run an extremely memory-intensive application and your limit is too low, your paging file will fill up and you will be out of luck in much the same way as when you completely disable your paging file.

The previous example illustrates why setting the correct paging file size is so important. An easy way to calculate the maximum size of your page file is to take the recommended size of the page file from the Virtual Memory Settings window, as shown in Figure 15-6, and multiply it by 2. If you are having problems finding where your computer states the recommended size, perform the following steps to change the paging file to a constant size because this value is on the same screen as the one on which you will be working.

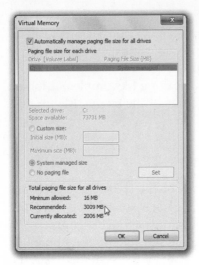

Figure 15-6: Virtual Memory settings showing the recommended Paging file size

Now that you are ready to optimize the paging file to a constant size, follow these steps:

1. Click the Start button, right-click Computer, and select Properties.

2. When System has loaded, click Advanced system settings.

3. Under the Performance section, click Settings.

4. Click the Advanced tab and then press Change under the Virtual Memory section.

5. This brings up all the page file settings. Modify the custom values so that the initial and maximum sizes are the same. To do this, you first need to enable the option to set a custom size so select the Custom size option.

6. Enter the value that you calculated in these two boxes, as shown in Figure 15-7.

7. Click the Set button and then click OK to exit.

After you restart, you will be using the new constant size paging file. You are now ready to run your defragmenter to defragment the paging file to ensure optimal performance.

CAUTION   The method that I use to calculate the size of the constant paging file is a very conservative and effective approach. However, if you feel the need for more free disk space, play around with the calculation, such as multiplying the recommended amount only by 1.75 or maybe even 1.5. If you do that, keep in mind that you will be increasing your chances of maxing out your paging file.

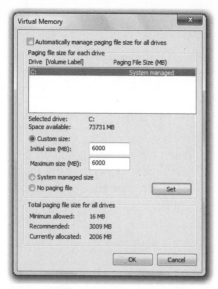

Figure 15-7: Setting the paging file to a Custom size

Changing the Location of the Paging File

The paging file can be placed on any storage device in your computer. If you really want to, you can even move the paging file to an external hard drive connected over USB. Although this would probably slow down your system because an external hard drive is often slower than a hard drive connected inside your case. However, if you have multiple hard drives in your system, and I am not talking about multiple partitions on the same drive, you may see a performance increase if you move your paging file off the main system drive.

Moving the paging file off your main drive will allow it to be accessed faster in situations in which your primary hard drive is busy. When users add hard drives to their computers, these new hard drives are typically faster than the hard drives that the computers came with because of advances in technology over time. Moving your paging file to the faster hard drive will also help performance.

Changing the location of the paging file is very easy. Just follow these steps and you will have it done in no time:

1. Click the Start button, right-click Computer, and select Properties.

2. When System has loaded, click Advanced system settings.

3. Under the Performance section, click Settings.

4. Click the Advanced tab and then press Change under the Virtual Memory section.

5. Now that you have the Virtual Memory settings displayed, select the drive on which your current paging file is located from the list of drives.

6. Before you make any changes, write down what the initial and maximum size text boxes contain. Then click the No Paging File option and press the Set button.

7. Select the hard drive on which you want your new paging file to be placed from the list of drives.

8. When the new hard drive is highlighted, select the Custom Size option and enter the numbers that you wrote down before. If you are not using the Custom Size mode, click the System Managed Size mode but reconsider what was talked about in the last section because it will help the performance of your hard drive.

9. Click the Set button, click OK, and you are finished.

After a reboot, your system will be using the paging file on the new hard drive. Feel free to delete pagefile.sys from your old hard drive location; it no longer is needed there.

Defragmenting Your Hard Drive

Fragmentation is everything when it comes to maintaining a traditional mechanical hard drive. Over time, as your hard drive fills up and you install and uninstall programs and games, the files on your hard drive can become fragmented, as Windows has to find open spots on your hard drive to place the file. Often the file is broken up into hundreds of little pieces and scattered all over the hard drive. This can cause a noticeable performance slowdown which can be easily cured by running a software program known as a *defragmenter*.

Disk Defragment software does the simple task of moving bits of the files around on the hard drives so that they are all placed together. This arrangement allows the hard drive to load a file faster since the head, which is the arm that reads the data off the plates inside the drive, does not have to scatter all over the place to read the data.

Before I go any further, it is important to point out that solid state hard drives (SSD) that are often included in high-end laptops and desktops and some Netbooks do not need to be defragmented. Solid state disks don't have any moving parts and as a result, very low random read times. It makes no difference if parts of a file are spread all over the drive because there is no mechanical head that has to move to different parts of the drive to read data. Because of the elimination of that delay, using defrag utilities on a SSD will have very little effect on its performance. If you have an SSD, I suggest you skip this section.

Using the Windows Defrag Utility

The defrag utility in Windows 7 has an updated interface but the functionality is the same. It does a good job of defragmenting your files using a basic optimization algorithm. Although it does not have all the bells and whistles of the third-party utilities, it is good enough for users that don't want to pay for slightly better performance.

The Windows defrag utility is called the Disk Defragmenter. There are two ways you can access the defrag utility — either in the Start menu or by right-clicking a drive in Computer and then selecting Properties. The utility can be found on the Tools tab of the drive properties. For this section I am going to use the Start menu shortcut:

1. Click the Start button, type in Disk Defragmenter, and hit Enter.

2. Select the drive you want to defrag and then click Analyze.

3. If the report shows your drive is fragmented, click Defragment disk and the utility will begin to defragment your drive with multiple passes, as shown in Figure 15-8.

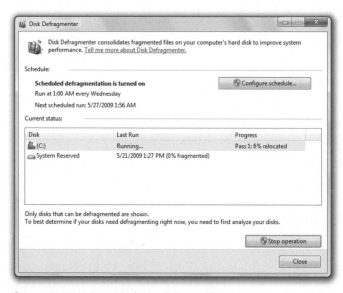

Figure 15-8: Using Windows defrag utility

Using Third-Party Defrag Utilities

As I mentioned in Chapter 12 there are a number of third-party defrag utilities that offer advanced features that they believe will do a better job than

Microsoft's included utility. All the utilities that offer advanced features such as automatic background defragmentation and boot time system defrag cost around $29 for home versions and $59 to $79 for professional versions. The major difference between the home and professional versions are additional value-added features. I will go into more detail about these with each following utility.

Using PerfectDisk 10

PerfectDisk is a popular defrag utility that has its own unique file placement and optimization strategy. In addition to the standard features such as automatic background defrag and boot time system file defrag it also has the ability to consolidate your free space. The professional version includes space management utilities that will help you manage what is on your disk and free disk space.

In Chapter 12, I showed you how to defrag the system files by running a system files boot defrag with PerfectDisk. When running in that mode, PerfectDisk only touches your system files and leaves the rest of your drive alone. Now I am going to show you how to do a full system defrag so all your files are optimized.

If you have not already done so, visit www.PerfectDisk.com and download and install the trial version. After you have it installed, follow these steps:

1. Click the Start button, type in PerfectDisk, and hit Enter.

2. When loaded, select the drive you want to defrag. You can select multiple drives by holding down CTRL and then clicking on each drive.

3. Select the type of defrag you want to do on the menu. You can select SMARTPlacement, Consolidate Free Space, or Defrag Only. I suggest using SMARTPlacement or Consolidate Free Space.

4. Click the green Start button and the defrag will begin as shown in Figure 15-9.

Using Diskeeper 2009

Diskeeper is another popular defrag utility that has a proprietary algorithm to optimize the location of files on your disk. Both a home and professional version are available with the professional version offering an improved file optimization feature called I-FAAST and a feature called Frag Shield that helps protect critical system files from becoming fragmented.

Unlike PerfectDisk there is no separate mode for optimizing boot files so if you used Diskeeper in Chapter 12 you already defragged your entire hard drive. If you have not already done so, download the disk defragmenter utility called Diskeeper, by Executive Software (www.diskeeper.com). If you do not remember how to do a boot defrag, go back to Chapter 12 and review the step-by-step instructions in the section "Boot-Time System Defrag with Diskeeper."

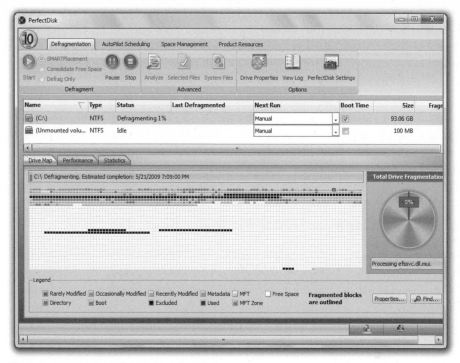

Figure 15-9: PerfectDisk 10 running defrag

Adjusting Your Application Priorities

Ever since the introduction of the multitasking processor, operating systems have been able to handle running multiple programs at once using the new task switching and segmentation features provided by the CPU. These new technologies made it possible for operating systems such as Windows to be created. Even though PCs today are able to multitask, they still really can do only one thing at a time per CPU core. For the operating system to support running dozens of applications at once, it has to slice up all the available processing time and give each application a turn. Although this is starting to change for consumers with the introduction of multi-core processors, each core can still do only one thing at a time. Previously this was only possible on expensive multiprocessor configurations typically only found in servers.

Operating systems use a variety of techniques to determine which application will get the next available time slot to use the CPU. One of the factors that determines this for Windows 7 is the priority level at which the application is running.

Every application that runs on your computer has a priority level attached to its runtime information. By default, the operating system starts each application at normal priority, which is right in the middle of the priority spectrum. Applications can run and be assigned six different priority levels, ranked from highest to lowest: Realtime, High, Above Normal, Normal, Below Normal, and Low. Because the CPU can do only one thing at a time, the different priority levels allow the operating system to decide which application will get the next CPU time slot. If an application is running at the High or Above Normal priority levels, it will get more CPU time than an application running at Normal level.

As you can see, the priority you give an application can affect how fast the program runs.

Using Task Manager to Adjust Priorities

Windows Task Manager is something that everyone experiences when they have problems with a frozen program. However, we learned that Task Manager is a very useful utility in Chapter 11, "Analyzing Your System." Another use of Task Manager is to change the priority at which an application is running. This capability can be very useful when you have a lot of programs running on your computer.

> **CAUTION**   Setting any application to Realtime can be dangerous because doing so allows the application to hog all the CPU time. Trying to exit a program that is running at this high priority is next to impossible if for some reason it crashes or is stuck in a loop. It takes a very long time to load Task Manager to end the application because the program is hogging all the CPU time.

If you have an application that has a high need for CPU operations such as rendering a video clip or a game, you can adjust the priority of the application by following these steps:

1. To load Task Manager, click the Start button, type **taskmgr** in the Search box, and then press Enter.

2. After Task Manager loads, click the Processes tab. Be sure to click Show processes from all users so you can see all processes running on your computer.

3. Right-click the name of the process for which you would like to adjust the priority, select Set Priority, and then select the level, as shown in Figure 15-10. Your change is now complete.

> **TIP**   Having problems identifying what process belongs to an application? While on the Applications tab of Task Manager right-click on any application and select Go To Processes. All processes that belong to the application will be selected on the Processes tab.

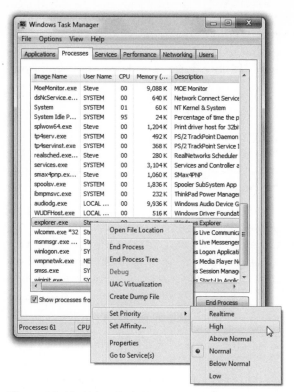

Figure 15-10: Using Task Manager to adjust
application priorities

TIP If your computer has multiple processors or multiple cores, or supports
hyperthreading, then you will notice an extra option, Set Affinity, when you
right-click a process. This option enables you to specify on which CPU core the
application will run (or which virtual CPU, in the case of hyperthreading users).

Using Task Manager to change the priority levels is great. However, there is
one downside. When an application on which you have altered the priority level
is closed, the priority level it was running at will be lost. The next time that the
program is started, the program will be running back at the default level. This
downside can be a pain in the neck for some users; however, a cool trick will
fix this problem, as discussed in the next section.

Starting Applications with a User Set Priority

A wonderful command built into Windows allows you to start any program
and specify its priority. This cool utility is called the Start command. Using the

Start command with priority flags followed by the executable enables you to start any program at a priority level of your choosing.

For the sake of demonstrating how to use the command, assume that the Calculator is set at high CPU priority. Follow these steps to set the command:

1. Open Notepad to type the command so that it can be turned into a batch script file. This can be done by starting Notepad from the Accessories item in the Start menu's All Program entry.

2. After Notepad opens, type **start /high calc.exe**. If you want to start the Calculator at a different priority, you can replace /high with **/low, /normal, /realtime, /abovenormal**, and **/belownormal**.

3. After keying in the priority level, click the File menu bar item in Notepad and select Save As. Change the file Save As Type to All Files and type **launchcalc.bat** in the filename box. You can call the file anything you want, but make sure that it has the .bat file extension so that Windows knows to execute the commands in the file.

4. Specify a location on your hard drive to save it, such as your desktop, and click the Save button. You are now finished and can exit Notepad.

Now that you have created the batch command file, you are ready to start your new shortcut.

The same technique can be applied to any program on your computer. Instead of typing calc.exe at the end of the command, type the name of the executable of the program that you want to start.

Additionally, this command can be used on nonexecutable files such as documents. For example, you can type **start /high mydocument.doc** to start Microsoft Word in the High priority level with your document opened.

Summary

You have now finished optimizing the core components of Windows 7. First you learned how to add more memory to your computer and about the new ReadyBoost feature of Windows 7 that allows you to gain some of the benefits of adding RAM without even opening your case to speed up memory access. Then you learned how you can adjust your paging file to speed up your hard drive access and adjust application priorities.

Next, I show you a way to speed up your network connection. I start with browsing the network and your network card and work outward to speeding up your Internet connection.

CHAPTER 16

Optimizing Your Network

Your browser and network subsystem play a major role in the use of your computer. People are spending more and more time using their web browsers and the Internet, making the web browser the most used application on many users' computers. Now that you have optimized almost every major component of the operating system, let's cover the most used application and components on which it is dependent, the web browser and the network that connects you to the Internet.

First, you optimize the speed of both Internet Explorer and Firefox by tweaking the number of active downloads. Then I show you some great utilities that will increase the speed of downloads, followed by tweaks that will speed up your network.

Optimizing Your Web Browser

On my computer, the web browser is the most used application. For society in general, the web browser has become the most used application on the computer. Considering that you have already optimized, tweaked, and hacked almost every other component of the operating system for speed, it's important to cover the most used application as well. Using the following tweaks, you can make your web browser work faster than ever before. How is this possible? Both Internet Explorer and Firefox have to adhere to web standards that specify how many connections a browser can make to a web server. By default in both Internet Explorer and Firefox, that amount is between two and six at a time. The following tweaks will show you how you can dramatically increase that number to speed up and increase the parallel downloading of files your web browser needs to display a web page.

Speeding Up Internet Explorer

Microsoft has made sure that Internet Explorer follows Internet standards by allowing you and your browser to download only six files at a time from any server. If you visit a web page with a lot of images and required files, such as CSS styles and JavaScript, you can easily end up with a scenario where your web browser has to make more than 40 requests to the web server to download all the files and then assemble the web page. Requesting only 2 of these 40 files at a time is going to be a lot slower than downloading, say, 10 of them at a time.

By tweaking hidden registry values, you can direct Internet Explorer to break Internet standards and download more than just two files at a time. Modifying this setting is simple to do, but be careful; the standards police will be after you. Follow these steps to speed up IE:

1. Click the Start button, type **regedit** in the Search box, and then press Enter.

2. After Registry Editor loads, navigate through `HKEY_CURRENT_USER\ Software\Microsoft\Windows\CurrentVersion\Internet Settings`.

3. Right-click in open space and create a new DWORD (32-bit) Value, as shown in Figure 16-1.

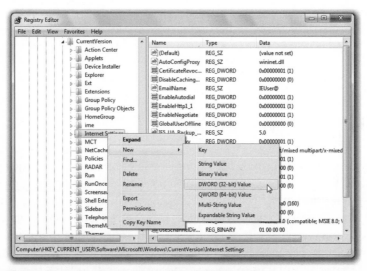

Figure 16-1: Creating a new registry DWORD Value

4. Type **MaxConnectionsPerServer** as the name of the new DWORD key.

5. Right-click this key and select Modify.

6. Set the base to Decimal and enter in a value greater than 6, as shown in Figure 16-2. I like to use 15 as my value here. Press OK when you are done.

Figure 16-2: Setting the value of MaxConnectionsPerServer

7. Create a new DWORD key and type **MaxConnectionsPer1_0Server** as the name.

8. Right-click this key as well and select Modify.

9. Set the base to Decimal and enter in the new value. Use the same value as used in Step 6. Click OK when you are finished.

10. Exit Registry Editor and reboot your computer.

After your computer has rebooted, your new Internet Explorer settings are active. If you ever feel like undoing this tweak, just go back into the registry and delete the MaxConnectionsPerServer and MaxConnectionsPer1_0Server keys that you created and reboot. Congratulations, you are now speeding on the information superhighway.

Speeding Up Firefox

Firefox suffers from the same limitation on file downloads imposed on it as Internet Explorer by Internet standards. Thankfully, there is an easy way to modify the number of simultaneous downloads in Firefox as well. Additionally, you can do a few other things to speed up Firefox, such as reducing delays and enabling parallel downloads (which Firefox calls *pipelining*). Instead of editing the registry, you can use a cool hidden feature in Firefox to hack the raw configuration settings built into the browser. Follow these steps to speed up browsing with Firefox:

1. Open a copy of Firefox if you do not already have it open.

2. Type **about:config** in the address bar and press Enter.

3. Click the I'll be careful, I promise! Button to view the settings.

4. Scroll down the list and locate network.http.max-connections-per-server, as shown in Figure 16-3.

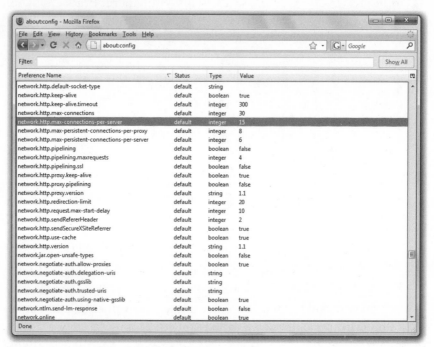

Figure 16-3: Modifying the configuration of Firefox

5. Right-click this setting and select Modify. Enter a higher value, such as 20, and press OK.

6. Enable parallel downloads, which is known as pipelining in Firefox. Scroll further down the list and locate network.http.pipelining.

7. Right-click this setting and select Toggle to set it to true.

8. Scroll down and modify network.http.pipelining.maxrequests. Set this to a value of at least 15 and press OK.

TIP If you use a proxy server to connect to the Internet, you will also want to toggle network.http.proxy.pipelining.

9. Now let's increase the max number of total connections. Locate **network .http.max-connections**.

10. Right click and select Modify. I like to set this value to 50 on my computer.

11. Finally, locate **network.http.max-persistent-connections-per-server** and select Modify. I set this value to 15.

12. Close and restart Firefox to activate your new optimized settings.

Accelerating Your Downloads

The most popular web browsers do not currently include advanced download managers that have the ability to speed up your downloads. Have you ever noticed that when you download a file from a server, it almost seems that the server you are downloading from is setting a maximum speed on the file you are trying to get? I run into situations like this all the time. I am downloading a file and it seems to be stuck at some slow speed for my broadband connection. While that file is downloading, I start downloading another file from the server and this one also is downloading at nearly the same speed. No matter how many additional files I download at the same time, they all seem to be stuck at the same speed, as if there is a maximum speed set for downloads.

Some web servers set a maximum download speed for file downloads, whereas other servers use various technologies to share their bandwidth among the other visitors, and others just seem to be inconsistent. All these situations can be helped with the use of a download accelerator application. Download accelerators work in much the same way as if you were downloading multiple files from the same server at once, only they download multiple chunks of the same file from the server at once. For example, in the scenario outlined previously, using a download accelerator divides the file I am trying to download into four equal chunks. I am able to download the file almost four times faster than if I were to download it in one big chunk. There is no magic going on here; the download accelerator is just breaking up the file, which results in more actual connections. If a web browser has a set maximum download connection speed, when you have four connections downloading at once versus just one, the combined speed of four is always going to be much faster, which means your download finishes more quickly.

Some of the more advanced download accelerators do more than just split up your files. They search the web for other servers that also have the same file you are downloading and then determine the speed at which the files can be downloaded from the alternative sources. If the other sources are faster, the accelerator will switch and download the file from the faster server.

Various download accelerators are available. Some are free and others are shareware. Take a look at Table 16-1 for a list of popular download accelerators. For this section, I use the Free Download Manager to speed up downloads.

Table 16-1: Popular Download Accelerators

APPLICATION NAME	URL	PRICE
Star Downloader	www.StarDownloader.com	Free or $19.95 for advanced version
GetRight	www.GetRight.com	$29.95 for basic version
Free Download Manager	www.FreeDownloadManager.org	Free
Internet Download Manager	www.internetdownloadmanager.com	$29.95
Download Accelerator Plus	www.SpeedBit.com	Free; ad supported

Using the Free Download Manager to Speed Up Your Downloads

The Free Download Manager is a very comprehensive download accelerator that includes many additional features that will help you manage your connection and find files on top of just downloading them. All you are interested in right now is finding ways to speed up downloads, so I am going to get right to the point. If you have not already done so, visit www.FreeDownloadManager.org now and download the latest version of the Free Download Manager.

After installing the latest version of the Free Download Manager and rebooting your computer, you are almost ready to get started using the download accelerator. First, you need to configure the Free Download Manager to allow you to split files into chunks greater than four so that you can maximize the speed of your downloads. Follow these steps:

1. Click the Start button and then type **Free Download Manager** in the Search box. After a few seconds the shortcut will appear at the top of the selection of choices. Click it to start the download accelerator.

2. After the Free Download Manager loads for the first time you will need to specify your connection type and click Finish.

3. Press and hold the Ctrl key and press the number 3. This will change your traffic usage mode to Heavy mode and will prompt the traffic mode change box if your computer is not already in Heavy mode. Heavy mode will allow you to download up to 5 files at once and split a single file a maximum of 12 times.

4. Click OK in the Confirmation window and you are finished. If you are not shown a confirmation window Free Download Manager may already be in Heavy mode based on your connection type selected.

You are now ready to begin downloading files with the Free Download Manager. Open a copy of Internet Explorer and browse to a web site from which you frequently download a lot of files. Free Download Manager integrates with your web browser so that when you click a file to download, the Free Download Manager automatically takes over. Follow these steps to download files with the Free Download Manager:

1. When you click a link to download a file, the Free Download Manager will take over and prompt you, as shown in Figure 16-4. This is where you will select to where you want the file to be downloaded and other advanced settings. Locate the Advanced button on the bottom of the window and click it. This brings up the Advanced Properties window.

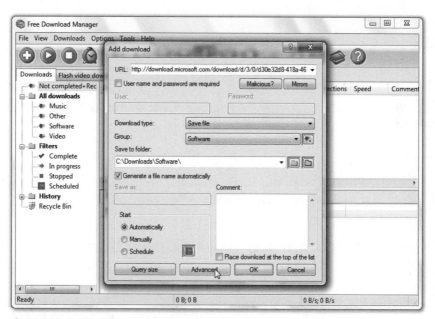

Figure 16-4: Free Download Manager prompting you with the Add download window

2. You need to adjust the number of chunks into which the download accelerator splits the file. Locate the Sections group on the Connection tab and increase the maximum number to a higher number, as shown in Figure 16-5. I like to set my maximum number to 15. When you are finished, press OK to return to the Add download window.

3. After you have the Save to folder specified, make sure the Start property is set to Automatically and press OK.

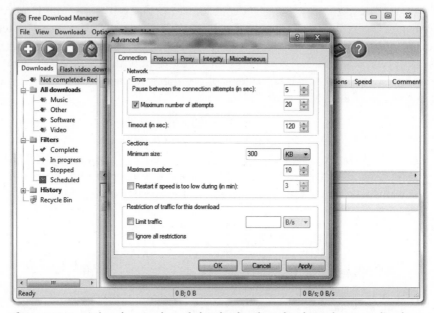

Figure 16-5: Setting the number of chunks the download accelerator splits the file into

Your file download will now begin. When the Free Download Manager is open and your file is downloading, click the Progress tab to see a graphical view of what parts of the file have already been downloaded.

Speeding Up Your Network Connection

The speed of your network connection does not just depend on the speed of your hardware. Windows is an operating system that is designed to work on a variety of different hardware and network setups. Because of the abstract nature of the operating system, it cannot be optimized for user-specific hardware setups.

Depending on the type of network connection you have, you might be able to tweak your connection so that the speed of your Internet connection as well as your local area network will be faster. These tweaks can help the auto-tuning network settings included in Windows 7 narrow in on a smaller range to find the optimal value.

Tweaking Auto Tuning

The network stack in Windows 7 is very intelligent compared to previous versions of Windows such as XP. Instead of using static transmission and receiving settings it will adjust to optimal values for the current network condition. Some of these values have a very wide range of possible settings so it can help to narrow the range. Also, depending on what your hardware supports, you may be able to increase the performance of your network significantly by disabling auto tuning completely.

All the auto tuning settings can be configured with the netsh command in conjunction with the auto tuning level you want to use. By default your system will run in Normal mode but there are a number of options available:

- Highly restricted — Allows the receive window to grow but is the most conservative.

- Restricted — Allows the receive window to grow but is less conservative.

- Normal — Allows the receive window to grow at the normal rate.

- Disable — Complexly disables the auto tuning feature.

Open up an administrative level command prompt to change the setting:

1. Click the Start button and type in **command prompt**.

2. When you see the shortcut appear, right-click it and select Run as Administrator.

3. Type in **netsh interface tcp set global autotuninglevel=<level>** and then hit Enter. Replace <level> with either highlyrestricted, restricted, normal, or disable. For example, a complete command would look like "netsh interface tcp set global autotuninglevel=disable."

I find it best to experiment with all the different levels to see what level works best in your environment. If you want to revert back to the default settings, set autotuninglevel=normal.

Disabling Unneeded Protocols

Every computer comes with programs installed that you do not need. As with extra programs taking up space, extra protocols are just wasting your network connection and can actually slow it down. How is this possible? By default, a few different protocols are installed on your computer to allow for maximum compatibility with other computers on a network; these protocols each require bandwidth to operate. Most users will not use too many protocols, and their computers will use up a portion of their connection as they respond and transmit information for these protocols.

Additionally, with extra protocols installed on your network adapter connected to the Internet, you increase the risk that you will have security-related problems. One of the most common risks for broadband users is having the Client for Microsoft Networks networking protocol enabled on their connections and no firewall to block the public from their computers. This protocol allows everyone on their networks, or local neighborhoods if they have a cable connection without a firewall or router, to connect to the users' computers and view any files that they may be sharing. This fact alone should be a good enough reason for you to turn off the extra protocols, but with them disabled, you will save a little bandwidth as well.

Viewing Protocols on Your Network Adapters

Viewing the protocols installed and active on your various network adapters is very easy. Just follow these quick steps and you will be viewing them in no time:

1. Click the Start button, type in Network and Sharing center, and hit Enter.

2. On the side menu, click Change adapter settings. This will show a list of all the network adapters installed on your computer.

3. Right-click any of the adapters and select Properties. This will bring up a list of the protocols installed as well as active on your adapter (see Figure 16-6). The protocols that are installed but are not active are indicated by the absence of a check in the box.

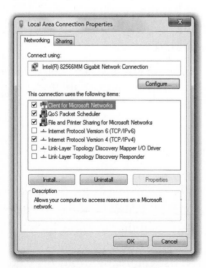

Figure 16-6: Network adapter protocol list

Disabling a Specific Protocol

Now that you have the list of installed and active protocols on your screen, you are ready to disable a protocol. To do so, just click the check box to remove the check. Then click OK and the protocol will no longer be active on the network adapter. Take a look at Table 16-2 for help with the default Windows protocols. Any other protocols you may have listed that are not in Table 16-2 should be researched online before disabling.

Table 16-2: Windows Vista's Networking Protocols

PROTOCOL NAME	FUNCTION
Client for Microsoft Networks	Used to access other shared resources on your local network running the File and Printer Sharing for Microsoft Networks protocol.
QOS Packet Scheduler	Used to provide traffic management on your network for applications that support the protocol.
File and Printer Sharing for Microsoft Networks	Used to share your printer and files on your computer with other computers on your local network.
Internet Protocol Version 6 (TCP/IPv6)	New version of the IPv4 protocol that is not very widespread. Unless you are connected to an IPv6 network (99 percent of you are not), you can safely disable this protocol.
Internet Protocol Version 4 (TCP/IPv4)	Primary network communication protocol. Do not disable this protocol.
Link Layer Topology Discovery Mapper I/O Driver	Used to discover other computers connected to your local network.
Link Layer Topology Responder	Used to identify your computer to other computers connected to your local network.

For optimal speed configuration, disable all protocols except for Internet Protocol Version 4. Note, however, that by doing so you will no longer be able to share or access shared files and resources, and certain programs and features that rely on other protocols may not work.

Also keep in mind that if you have multiple network adapters in your computer — such as a wireless adapter, a wired network adapter, and a dial-up modem — you will have to repeat the preceding instructions for each device.

Summary

This chapter completes the final chapter in Part III, "Increasing Your System's Performance." I covered speeding up every aspect of Windows 7, from the moment you press the power button to using your most frequent applications. In this chapter, I went over how to speed up your web browser and download files faster. Then, I went back to optimize the system components that you need to browse the Web and the network.

The next part of *Windows 7 Tweaks* covers securing your computer. Windows 7 has a lot of new security features that will help protect your computer better than ever before. The next few chapters show you how to use those new features as well as many additional security tweaks that will help make spyware, adware, and hackers a distant memory.

Part

IV

Securing Windows

In This Part

Windows Security

Security is one of the most important issues in the Windows computer world. Over the years, as Windows gained popularity and as it became the dominant operating system on the market, it became the primary target for hackers and other individuals who want to compromise your system. Additionally, you use your computer for more and more activities, which result in a massive amount of highly valuable and confidential information stored inside. Today it is not uncommon to have personal financial information, hundreds of personal documents, and thousands of priceless digital photos all stored on your computer. As the amount of personal data stored on your computer increases, the reward to compromise a system increases as well. This creates an enormous need for a secure operating system that will keep your data safe.

According to Microsoft, Windows 7 is the most secure version of Windows released in history. Building off the major security changes introduced in Windows Vista, Windows 7 is technically superior but it is far from perfect. Security patches are still released to protect users from new attacks and a lack of education on the new security features results in many users not using them.

This chapter helps you get the most out of security features and locks down your computer using common industry best practices to protect your computer from getting compromised.

Actively Protecting Your Computer

The days when running an antivirus program on your computer alone was enough to protect it are long over. Now you need to play an active role in the process of protecting your computer. The types of threats are changing very quickly. Currently, the most effective way to compromise a computer is by taking advantage of the human factor — that is, tricking you into running some code that will install a malicious program on your computer to help someone steal your data or take over your machine. Another effective method to compromise a computer is to exploit a known vulnerability in the operating system. In this situation, a user is not up-to-date on their security patches and they are basically leaving the door unlocked so that anyone with limited computer knowledge can step right in and install and steal anything they want.

Taking an active role in securing your computer involves keeping up-to-date on the latest security news so that you know about new vulnerabilities and methods hackers are using to compromise your computer. Additionally, you need to know what to look out for so you don't fall for any undocumented hacks or tricks, as well as make sure the known vulnerabilities are fixed on your computer.

This section helps you with all the aspects of actively protecting your computer. First, I show you some great ways to keep up-to-date on the latest security news. Then I show you how to make sure that Automatic Updates in Windows 7 is working properly and that your computer has all known vulnerabilities fixed. Finally, I give you some pointers that will help protect you from falling for most undocumented and unknown hacks and tricks to compromise your computer.

Staying Up-to-Date

One of the largest parts of taking an active role in protecting your computer's security is keeping up-to-date with the latest trends and news on active vulnerabilities. There are various web sites and newsletters that can help you stay on top of the latest Windows security news. Take a look at the following sites and sign up for some of the newsletters to stay on top of the latest security threats:

Microsoft's Security at Home Newsletter: This newsletter is targeted at less-technical home users and has a lot of information about good techniques for better "human" security, as I mentioned earlier. The newsletter is free and you can sign up at `www.microsoft.com/athome/security/secnews/default.mspx`.

TechNet's Microsoft Security Newsletter: This newsletter, which targets advanced computer users, goes into more depth concerning the latest security patches released, in addition to general security news. This newsletter is also free and you can sign up at `www.microsoft.com/technet/security/secnews/default.mspx`.

TrendMicro's Security Info: This is a security web site that helps you find out about the latest viruses, malware, and vulnerabilities for Windows 7 and popular applications that run on it. Visit `www.trendmicro.com/vinfo/` to get the latest news.

McAfee Dispatch: This newsletter alerts you to the latest virus threats as well as keeps you up-to-date with general virus-related news. The newsletter is free and can be subscribed to at `http://dispatch.mcafee.com/us/`.

US-CERT: This is the federally funded Computer Emergency Readiness Team web site, which provides information on the latest security news and vulnerabilities for Windows 7 and every other computer software product, including applications that run on Windows. US-CERT is a very comprehensive web site that has several RSS feeds that you can subscribe to with your favorite RSS reader or with Internet Explorer. Visit `www.us-cert.gov` to use this massive resource.

Updating Windows 7

Another key part of actively protecting your computer is to make sure that all known vulnerabilities have been fixed. Every month, Microsoft releases new security patches for all their products that fix security holes and increase the security of Windows. It is very important to make sure that your computer is set up to download these new security patches automatically and that it is working properly. With the integrated Windows Update feature in Windows 7, this is easier than ever before.

Follow these steps to make sure that Automatic Updates in Windows 7 is working properly and you have the latest security patches installed:

1. Click the Start button, type in Windows Updates, and hit Enter.

2. Make sure that your computer has the latest security patches installed. Click Check for updates from the top of the left menu, as shown in Figure 17-1. If any updates are available, make sure you install them right away by clicking Install Updates.

3. Now that your computer is up-to-date, make sure it stays that way by making sure Automatic Updates is set up and running. Click Change Settings to bring up the Automatic Updates details.

4. Make sure that the Install updates automatically box is selected, as shown in Figure 17-2. I also like to adjust the install time from 3:00 AM to a time I know my computer is going to be on. Because my computer is usually on when I am at lunch, I use 12:00 PM for my update time.

5. After everything is set, click OK to save your changes.

Windows is now up-to-date and will remain up-to-date when Microsoft releases new security patches for Windows 7.

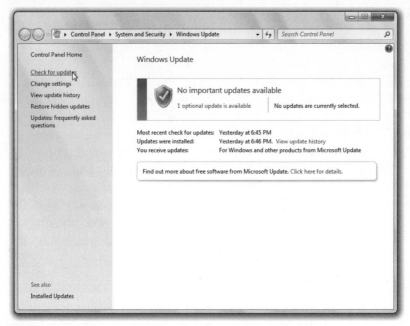

Figure 17-1: Updating Windows 7 with Windows Update

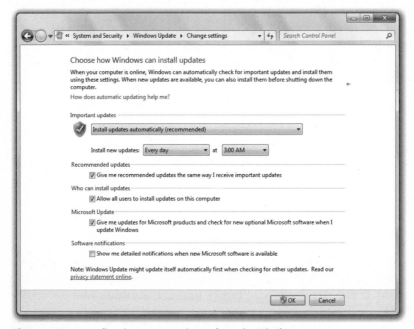

Figure 17-2: Configuring Automatic Updates in Windows 7

Active Security Tips

As I mentioned earlier, one of the easiest ways to break into a computer to install malware or steal data is through the human factor. This works by taking advantage of the fact that we do not usually read the fine print for an application that we download or are just click-happy and click Yes on any dialog box that pops up. If you exercise a little caution and follow the upcoming recommendations, you can take the human element completely out of the picture.

Don't Get in the Habit of Clicking Yes/Continue/Allow

In Windows 7, User Account Control provides more control over what applications automatically get installed on your computer. The days of visiting a web site and getting junk automatically installed on your computer are over. In Windows 7, User Account Control, when configured properly, requires you to authorize almost all changes to your computer, including system configuration changes and installing new programs. To some, these prompts can become overwhelming and result in the habit of just clicking Continue on all of them that pop up. Such behavior completely bypasses the new security features in Windows 7, allowing almost anything to take over your system completely.

The next time you get a User Account Control pop-up, click the Details arrow, as shown in Figure 17-3, to find out exactly what you are allowing.

Figure 17-3: Viewing details on a User Account Control pop-up

Watch Out for the Internet Explorer Plug-Ins You Install

Internet Explorer plug-ins are notorious for bundling all sorts of extra junk along with the application, especially those by web sites that offer some free application. There is usually a reason why the application is free. Most companies are in business to make money and they have to make money some way. They usually get paid for bundling additional software with their software. This can result in a bunch of new applications popping up on your computer when you thought you just installed one.

Most of the more popular web sites are a little more forthcoming about what extra junk they are going to install on your computer. You can find if they are going to install any other applications by reading the user agreement that everyone just clicks past and by paying attention to the installation options. There are usually check boxes that enable you to prevent other applications from being installed. If you are visiting a lesser-known web site or a web site that may have illegal or adult content, I highly recommend not installing any plug-ins unless you do research and can verify it is a legitimate plug-in.

If You Didn't Start It, Be Cautious

If you are using your computer and you are hit with a surprise User Account Control pop-up, one that you did not expect, be very cautious about clicking Continue and allowing the request to be granted. For example, let's say you are typing a document and all of a sudden User Account Control wants you to approve a system change. This may be a big indication that your computer is infected with some sort of malware or virus that is trying to change your system settings. I recommend doing a full system virus and malware scan immediately to make sure that your computer is clean.

Secure Your Network Connection

One of the best ways to secure your computer is to place it behind a firewall or a router device that will protect it from malicious Internet traffic. By blocking the public access to your internal network or wide open access to your computer, you can effectively kill the potential for certain types of direct attacks.

In the next chapter I show in greater detail how you can use firewalls to protect your computer.

Protect Your Accounts

Your account is safe only as long as no one has or can guess your password. Make sure that you have a password on all your accounts and that it is never written down in any place. The next section will help you secure your computer accounts and pick complex passwords that will be hard for anyone to guess and hack with brute force techniques.

Controlling Your Computer Accounts

Your computer's physical security, as well as online security, depends on how easy it is to access your accounts. This book shows you many ways that you can protect your computer, but almost all of them can be defeated by an account on your computer that has a poor password or no password at all. This is why it is critical to ensure that your computer is protected by accounts with strong passwords. Anything less will weaken your entire security defense.

This section shows you how you can manage your user accounts in Windows 7 to make sure they are all well protected.

Managing User Accounts

Windows 7 includes various accounts that are set up when you install or buy a Windows 7 computer. These accounts are usually disabled by default, but there are a few quick tips that will ensure they can never be used again. The other accounts on your computer can be protected, too. Follow the next few sections to secure all your accounts.

Using Complex Passwords on All Your Computer Accounts

All the accounts on your computer should have a complex password associated with them in case your computer is ever exposed to the Internet. Passwords such as easy-to-remember words and predictable key combinations, such as "asdf," just don't cut it. These types of passwords are vulnerable to brute force dictionary attacks where an intruder can use special software to try hundreds of combinations to hack into your account.

A complex password is a password that has at least eight characters and consists of uppercase and lowercase letters, as well as numbers or other symbols. "Ftm3D8&-" is an example of a complex password. Something such as this is very difficult to guess and will take quite some time for a brute force technique to crack it.

Using complex passwords on all your accounts might not be easy at first, but after a while they will grow on you and you will have no problem remembering them. To prevent losing access to any encrypted files, it is best to log on to each account that does not already have a complex password and change them. If you use the Set Password function in Computer Manager, as you did for setting the passwords for the Guest and Administrator accounts, you risk losing access to any files that were encrypted under the user's account.

Follow these steps to safely change a user's account password:

1. Log on to the user's account that needs a password change.

2. Press and hold Ctrl+Alt+Delete so that the secure desktop is shown (see Figure 17-4).

3. Click the Change Password button.

4. Type the old password once and then the new password for the user twice, and click the blue arrow button.

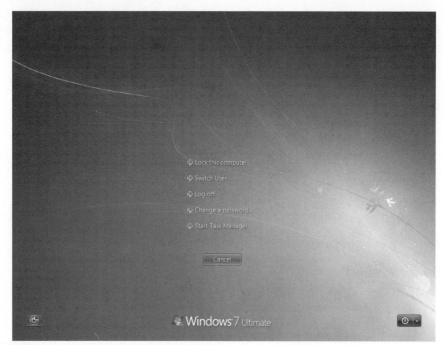

Figure 17-4: Windows 7's secure desktop

The password for the account has now been changed.

Assigning a Password and Renaming the Guest Account

One of the default accounts set up in Windows 7 is the Guest account. This account can be useful if your computer is in a public place such as a library and a low rights account is needed. However, for most of us, this account is just another possible security hole because it cannot be deleted. It is disabled by default but it could be enabled again by a virus or malware if your computer ever gets infected. The best way to neutralize this account is to give it a random password and rename it to eliminate the chances that some script will be able to use it.

Follow these steps to protect this account:

1. Click the Start menu, right-click Computer, and then select Manage.

2. After Computer Manager loads, expand Local Users and Group and select the Users folder. All the local computer accounts will be listed, as shown in Figure 17-5.

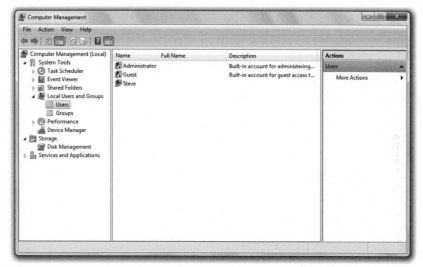

Figure 17-5: Computer Management listing local computer accounts

3. Right-click the Guest account on the list and select Set Password.

4. A warning screen will appear telling you about what may happen if you proceed. Disregard this message and click Proceed.

5. When the Set Password window appears, type in a completely random password that is a complex password. It must also be at least 20 characters long in both boxes, and click OK. The new password will now be set.

6. Rename the account to confuse any malicious scripts that might be looking for it. Right-click the Guest account again and select Rename.

7. Type a new name for this account that has some random letters and numbers in it. You just want to make it different from Guest.

8. When you are done renaming it, click Enter and you are finished.

Your Guest account is now more secure than ever.

Secure the Administrator Account

The Administrator account is the most important account on the computer because it has the highest permissions and can do anything it wants to the configuration and settings of your computer. Securing this valuable account is critical to the overall security of your computer.

This can be accomplished by ensuring the account is disabled, setting a strong password, and renaming it so that it is harder for malicious scripts and viruses to try to use. Doing this is very similar to securing the Guest account as you just did in the last section.

Follow these steps to protect your Administrator account:

1. Click the Start menu, right-click Computer, and select Manage.

2. After Computer Manager loads, expand Local Users and Group, and select the Users folder.

3. Right-click the Administrator account and select Properties.

4. Check the Account is disabled option if it is not already selected, as shown in Figure 17-6. Then click OK to save the changes.

Figure 17-6: Disabling the Administrator account

5. Right-click the Administrator account and select Set Password.

6. A warning screen will appear telling you about what might happen if you proceed. Disregard this message and hit Proceed.

7. When the Set Password window appears, type a completely random, complex password that is at least 20 characters long in both boxes and click OK. The new password will now be set.

8. Rename the account to confuse any malicious scripts that might be looking for it. Right-click the Administrator account again and select Rename.

9. Type a new name for the account that has some random letters and numbers in it. I like to use AdminDisabled [random numbers] as a new name.

10. Press Enter and you are finished.

Now both of the built-in Windows 7 accounts are secured.

Hiding Usernames on the Logon Screen

If you use your computer in a high-security environment it is very important to hide your username from the logon screen so that potential intruders are not able to figure out your username — before they even try to break your password. Using the Local Security Policy to your advantage, you can configure a setting that will automatically clear the username of the last person that logged in. This will add another layer of protection on your account by putting it in stealth mode.

Follow these instructions to turn on this setting:

1. Click the Start button, type **secpol.msc** in the Search box, and then press Enter.

2. After the Local Security Policy editor has loaded, expand Local Policy, and then select Security Options.

3. Scroll through the list and right-click Interactive logon: Do not display last user name, and then select Properties.

4. Select the Enable box, as shown in Figure 17-7, and then click OK.

5. Close the Local Security Policy editor and you are finished.

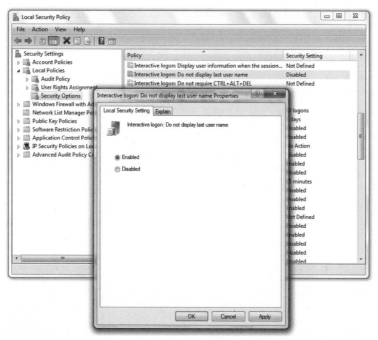

Figure 17-7: Hiding your username with the Local Security Policy editor

The next time you reboot, your username will be hidden.

Setting the Account Lockout Policy

To complement the new complex password that your accounts now have, I recommend configuring the Account Lockout Policy to add even more security to your accounts. The Account Lockout Policy enables you to protect your account from an intruder trying dozens or even thousands of possible password combinations to try to guess your password. When configured, after the intruder has entered the wrong password a set number of times, the account will then be locked for a set amount of time. After that time interval has passed, the account is unlocked and the whole process is reset.

This provides valuable additional security for your accounts that will eliminate the effectiveness of certain brute force tools that will try every possible combination to hack into your account. By using the Account Lockout Policy, you can increase the amount of time required to try every possible combination to something unfeasible.

Setting the Account Lockout Policy is very similar to configuring your computer not to show the last username that was used to log in with. Follow these steps to configure the lockout policy for your computer:

1. Click the Start button, type **secpol.msc** in the Search box, and then press Enter.

2. After the Local Security Policy editor has loaded, expand Account Policies and then select Account Lockout Policy.

3. Right-click Account lockout threshold and select Properties.

4. Increase the number of invalid logon attempts from 0 to a higher value to enable the feature. I like to use 5 as my number of invalid logon attempts before my account is locked out.

5. Click OK to save the setting. A Suggested Value Settings window pops up that will automatically populate the two other settings: Account lockout duration and Reset account lockout counter after. Click OK here as well to use the default values.

6. If the 30-minute duration of the account lockout and before the account lockout counter reset is too long for you, just right-click each setting, select Properties, and modify the value. I typically use 10 minutes for both of these settings because I think it is a nice balance between added security and inconvenience when I may be using my computer half asleep and type in the wrong password more than five times.

Your Account Lockout Policy is now set up and will begin protecting your computer immediately.

Tweaking User Account Control

User Account Control (UAC) made its debut in Windows Vista and has been annoying and protecting users ever since. According to Microsoft, User Account Control decreased malware infection rates significantly in Windows Vista compared to Windows XP. On paper, UAC has been a great success but in practice it annoyed users a little too much. In Windows 7, UAC was fine-tuned to minimize interruptions and is significantly less annoying.

For the majority of you who skipped Windows Vista, User Account Control provides total control over all changes to your system. If you try to install a program, install a plug-in, or access any application that has the capability to change critical system settings, UAC goes into action and makes sure that you really want to do what an application is trying to do on your computer. In terms of the security of your computer, UAC is great because it catches when applications, scripts, and even web sites try to do things to your computer that cause a critical change. However, if you initiate the change, such as trying to install a program or modify a Windows setting, you also have to deal with the pop-ups because of the way UAC is designed.

User Account Control works by monitoring the Windows Application Programming Interface (API), system components, and application configuration files, to find out whether an action needs higher privileges. If an action is found, then it prompts a UAC box for your authorization.

Controlling User Account Control

The new User Account Control in Windows 7 plays a big role in the overall security of the operating system. No longer do you have to worry about software secretly getting installed or scripts running that change critical system data running without your knowledge. Instead, you have to worry about getting bombarded with UAC pop-ups that require you to authorize almost every change this book asks you to do. Thankfully, Microsoft did not implement this feature without adding the ability for power users to tweak it to make their lives easier while still benefiting from some of the protections of UAC.

User Account Control Levels

In Windows 7, Microsoft included a new User Account Control Settings feature that allows you to modify the level of protection UAC provides. For the first time you can choose between four different levels of UAC protection, as shown here:

- Always Notify when programs or a user attempts to make changes to the computer.

- (Default) Notify only when programs attempt to make changes to the computer.

- Notify only when programs attempt to make changes to the computer and do not use secure desktop.

- Never notify.

The new feature allows you to define the balance between security and annoyance that is right for you. Modifying the setting can be done with just a few clicks:

1. Click the Start button, type in **User Account Control Settings,** and hit Enter.

2. When the Settings screen is displayed, drag the slider to the settings you want to use, as shown in Figure 17-8.

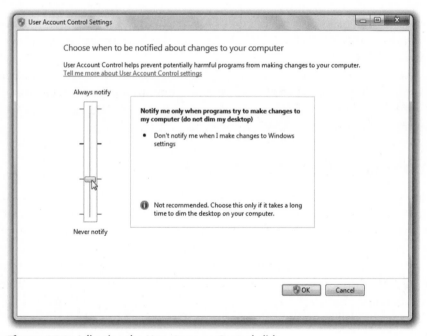

Figure 17-8: Adjusting the User Account Control slider

3. Click OK to save your settings.

Fine-Tune User Account Control with Local Security Policy

Although I prefer using the User Account Control Settings window to tweak UAC, you can also configure UAC through your Local Security Policy. There, you can tweak 10 different settings for the UAC, as described in Table 17-1.

Table 17-1: User Account Control Settings

SETTING NAME	FUNCTION
User Account Control: Admin Approval Mode for the built-in Administrator account.	This determines whether an Administrator who is logged on and working will get UAC prompts. This account is usually disabled, so this setting is useless.
User Account Control: Allows UIAccess applications to prompt for elevation without using the secure desktop.	This setting allows remote control applications such as Remote Assistance to receive UAC prompts without switching to the secure desktop.
User Account Control: Behavior of the elevation prompts for Administrators in Admin Approval Mode.	This determines which type of prompt an Administrator receives. You can choose between just prompting for consent, a prompt asking for the admin password, or disabling the prompting all together.
User Account Control: Behavior of the elevation prompt for standard users.	This determines the type of UAC prompt standard users receive. By default, this is set to prompt for credentials, but it can be set to disable prompting.
User Account Control: Detects application installations and prompts for elevation.	This allows you to disable UAC prompts for installing new applications.
User Account Control: Only elevates executables that are signed and validated.	This setting is disabled by default, but if you want a super-secure system that can run only applications that are signed with a certificate, you can enable this.
User Account Control: Only elevates UIAccess applications that are installed in secure locations.	This allows UAC to elevate only those applications that are in secure locations such as your local hard drive. An unsecured location may not be a trusted network drive.
User Account Control: Runs all administrators in Admin Approval Mode.	Similar to the Admin Approval Mode for the built-in Administrator account, this setting applies to all accounts that are a member of the Administrator security group.
User Account Control: Switches to the secure desktop when prompting for elevation.	Allows you to specify whether you want to switch to a secure desktop — one where other applications and scripts do not have access — to protect the UAC prompts from being manipulated by scripts and applications instead of end users.
User Account Control: Virtualizes file and registry write failures to per-user locations.	Provides the ability for users running as standard users to be able to still run applications that might previously have required administrative rights. This redirects system registry entries that are protected by admin permissions to local user locations so the application will still run.

Changing the UAC settings is easy to do with the Local Security Policy editor. Just follow these steps to modify the settings:

1. Click the Start button, type **secpol.msc** in the Search box, and then press Enter.

2. After the Local Security Policy editor loads, expand Local Policy and select Security Options.

3. Scroll to the bottom of the list to see all the UAC security policies. Right-click a policy and select Properties to modify.

4. When finished, click OK to save the changes.

As you can see, editing the User Account Control's settings is very simple. If you are fed up with the User Account Control and want to disable it completely, all you need to do is set both the "User Account Control: Behavior of the elevation prompt for administrators in Admin Approval Mode" and "User Account Control: Behavior of the elevation prompt for standard users" policies to no prompt and you will no longer have any annoying prompts. However, you will have just killed one of the best security features in Windows 7. That is why I believe that it is still possible to use User Account Control while decreasing some of the annoying prompts. The next section will show you how I like to configure my UAC settings for a good balance.

A Good Compromise Between User Account Control and Security

Although many people want to disable UAC completely, I am against this because of the added security it provides to Windows 7. Instead, I like to configure my computer in a way that I can get the best of both worlds — being able to install applications and freely configure Windows settings without getting bombarded with UAC prompts, while still getting the security of UAC. How is this possible? Use two accounts!

All too often people like to use their computer logged on with a user that is a member of the Administrator group. They do this accidentally or without even knowing it because when an account is created as part of the end of the Windows 7 setup, it automatically adds it to the local Administrator security group. The end result is a situation in which you have to be treated as a standard user and authorize every single change to secure the system. I offer a better solution to secure the system that will greatly reduce the number of prompts you see that is very simple and almost easier to use after you get the hang of it.

This is how it works: You will have two accounts on your machine. One for your day-to-day use that will be a low-rights standard user account with UAC running, and another account that will have full admin rights with UAC disabled so that you can easily install and change system settings with it when needed.

To do this, you need to convert your Administrator level account down to a standard user account. Next, create a new Administrator account that is for the sole purpose of installing and managing applications and changing system settings. You will then configure UAC not to prompt authorizations on that special admin account so that you can be free of the UAC annoyances when using it.

After creating your two accounts, you will have your standard user level account that you will use 99% of the time for your day-to-day work that is protected with UAC, ensuring your computer is secure. Then, when you need to make a bunch of system changes or install a bunch of applications, you can use fast user switching to switch into the system configuration admin account you created to quickly make your changes without having to worry about UAC.

Follow these detailed steps to get the best of both worlds:

1. Convert your account to a standard user account. Click the Start button and select Control Panel.

2. Under the User Accounts and Family Safety section, select Add or remove user accounts.

3. Select your account from the list of accounts.

4. Under Make changes to your user account, select Change the account type.

5. Select Standard user instead of Administrator and click Change Account type You have now finished converting your account into a standard user account. If your account is the only administrator account on the system you will not be able to change the account type.

6. Create a new account that you are going to use only for installing and managing applications and changing system settings. Go back to Control Panel and select Add or remove user accounts again. This time select Create a new account.

7. Type the name of the account; I like to use System Configuration as the name of my account. Then, select Administrator as the type of account and click Create Account. You are now finished creating the separate Administrator account. Now, the only part left to do is configure UAC to not show prompts to your new admin configuration account.

8. Go back into the Local Security Policy editor by clicking the Start button, typing **secpol.msc** in the Search box, and pressing Enter.

9. Navigate through Local Policies and Security Options and locate User Account Control: Run all administrators in Admin Approval Mode. Right-click this policy and select Properties.

10. Select Disable and click OK to save the changes. You are now finished setting up UAC to not run for your system configuration account.

After you are finished with these steps, you can easily switch to the configuration account with higher rights by pressing and holding Ctrl+Alt+Delete. Then click Switch User and select the configuration account. When you are finished doing work that requires higher rights, press Ctrl+Alt+Delete again and switch back to your low rights session.

Using File Encryption

Do you have important documents on your computer that you don't want anyone else to see? Sure, you can set file permissions on files so that only your account can read them. Is that enough? Unfortunately, it is not, as there are many ways that file permissions can be manipulated and your account password replaced if someone has physical access to your computer. If your computer is stolen or if someone breaks into your office or home, the only way truly to protect important data is to encrypt it.

Windows 7 includes two different levels of encryption: file level and hard drive level. The file-based encryption is a feature of the NTFS file system, whereas the drive-level method is a feature in Windows 7 called *BitLocker Drive Encryption*. The main difference between the two is that BitLocker Drive Encryption can encrypt your entire drive or partition so that even the file system is protected. Everything on the drive, including the operating system, is encrypted so that no one will even be able to boot up the OS if they do not have access to the device where the encryption key is stored. The security of BitLocker Drive Encryption comes at the price of performance and requires certain hardware, which is why file level encryption is often preferred. Therefore, I am going to cover that first.

Encrypting Your Files

File level encryption in Windows 7 is very easy to do. However, there are some steps that are best taken before you start encrypting files to make sure that you can always decrypt your files at a later time no matter what events occur. This next section shows you why it is important to set up a Recovery Agent in Windows 7.

Setting Up a Recovery Agent

What happens to your data if some day you forget your password and someone has to set you a new one or if you are forced to reload Windows 7 because of a major Windows or hardware failure? In all these events you will end up losing access to any files you encrypted earlier because of the way the encryption system is safeguarded. If you encrypt files on your computer, you want to make sure that they are safe and no one but you can read them. Windows needs to make sure that your encrypted files can be decrypted only by the account that wanted them protected.

If someone else has an Administrator account on your computer, he is capable of setting a new password for your account and logging on using your username and password. Typically, anyone logging on to your account has full access to all your encrypted files; however, in the preceding scenario, to protect your files Windows removes access to them so that even your account can no longer access the files. This feature has both good and bad effects. It is very good because it is smart enough to protect your data; however, you can also lose access to your own documents. There is, however, a solution to this dilemma. By using local group policy, you can specify a Recovery Agent that will always give you the ability to decrypt your own files.

This works by instructing the encryption system to add an extra certificate reference to the file when it is in the process of encrypting. This extra certificate reference belongs to what is commonly called the *Recovery Agent*. Setting up the Recovery Agent is two-fold. First you must generate the certificate assigned to the Recovery Agent. Then you need to set up the encryption system to use it. Follow these steps to get your Recovery Agent up and running:

1. Log on to an account on your computer that is a member of the Administrator group.

2. Click the Start button, type **cmd** in the Search box, and then press Enter.

3. Once Command Prompt is shown type in **cipher /r:rafile** and hit Enter.

4. When prompted, type a password to protect the Recovery Agent certificate, and then press Enter. You will have to do this a second time to confirm the password was entered correctly. When the command is finished, it will have generated two files: rafile.cer and rafile.pfx. I will go into more detail on these files later.

5. You are going to use rafile.cer to set up the Recovery Agent on your computer. First, you need to move that file to a location that is accessible by all users on your computer. Click the Start button and then click your username on the top-right side to bring up your home folder. This is where the files generated were placed. Right-click rafile.cer and select Cut.

6. In Computer, go to your C: drive and create a folder called RA. Paste rafile.cer into that folder. Now you are ready to set up the encrypted file system to use that Recovery Agent certificate.

7. Click the Start button again, type **secpol.msc** in the Search box, and then press Enter.

8. Expand Public Key Policies, right-click Encrypting File System, and then select Add Data Recovery Agent.

9. Click Next on the wizard welcome screen and then click Browse Folders to specify the location of rafile.cer. It should now be in `c:\ra\` if you followed Steps 4 and 5 correctly.

10. After the file is selected, click Yes on the Install confirmation screen. Your window should now look similar to Figure 17-9.

11. Click Next again, click Finish, and then you are done. The Recovery Agent is now set up.

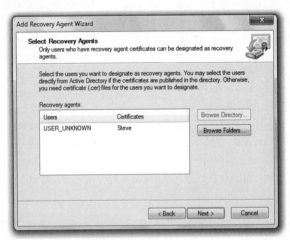

Figure 17-9: Adding a Recovery Agent to Windows 7's encrypted file system

It is very important to remove the other file, rafile.pfx, from the computer and burn it to a CD or store it on a USB thumb drive. Then place the CD or USB thumb drive in a safe or safety deposit box to ensure it does not get into the wrong hands. If you ever need to decrypt your encrypted files, you will use rafile.pfx. If anyone gets a hold of that file and can then guess your password, all your files can be decrypted. That is why it is so important to remove that file from your computer and put it in a very safe place.

If you ever have a need to decrypt your own files after losing access to them for any reason, copy the rafile.pfx back to any computer (one that you want to decrypt your files on) and double-click it. Then go through the wizard to import the certificate and enter your password when prompted. You will now be able to access and decrypt any files needed.

Setting Files to Be Encrypted

Now that you have your Recovery Agent set up and the PFX file removed from the computer and placed in a safe location, you can safely and securely encrypt the files on your computer. To do so, just navigate to a file or folder that you want to encrypt on your machine and follow these steps:

1. Right-click a file or folder and select Properties.

2. On the General tab, click the Advanced button.

3. Check the Encrypt contents to secure data box and click OK, as shown in Figure 17-10.

4. Click OK to exit file Properties, and you are finished.

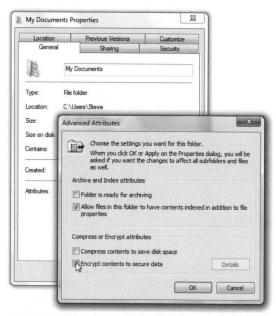

Figure 17-10: Encrypting files with the encrypted file system

If you ever want to decrypt a file, just uncheck the Encrypt contents to secure file box that you just checked previously and click OK.

Using BitLocker Drive Encryption

BitLocker Drive Encryption is another improved feature from Windows Vista that allows you to encrypt an entire drive or partition. This drive-layer encryption even encrypts the file system and operating system files so everything is secure. BitLocker Drive Encryption is the most secure Windows security option. This feature is ideal for laptop owners who have sensitive data on their drive as well as desktop users who can't risk their information getting into the wrong hands.

BitLocker Drive Encryption works by encrypting the entire partition, including the file system, with a 256-bit encryption algorithm. Using a Trusted Platform Module (TPM) chip, USB thumb drive, or a typed-in passkey, BitLocker protects your encrypted partition. When you boot up your computer, BitLocker starts to load from a small unencrypted partition, prompting you to insert your USB key or passcode to begin booting Windows 7. If everything checks out, BitLocker unseals the encrypted partition and starts running the normal boot code. Failure to insert the USB key or correct passcode will result in a failure and even an inability to boot Windows.

Using BitLocker Drive Encryption in Windows Vista is very difficult. The user needs to partition the drive in a specific format before Windows is even installed to use the feature. Windows 7 integrated the Windows Vista drive preparation tool so now you don't need to reinstall Windows to enable BitLocker.

Hardware Requirements

For the most secure setup, BitLocker Drive Encryption requires either a TPM chip version 1.2 or newer built into your computer. It is possible to set up BitLocker Drive Encryption on a computer without a TPM device or using a USB drive, but your only source of protection is a passcode and the physical USB drive.

Enabling BitLocker Drive Encryption

TIP If your computer does not have a compatible TPM chip, you can still use BitLocker Drive Encryption with a USB storage device. However, Microsoft has recently decided to hide this option from users. A local group policy change must be made to turn this option back on. Click the Start button, type gpedit. msc in the Search box, and hit Enter. When Group Policy editor has loaded, navigate through Computer Configuration, Administrative Templates, Windows Components, BitLocker Drive Encryption, and Operating System Drives. Right-click Require additional authentication at startup and select Edit. Select the Enabled option and hit OK. You can now use a USB storage device with BitLocker Drive Encryption again.

Using BitLocker Drive Encryption is easy when you have your hard drive configured properly and have reinstalled Windows 7. Just follow these steps to get BitLocker up and running for you:

1. Click the Start menu and select Control Panel.

2. When Control Panel loads, click the System and Security heading.

3. Click BitLocker Drive Encryption.

4. If your computer is configured properly, you should see a Turn On BitLocker link, as shown in Figure 17-11, next to your operating system drive. Click that link now. If your computer does not have a TPM device, make sure you follow my previous tip.

5. Select the type of device you will be using to protect your computer and follow the onscreen steps for your method of protection.

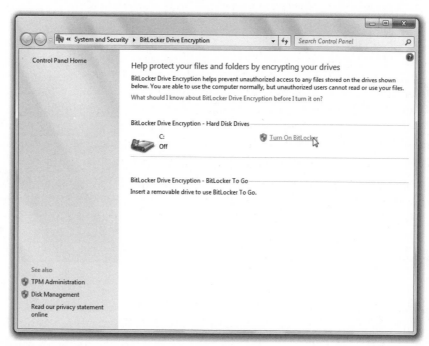

Figure 17-11: Enabling BitLocker Drive Encryption

After you complete all the steps the wizard guides you through, your computer will begin encrypting the hard drive automatically.

Congratulations, your computer is now even more secure. Keep in mind that you will need to insert your USB drive every time you want to boot your computer if you choose the non-TPM option. Failure to insert it will result in your computer not booting. Make sure that you keep your emergency recovery passcode stored in a safe place, as well as your USB drive, in the event you choose to use that option.

If you want to fine-tune the BitLocker settings, you can find dozens of group policy settings by clicking the Start button, typing in **gpedit.msc,** and hitting Enter. Then navigate through Computer Configuration, Administrative Templates, Windows Components, and BitLocker Drive Encryption.

Enabling BitLocker To Go Drive Encryption

Just about every computer user I know has a number of USB storage devices that are used to move and share files. With the storage size of USB flash devices sky-rocketing and the amount of data we store on the small, easy to lose, devices increasing, the need to protect our data is becoming critical. Many users have all their personal documents stored on a tiny USB storage device. What would happen if you lost one of your drives? Anyone that finds it can plug it into their computer and have full access to all your private data.

Thankfully Microsoft has addressed this growing issue in Windows 7 with a new version of BitLocker Drive Encryption designed for USB storage devices called BitLocker To Go. The portable version of BitLocker provides a very simple but effective way to protect your data with encryption.

Best of all, BitLocker To Go is compatible with all versions of Windows. Just take your encrypted USB storage device to any other Windows 7 computer and you will be prompted for the password of your device. After you enter the password you will have full read and write access to your drive. If you use your device on older versions of Windows, a special program will launch that will ask for your password and then provide you with read-only access to your files.

Enabling BitLocker To Go is the easiest of all the security features to turn on. Just open Computer to view the drive, right-click it, and select Turn on BitLocker. You will be asked for a password — just follow the wizard as it encrypts your device.

Summary

This chapter was about making what Microsoft is calling "the most secure operating system ever released" even more secure. First, I talked about active ways to protect your computer by keeping up on the latest news and trends and making sure that your computer is up-to-date on the latest security patches. Then I showed you how to configure User Account Control in a way that balanced both usability and security by creating a separate configuration administration account while running as a standard user the majority of the time. Finally, I covered the two different types of encryption available in Windows 7: file level and drive level with BitLocker Drive Encryption.

The next chapter builds on the secure foundation this chapter created by securing your computer from attackers getting in from over the Internet. I show you how you can configure hidden firewall settings to turn on the two-way firewall that is normally turned off. Then I go over the latest tools to fight spyware and viruses.

CHAPTER 18

Internet Security

The Internet is the primary source for almost all the attacks on your computer. Someone may be trying to break in to steal information or a worm from another infected computer may be trying to use the latest exploit to infect your box as well. So how do you protect your Internet connection? I show you how you can test your computer and see how vulnerable it actually is. Then you find out how you can use the firewalls to build a "brick wall" around your computer. Additionally, you discover how to protect yourself from other Internet threats such as spyware and what to do to clean up an infection.

Analyzing Your Security

The first step in securing your Internet connection is detecting where you are vulnerable. Your specific network setup (for example, if your computer is behind a hardware firewall or router) will affect how exposed your computer is. For example, if you have a high-speed broadband connection and share it with more than one computer in your home using a router, your computers are already better protected than a computer that is just directly connected to the Internet. By default, most routers act as a firewall by blocking all external Internet traffic from coming into your home network. However, if your laptop is infected and you plug it into your home network, all the machines become vulnerable because the threat is now inside your firewall. I go into more detail of how firewalls work in the next section, but first, let's test your connection to see how exposed your computers are to attacks from both the Internet and from other machines on your internal network.

Testing Internet Security

Ports are the gateways inside your computer. When a computer program wants to communicate with a remote computer, it makes a connection to the remote computer through a port that it will use to talk with the computer. Each computer has thousands of ports — 65,535 to be exact. You can think of the different ports as a bunch of different mailboxes. When a program wants to send data to a remote computer, it sends it to a specific port (mailbox) number. Then, provided that a program is on the remote computer that is set up to receive data at a particular port (mailbox), the remote computer can then work with the data it was sent.

Theoretically, nothing is wrong with this scenario. In the real world applications don't always work this way. Sometimes, applications are sent data they are not programmed to receive. This can cause errors and unexpected behavior that may execute code a remote attacker is sending it. The result is that a remote attacker can gain access or infect your computer using a flaw in the application. The technical name for data sent to a program that results in bypassing security is an *exploit*.

Now that you know the basics of how attacks work, you will use various utilities to check for open ports that allow other users to connect. In theory, if you have no ports open, then it is next to impossible to break into your computer. To detect the ports on your computer that are open to the entire Internet, it is best to use a web-based port scanner. If your computer is on an internal network and is behind a firewall or router, a software-based port scanner will show you what ports are open internally.

First, check your external port exposure, which everyone on the Internet can see. To do this, you will use a web-based port scanner. Various web sites offer such scanners and are also free of charge. I personally like to use GRC.com to do my testing. Follow these steps to test your external connection:

1. Open a copy of either Internet Explorer or Firefox and navigate to www.grc.com/x/ne.dll?bh0bkyd2.

2. When the page loads, click the Proceed button.

3. Click All Service Ports to begin the scan.

4. When viewing the results, make sure that everything is in the green or blue. You do not want any ports to be open, which is indicated with red. Green indicates your computer did not respond at all giving your computer a stealth look. Blue indicates your computer responded that the tested port was closed.

Depending on the results of your test, if you have any ports that are open, you can find out how to close those in the Firewall section, but first, if you are connected to an internal network, it is a good idea to test your internal vulnerability. As I mentioned earlier, it is best to use a software port scanner for testing your internal vulnerability. For this test, you learn how to use Axence NetTools, a comprehensive network tools suite with a fast port scanner. To get started, visit www.axencesoftware.com/index.php?action=FreeNT and download the latest copy of NetTools. Then follow these steps to scan your computer's local ports:

1. After you have downloaded and installed Axence NetTools, click the Start button, type **nettools** in the Search box, and then press Enter.

2. After NetTools starts, click the Scan host option on the far right of the icon bar.

3. In the address box, type **localhost**. If you want to scan a different computer, you can type the IP address of any computer in this box.

4. Set the port range for it to scan. In NetTools you have five options: Services, Ports (well known), Ports (well known-extended), Ports (range), and Ports (trojans). For this section you are going to use Ports (range) to scan all possible ports. The other selections scan only the more popular ports where known applications are running. If you want a quicker scan, I recommend using Ports (well known-extended). Because you want to do a complete scan here, select Ports (range). The two ports boxes will be enabled. Enter **65535** in the end Ports box so that it goes through all possible port numbers.

5. Press Scan next to the Address box and watch the results appear, as shown in Figure 18-1.

It can take more than an hour to scan all 65,353 ports on your computer, depending on your hardware. After it is finished, you will have a list of all ports that are open in your computer. You will find out how to close these ports later in the "Using a Firewall" section.

Watch the Action Center

The new Action Center in Windows 7 is another easy way to find out if all your "essential" protection software is installed and running. It is important to have your firewall running, virus software, spyware protection, and other security features set up and running at all times to defend your computer against anything that might try to attack it.

Using the Action Center is very simple. Just click the Start button, type **Action Center** in the Search box, and then press Enter. When it loads, any alerts will be expanded for you to see as shown in Figure 18-2. If everything is in the green, you are set. If not, pay attention to the recommendations so that your computer is as secure as possible.

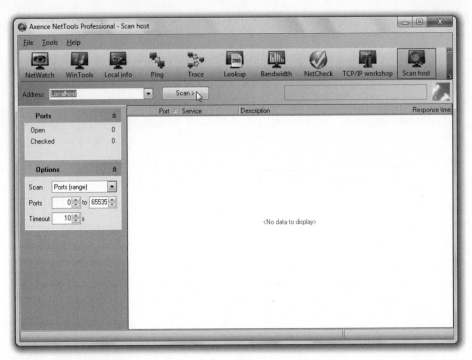

Figure 18-1: Using NetTools to find open ports on your PC

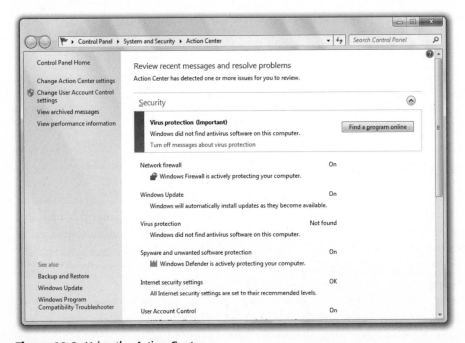

Figure 18-2: Using the Action Center

Using a Firewall

In the last section, you found out how potentially vulnerable your computer is to viruses and attackers from the Internet and your internal network. You also know that one way to help fight those attackers is to block access to your computer on all the ports, which can be gateways into your computer. How exactly do you block all the ports? Use a firewall. A firewall is a special application that acts as a brick wall that is protecting all the ports on your computer.

When a remote computer attempts to access a computer that is protected by a firewall, it is not able to connect and the data that was sent is ignored and discarded. Depending on the way the firewall is configured, when data is sent to a blocked port on your computer, the firewall will either respond to where the data was sent from with a message that the port is closed or it will do nothing, giving your computer a stealth presence. Most firewall applications are set up by default to run in stealth mode, which provides the maximum amount of protection. Any remote computer trying to connect or send data to your computer with a firewall installed and running in stealth mode will think that your computer has gone offline because it is not getting a response.

So far, I have talked only about firewalls that block incoming attacks from the Internet. Firewalls can also block traffic originating from your computer going out to the Internet. Why would you want to do that? What if someone installed a key logger on your computer that sends all your information to a remote computer for him to use? Or how about a media player that sends a history of everything that you played to a server for their tracking purposes? With a two-way firewall, you can block outgoing traffic that you haven't authorized.

Firewalls can be a very powerful security device. In Windows 7, a firewall configured properly can completely eliminate one way an attacker may try to gain access to your computer. The next section shows you how you can use the new and improved firewall in Windows 7 to block incoming attacks and prevent unwanted applications from sending information out.

Using the Windows 7 Firewall

The firewall included in Windows 7 is much more advanced than previous Windows firewalls. Microsoft actually calls it, "Windows Firewall with Advanced Security." It has three different location profiles that allow you to customize your firewall rules based on where your computer is. If it is in a public place, you are going to want to have very strict firewall rules compared to if you are in a corporate domain at work or at a private network at home. On top of the location profiles, the firewall has a very complex rule structure that allows maximum flexibility to create very specific openings in your firewall to permit application or service-related network traffic. Most importantly, Windows Firewall now has to block outgoing traffic as well.

The upgrades to Windows Firewall really make it a very powerful security solution that was once provided only by advanced third-party firewall software. The next two sections guide you through the basics of using the advanced firewall configuration tool and enabling the outbound firewall.

Configuring Windows Firewall

The Network and Sharing Center is where you configure all the network-related settings on your Windows 7 PC. The Windows Firewall can also be accessed from the Network and Sharing Center but only the basic controls are exposed. Instead, the best way to manage the Windows Firewall is through the Windows Firewall with Advanced Security Management Console. Click the Start button, type **wf.msc** in the Search box, and then press Enter. When Windows Firewall with Advanced Security window loads, you will see the complexity and the power of the new firewall. Maybe it was a good idea Microsoft decided to hide this from inexperienced users after all. On the main screen you will see a list of the profiles, as shown in Figure 18-3.

Figure 18-3: Using Windows Firewall with Advanced Security

This main screen is where you can see an overview if the firewall is on and if the Inbound and Outbound Rules are active. The next step is to view the specific rules. You can do that by simply selecting Inbound Rules or Outbound Rules from the list on the left. Go ahead and click Inbound Rules now.

Shortly, you will see all the rules currently set up on your computer. If they are enabled, they will have the green icon. If not, the icon will be gray. You can also see what firewall profiles the rule is used in, as shown in the Profile column in Figure 18-4. If you ever need to enable or disable a rule, just right-click it and select Enable or Disable. You can also edit an individual rule's properties by right-clicking the rule and selecting Properties. Working with the Outbound Rules is exactly the same as working with Inbound Rules; Outbound Rules just control a different direction of traffic.

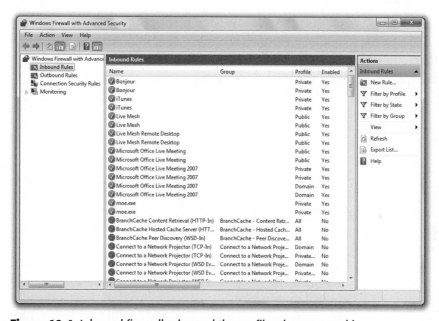

Figure 18-4: Inbound firewall rules and the profiles they are used in

For the sake of demonstrating how to add a new rule, say that you just installed some type of server on your computer that users will connect to on TCP port 800. Follow these steps to open up a hole so that your users can connect:

1. If Windows Firewall with Advanced Security window is not already open, click the Start button, type **wf.msc** in the Search box, and then press Enter.

2. After the management console loads, click Inbound Rules.

3. Under Actions in the right pane, click New Rule.

4. The new Inbound Rule Wizard loads and asks you for the type of rule you would like to create. For this scenario, you are going to select Port. Click Next when you have selected Port.

5. You are asked to specify what type of port to open. Unless you have an application that specifically requires a UDP port, almost every time you will be selecting TCP. For this scenario, select TCP. Also on this screen, type **800** in the specific port box because you want to open up only port 800. Click Next when you are done.

6. The next screen asks you to define the action of the rule. You can choose to Allow the connection, Allow the connection if secure (on a network with IPSEC), or Block depending on what you want to do. Select Allow the connection and click Next.

7. You will need to select what profiles this rule will be part of. By default, all the profiles are checked; uncheck any profiles you do not want your rule to be part of and click Next.

8. The last step is to name your new rule. Type a name and a description if you want and click Finish.

Your new rule will now appear on the Inbound Rule list. It will automatically be enabled when you click Finish.

Enabling the Outbound Firewall

In Windows 7 Microsoft decided it was best to disable the outbound connection filtering because it can cause headaches for many inexperienced computer users. This may have been the right choice, but not filtering your outbound traffic can increase the possibility that an application can steal important personal information and send it to a remote computer. If this application is malicious, it can be used to steal personal information such as passwords and bank account numbers. Turning on the outbound firewall filtering and enabling only the rules that grant your normal applications access to the Internet will greatly increase the security of your computer.

Enabling the outbound firewall rules on your computer is easy to do after you know where Microsoft hid the setting. Follow these steps to turn the outbound firewall back on:

1. If Windows Firewall with Advanced Security window is not already open, click the Start button, type **wf.msc** in the Search box, and then press Enter.

2. When the management console is loaded, click Windows Firewall Properties right in the middle of the opening screen.

3. When the settings window loads, you will see a tab for each of the different firewall profiles. Select the tab for the profile on which you would like to enable outbound filtering.

4. Under the State section, locate the Outbound connections drop-down box and change it to Block.

5. Click OK when you are finished to activate the outbound firewall on the profile you specified.

Windows automatically detects any applications that try to access the Internet or other network resources that are now blocked with the outbound firewall turned on and will prompt you automatically to authorize the application to send information out to the Internet.

Web Browser Security

Now that you have eliminated one method that attackers use to enter your computer, by blocking your ports with a firewall, it is time to secure the other entry point — the web browser. An attacker can also get into your computer by using an exploit in a web browser by tricking you into installing a web component that has malicious code inside. Internet Explorer has many security settings built in that will help you keep safe. However, there are often tradeoffs including ease of use and convenience. For example, you can disable the installation of all web components for maximum security, but when you really need to install one, it can take longer and require more work than normal.

Internet Explorer 8

Internet Explorer 8 is a refined upgrade that builds on the security features of Internet Explorer 7 such as Protected Mode. Possible only when using Internet Explorer 8 on either Windows Vista or Windows 7, Protected Mode still is the most important security feature that all browsers should have.

In the past, Internet Explorer was prone to various attacks, leaving it one of the weakest parts of the entire operating system. Microsoft tried to stop automatic downloading and installation and web site exploits, in its release of Service Pack 2 for Windows XP, but we all know that worked only a little. Flaws are still being discovered in Internet Explorer every once in a while and attackers are trying to find new ways to trick users into installing malicious code. How do you fix this problem? Simple — you isolate Internet Explorer into a secure environment so that in the future, if exploits are found, they will not work because IE cannot access resources other than its own. That new protection is called *Protected Mode*.

Protected Mode, the new SmartScreen bad web site filter combined with other security features in Internet Explorer 8, will help secure the other major point of entry for spyware, malware, and attackers. The next section shows you how to get the most out of these new features.

Fine-Tuning Security Settings

You can adjust the security settings in Internet Explorer within Internet Options. Follow these steps to adjust the security settings in IE8:

1. Open Internet Explorer 8.

2. Click Tools and select Internet Options on the bottom of the menu.

3. After Internet Options loads, click the Security tab. The Security tab enables you to manage the individual settings for what is allowed in each of the browser zone settings — for example, if ActiveX controls are allowed to be automatically downloaded and installed in the Internet zone. You can adjust these zones by selecting the zone and then clicking the Custom level button, as shown in Figure 18-5.

Figure 18-5: Adjusting Internet Explorer 8 security zones

4. After the security settings for the zone selected load, you can scroll through the list of settings and select either Disable, Enable, or Prompt for most settings. For optimal security, I recommend disabling a lot of these features beyond what is normally disabled. Take a look at Table 18-1 for the settings I recommend that you change for best security practices. When you are finished modifying all the settings, click OK to return to Internet Options.

5. After you are back on the Security tab of Internet Options, make sure that the Enable Protected Mode box is checked for each of the zones. This is one feature that I believe should be enabled for all zones.

6. You are now ready to move on to the Advanced tab to adjust more security settings. Click the Advanced tab and scroll down the list to the Security section, as shown in Figure 18-6.

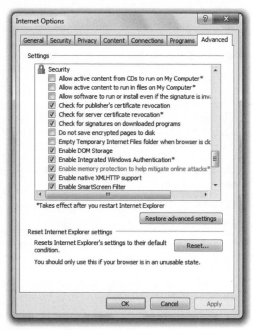

Figure 18-6: Adjusting advanced security settings in Internet Explorer 8

7. In the Security section, I recommend selecting Do not save encrypted pages to disk and Empty Temporary Internet Files folder when browser is closed. These two settings will help protect your privacy as well as keep your important online data safe from web sites, such as banking information.

8. When you are finished, click OK to save your changes.

You are now finished configuring Internet Explorer to run more securely and protect you even better when you are online.

Table 18-1: Internet Explorer Security Zone Settings

SETTINGS NAME	FUNCTION
Loose XAML	I like to select Disable for this option because few sites use it and disabling it means one less feature to worry about getting exploited.
XAML browser applications	I disable this setting as well because it's not used much either.
XPS documents	Disable this option for tighter security. If you don't use this document format, you should have no problems disabling it.
Run components not signed with Authenticode	For tighter security, select Disable.
Font download	Consider yourself very lucky if you ever run across a web site that uses this feature. Disable it to be safe.
Enable .NET Framework setup	Disable this setting. I do not understand why this option is even listed here.
Include local directory path when uploading files to a server	I like to disable this option for privacy and because it should never be needed.
Launching programs and files in an IFRAME	Disable this feature. Really, this should never be done.
Logon	I usually set this option to Prompt for username and password for maximum security.

Defending Against Spyware and Malware

Spyware has become the largest annoyance on Windows for the last few years. Often hidden in downloads that appear innocent, these programs can spy on your computer activities and report home various information about your computer habits. Adware is another menace that is closely related to spyware. Just as with spyware, it can be secretly installed on your computer and will monitor what you do. Then, when the time is right, it will display relevant advertisements. Did you ever visit eBay.com and then notice an advertisement for Ubid.com, one of eBay's competitors, pop up on your screen? If so, then you are infected with adware.

Your computer can become infected in a number of ways. The most common is by visiting a web site and downloading a free game, emoticons for an instant messenger, or a browser utility such as a search toolbar. Often these utilities are spyware themselves and are also bundled with other spyware and adware.

Unfortunately, users never seem to read the terms of service agreements that are presented when they install these free apps on their computer, and pass right over the notices that this software will display ads and will monitor your browsing habits.

In Windows 7 it is getting much more difficult for outsiders to install software on your computer that you don't want because of User Account Control. If something is installed, it is because you authorized it when you clicked Allow in the UAC authorization box. What do you do if you made a mistake? The next section shows you how to use the new anti-spyware and anti-malware application called Windows Defender to protect your computer and clean it of any spyware threats.

Using Windows Defender

Because spyware has been an increasing problem for so many Windows users, Microsoft has included free spyware protection in Windows 7 called Windows Defender. Windows Defender works by scanning the files and registry on your computer for signatures of known adware and spyware applications. The signature definitions that it uses are updated very often and are also assisted by Microsoft SpyNet to find out about new, unknown spyware that is not yet widespread. When Windows Defender finds a file that looks suspicious but does not know exactly what it is, it sends that information back to the Microsoft SpyNet computers for tracking.

Windows Defender does more than just detect and monitor spyware files. It also monitors applications that are installed in your startup and processes currently running in memory. Using the Software Explorer feature located under Tools, you can harness the power of Windows Defender to fight malicious software that has infected those areas as well. To get started, you learn the basic uses of Windows Defender.

Scanning Your Computer

Windows Defender is very effective at scanning your computer for spyware. By default, Windows Defender is configured to scan your computer once a day in the early hours in the morning. If you ever notice something strange happening to your computer and suspect spyware, you can perform the following steps to do a full system scan with Windows Defender:

1. Click the Start button, type **Windows Defender** in the Search box, and then press Enter.

2. After Windows Defender loads, click the down arrow next to the Scan button and select Full scan, as shown in Figure 18-7.

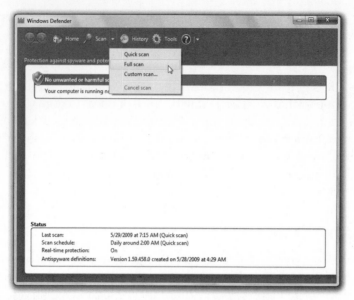

Figure 18-7: Starting a full system scan with Windows Defender

3. When the scan is finished, the results are shown. If any spyware is found, click Review Items detected by scanning to find out exactly what was found.

4. On the Scan Results screen, all the malicious software detected by Windows Defender is shown, along with details on what each application is. Click the Remove All button, as shown in Figure 18-8.

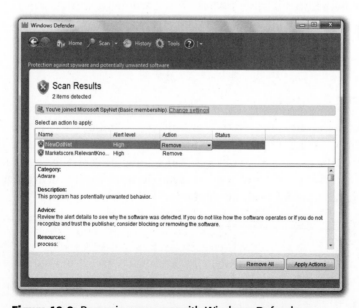

Figure 18-8: Removing spyware with Windows Defender

Using Other Anti-Spyware Software

Sometimes Windows Defender just doesn't detect all the spyware on your computer. You can try to kill it manually using the Software Explorer feature and disable the startup programs, but there is an easier way. Before going for the manual approach, give these two proven spyware utilities a try:

- **Lavasoft's Ad-Aware Free Version:** `www.lavasoft.com/products/ad_aware_free.php`
- **Spybot — Search & Destroy:** `www.safer-networking.org`

Using Antivirus Software

Antivirus software is the classic PC utility that has always been thought of as absolutely necessary if you own a computer. The fact is, in Windows 7, the need for antivirus software when User Account Control is turned on is significantly lower than previous versions of Windows because UAC prevents most events from happening that you have not authorized. For example, if you open an e-mail that contains a virus and the virus attempts to reformat a drive, a UAC prompt will pop up asking you to confirm the reformat request. UAC stops the virus dead in its tracks in this situation.

Unfortunately, many people choose to disable or run UAC at a low protection level so they are not bombarded by prompts for every little thing they do. Additionally, some users click Authorize on every UAC prompt they see, which makes UAC useless. For this reason, I feel it is still a good idea to run some type of basic antivirus program on most computers — especially if you have UAC disabled or if your computer is being used by a beginner computer user.

Using avast! Antivirus Software

There are many free antivirus utilities that work well with Windows 7. My favorite is avast! Home Edition, which can be downloaded for free if it is for non-commercial use. This saves a lot of money that you may be spending on mainstream antivirus products and their yearly signature update fees. With avast! Home Edition, all the signature updates are free. All you have to do is register on avast!'s web site to get a free registration key within 60 days of installing the software.

Similar to other popular virus scanners, avast! has various on-access scanners that automatically scan files when they are opened on your computer. This makes it less necessary to do a full system scan to find files because you can be sure that a file is scanned before it is executed. Additionally, avast! includes support for all the popular mail applications, so you can be confident that your messages will be safe as well.

Using avast! is similar to other antivirus programs. Follow these steps to get it up and running on your computer and to perform a full system scan:

1. Visit www.avast.com/eng and download the free version of avast!

2. After you have it installed, reboot.

3. Click the Start button, type **avast** in the Search box, and then press Enter.

4. Then click on the Scan Computer button on the left menu.

5. On the Scan Now screen click Full System Scan and the scan will begin as shown in Figure 18-9.

Figure 18-9: Selecting a full system scan in avast!

After the scan has completed, you will be presented with the results and the option to take action on any discovered viruses. With the real-time scan features of avast!, you do not need to run a full disk scan very often. If a file becomes infected and you attempt to open it, the on-access scan will catch it.

Summary

This chapter has shown you how you can protect your computer from attacks that arrive via the Internet by using exploits and open ports on your computer and through your web browser. I showed you how you can use Windows Firewall to protect your computer and also defend against attacks and increase the security of Internet Explorer. Then I wrapped up the Internet security chapter by protecting your computer from spyware and viruses. The next chapter is all about protecting your privacy in Windows. Windows 7 tracks more information about what you do than any other version of Windows. Sure, that information can be useful, but it also can be embarrassing. Find out how to clean it up in the next chapter.

CHAPTER 19

Protecting Your Privacy

Windows 7 keeps track of all activities you do on your computer. It records the web sites that you visit, the addresses that you type in, the applications that you launch, and even the files that you open. Why does it do this? All the information is used to tailor your computer experience and power features designed to make Windows easier to use, such as the frequently run programs or recently opened documents lists. Your browser history is used to suggest web sites when you start to type the URL to save you a few keystrokes. These features can be very useful, but they also expose what you do on your computer to anyone that sits down in front of it.

The documents you open, personal letters you write, the web sites you visit, and the applications you use equate to an enormous amount of personal data that most users would like to keep private. Maybe you want to keep what you do online secret or just keep financial documents away from the kids — either way this chapter is for you. I show you how to configure Windows 7 so it is easy to use but mindful of your privacy.

Internet Explorer Privacy

Internet Explorer is one of the most difficult parts of Windows to clean because it stores your data in many folders and files across the computer. Every time you want to clean all your Internet Explorer history, you need to clear recent addresses, remove history files, erase temporary web files, and remove cookies. The first part of this section shows you how to clean all the required parts to remove your Internet Explorer history and protect your privacy.

The second part of this section shows you how you can protect your privacy further by configuring and using new Internet Explorer features.

Removing Address Bar Suggestions

Windows 7, as with past versions of Windows, includes a feature called AutoComplete that is always enabled by default for the address box. This is normally a very convenient feature because it can help you when typing in an address by presenting you with various suggestions based on your browser history. With the convenience comes the danger that it can reveal your online whereabouts. When I start typing "twe" in my address bar, it automatically suggests tweaks.com because I previously visited the site. Anyone who uses my computer and starts typing addresses in manually can see sites that I have visited. If they just type in www.s or www.t, they will be presented with a small list of all the sites that I have visited that have URLs that start with *s* or *t*.

How do you stop the suggestions? It depends if you want to remove just one entry or clear all.

Removing a Single Web Site from the Address Bar

Windows 7 includes a number of great new privacy features that gives control of your information back to you. When you come across an address bar suggestion in Internet Explorer 8, you can hover over the entry displayed in the drop-down list and a red X will appear on the right as shown in Figure 19-1.

Just click the red X delete button and the entry will be removed for good while preserving the rest of your browser suggestions. This is one of my favorite new features that you will see throughout Windows 7 that really allows you to control your information much better than previous versions of Windows.

Clearing All Address Bar Suggestions

In the past, clearing all the address bar suggestions was a big job in which you had to delete a file that was in use. With Internet Explorer 8 it will just take a few clicks:

1. When Internet Explorer is open, click Safety and then Delete Browsing History.

2. On the Delete Browsing History screen, uncheck all items except for History.

3. Click Delete, and all your address suggestions will be deleted.

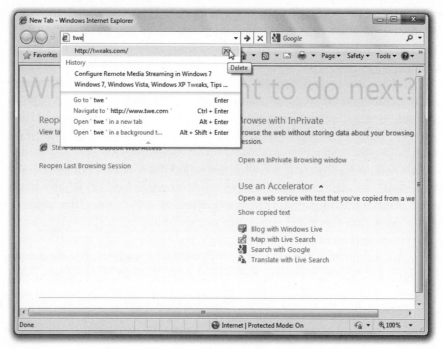

Figure 19-1: Removing a single entry from the address bar

Keep in mind that in IE8, address bar will also search your list of favorite web sites. If you want to prevent one of those sites from showing up in the address bar suggestions then it is best to delete the favorite.

Clearing Temporary Internet Files, History, and Cookies

Every time you visit a web site, the files for the web page (such as the HTML and the images) are downloaded and stored in a temporary directory known as Temporary Internet Files. Over time, this directory can become full of images and HTML from various web sites you visited. This directory can end up taking a lot of storage space. Additionally, a user can browse your Temporary Internet Files directory and find out exactly what sites you have been visiting just as if they were looking at your browser history. If you are concerned about your privacy, or just concerned about disk space, then clearing the temporary Internet files is a must.

The web browsing history is another area that users often like to clear. Internet Explorer, by default, is configured to record all the web sites that you visit for a 20-day period. If you are concerned about your privacy, your browsing history should be cleaned frequently and history settings configured best for your privacy. Doing so will ensure that any user of your computer will not easily be able to see what you have been doing.

Cookies are also created on your computer when you visit web sites. Contrary to popular belief, cookies are not all bad. Most web sites use them to save user data to a browser. An example of this is site automatic logon when you visit a web site. A web site you visit can detect if the web site has given you a cookie already that has your user ID stored in it. If it finds one, then it knows exactly who you are and logs you on automatically. Advertisers also use cookies to store personal data. Instead of showing you the same advertisement 50 times, they use cookies to keep track of how many times an advertisement is displayed on your screen.

However, some advertisers abuse what are called third-party cookies to track what web sites you visit and then deliver relevant ads based on what you do online. Because of the abusers it is best to just delete all your cookies because it is hard to separate them. I'll show you more about how to protect against third-party cookies in the next section.

Clearing the temporary Internet files, history, and cookies is a very simple task. Just follow these steps to clear these files:

1. When Internet Explorer is open, click Safety and then Delete Browsing History. Alternatively, you can use the keyboard shortcut CTRL + Shift + Delete.

2. On the Delete Browsing History screen, check all items except Preserve Favorites website data, as shown in Figure 19-2.

3. Click Delete and all will be deleted.

Figure 19-2: Clearing browser data in Internet Explorer 8

Now users will no longer be able to see what web sites you visit from the cookies and temporary Internet files that are stored on your computer. Additionally, you will have freed up some disk space by deleting these files.

Adjusting Your Cookie Security Policy

As mentioned, cookies are not as bad as some people in the computing world would like you to believe. Instead, the only real risk they present is a loss of some privacy, as I mentioned previously. If you allow your browser to be instructed to create cookies on your computer, over time your PC would have quite a collection of them. Anyone who used your computer would then know what sites you visited, if they knew where the cookie files were located.

The latest version of Internet Explorer includes many new enhancements. One of the enhancements includes a new way of accepting cookies. Now you have the capability to specify whether you would like your browser to block all cookies or just certain types of cookies. To be able to use this new feature, you need to understand the two different types of cookies:

- **First-party cookies:** Placed on your computer by the current site that you are visiting.

- **Third-party cookies:** Placed on your computer by remote sites, such as advertisement servers.

The difference between good and bad cookies is how they are issued. If you go to Tweaks.com, the web server will issue your browser a first-party cookie. That cookie contains harmless user session data so the web server knows whether you are logged in. The cookies that have the potential to be abused are called third-party cookies because they are not issued by the web server you are visiting but rather a third-party. These cookies are common among online advertising programs such as Google Adsense. The privacy concern that can make them a bad cookie depends on what the advertising company does with the cookie. With a third-party cookie, it is technically possible for Google to monitor what web sites you visit and then deliver advertisements that are relevant to what you do on the Web. This is possible because Google Adsense is used by about 1 out of 4 web sites online, which means 1 out of 4 web sites are making your browser connect to Google's servers to display an advertisement. When that call is made to Google's servers, it can read previous third-party cookies it placed on your computer from previous web sites that you visited that made the same call to Google to get an advertisement to display. Behind the scenes, Google's advertisement serving software can connect the dots and build a profile of what type of web sites you visit.

In theory, after you visit a number of web sites about training a puppy, for example, it is technically possible to be served advertisements about training puppies when you are on sites completely unrelated to dogs. All thanks to third-party cookies.

If you don't want to be tracked online with the help of third-party cookies it is possible to tweak your cookie acceptance settings. Just follow these steps:

1. Open Internet Explorer.

2. Click Tools and select Internet Options.

3. When Internet Options loads, click the Privacy tab.

4. You will see the up-and-down slider that allows you to select different levels of cookie security. I recommend that you bypass this and just click the Advanced button instead.

5. After you have clicked the Advanced button and see the Advanced Privacy Settings window, select the box that says Override automatic cookie handling.

6. Your settings for first- and third-party cookies will now be available for adjustment, as shown in Figure 19-3. I recommend that you always accept first-party cookies. You can decide whether you want to block all third-party cookies or be prompted to accept them. If you select the Prompt option, a dialog box notifies you that each cookie's request has been received.

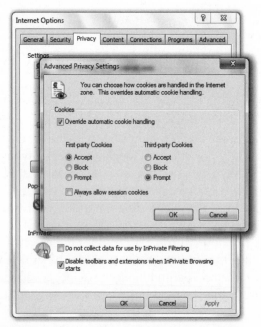

Figure 19-3: Adjusting cookie privacy settings

7. When you are finished with your settings, click OK to save your changes and return to Internet Options.

8. Click OK again to close Internet Options.

Now that you have set the cookie privacy setting manually, you can eliminate cookies from being stored on your hard drive in the first place. Doing so will allow you to protect your privacy and still be able to use web sites that need cookies.

Protecting Sensitive Online Data

If you manage your finances or shop online, then you probably have had experience with using secure web connections, otherwise known as *SSL*. These secure connections encrypt the data that is transferred to and from a web server and your computer. After the data gets to your computer, your browser has a special key that decrypts the information and displays it on your computer. During this process, when the file is decrypted, it is saved in the Temporary Internet Files directory so that the browser can display it.

This default appears to be harmless because the web page is saved on your computer only. If no one has remote access to your computer, the data would be safe, right? Not necessarily, because your data is now vulnerable to anyone who has physical local access to your computer. If that person is clever and lucky enough, he or she can sort through your Temporary Internet Files directory and just might find some confidential information such as your online banking information. All this information is saved by default on your hard drive for anyone to look at who knows how to get to it. They do not even need to know your password or even log on to your account on the bank's web site because a snapshot of the web page is stored locally on your computer.

What can you do to protect your computer from this vulnerability besides setting up better computer security such as complex passwords? There is a cool feature of Internet Explorer that you just have to turn on that will eliminate the problem completely. Simply called Do Not Save Encrypted Pages to Disk, this feature, when enabled, solves your problems. To enable it, follow these steps:

1. Open Internet Explorer.

2. Click Tools and select Internet Options.

3. Click the Advanced tab.

4. Scroll down through the list toward the bottom of the window until you see the Security section.

5. Locate Do Not Save Encrypted Pages to Disk, and check the box to the left of it.

6. Click OK to save and activate your changes.

Now you will no longer have to worry about pages that were encrypted being saved to your drive for anyone who has access to your computer to see.

Disabling AutoComplete

You already know about AutoComplete from the address bar. You have taken care of that privacy problem by clearing the file that stored the information, as shown in the section called Removing address bar suggestions. AutoComplete also tries to give a helping hand when you are filling in text boxes on web pages. In this situation, AutoComplete works exactly the same as it does with the address bar. As you begin to fill in the text box, several suggestions will appear based on information that you have already typed in.

To get an idea of how this works in action, visit any site with a text box such as a username or login field and start to type your username. When you do so, words similar to those you have typed in the box on other visits to the site will appear. This capability allows anyone that uses your computer under your account to see your username or anything else you entered into similar text boxes on web sites.

Clearly, having this feature enabled would be a big concern if you were concerned about your privacy. Disabling the AutoComplete feature is not very difficult and will completely take care of this privacy concern. Follow these steps to put an end to AutoComplete:

1. Open Internet Explorer.

2. Click Tools and select Internet Options.

3. Click the Content tab and then the Settings button under the AutoComplete section.

4. After the AutoComplete Settings window loads, clear all the boxes, as shown in Figure 19-4.

5. When you are finished, just click OK to save your changes.

6. Click OK again to close Internet Options and activate your changes.

AutoComplete is now a thing of the past. You no longer have to worry that people who use your computer will be shown all the things that you type into your address and text boxes.

Clearing Temporary Internet Files Automatically

Earlier I showed you how to clear your temporary Internet files so that they will not be a privacy concern. Over time, your Temporary Internet Files folder will fill up and will become a privacy concern. One easy way to fix this is to use this cool hidden feature of Internet Explorer that automatically deletes these files every time you close Internet Explorer. This way, you will not have to worry about clearing all the files every time that you use Internet Explorer. Follow these steps to activate the automatic empty feature:

1. Open Internet Explorer.

2. Click the Tools menu bar item and then select Internet Options.

3. Click the Advanced tab and scroll down almost to the bottom of the list.

4. Locate and select Empty Temporary Internet Files folder when browser is closed, as shown in Figure 19-5.

5. Click OK to close Internet Options and activate your changes.

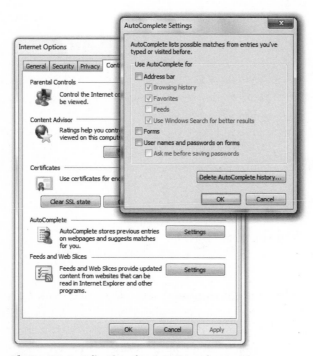

Figure 19-4: Adjusting the AutoComplete settings

Enabling the automatic empty feature is a great way to maintain a clean PC. Keep in mind that this will delete only your temporary Internet files, not your cookies. You will still have to delete the cookies the way that I mentioned previously in this chapter.

Running Internet Explorer 8 in Super Privacy Mode

New to Internet Explorer 8 is a new feature named InPrivate Browsing. Also known as "porn mode" this privacy feature prevents Internet Explorer from storing any data about your browsing session including cookies, history, and temporary Internet files. As soon as you close the browser there are no traces of what web sites were visited. Additionally, toolbars, extensions, and third-party cookies are disabled to further protect a third-party from spying on what web sites you visit.

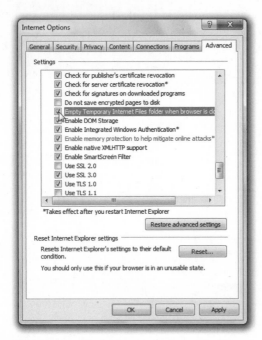

Figure 19-5: Setting up IE to automatically clear temporary Internet files

I personally like to use InPrivate Browsing when I do online banking to add an extra layer of protection. Keep in mind, though, that InPrivate Browsing is not anonymous browsing. Should you do something illegal within InPrivate Browsing, the browser does nothing to hide your IP address from a remote server. When an IP address of a visitor is captured in a server log it is easy to subpoena the ISP that owns the IP for the name and address of the user behind the IP.

Using InPrivate Browsing is very simple. While Internet Explorer 8 is running, click Safety and then select InPrivate Browsing. You can tell InPrivate Browsing is running by the distinct InPrivate logo as shown in Figure 19-6.

Windows Interface Privacy

After you have Internet Explorer under control, you can move on to cleaning the rest of the Windows interface. Just as with Internet Explorer, Windows Explorer keeps track of the applications that you run and files that you open. It does this so that it can tailor your computer to your personal use with features such as the frequently run programs list on the Start panel. Features such as this are designed to speed up the use of your computer. However, the side effect of the convenience is a loss of privacy. These next few sections show you how to recover your privacy, albeit at the expense of convenience.

Figure 19-6: Internet Explorer 8's InPrivate Browsing

Clearing Frequently Run and Opened Files Lists Including Jump Lists

One of the great new features of Windows 7 can also be a pain when you are concerned about your privacy. The capability to select the programs that you use frequently directly from the Start panel instead of having to navigate through the entire Start menu can save you some time. However, over time, this list can become cluttered with programs that you don't want to be there. Additionally, anyone who uses your computer can easily see what programs you use.

Windows 7 also does something similar with the files that you open. Every time you open a Word document, a digital image, or any other file, an entry is created in the Recent Files list that also is displayed in the jump list when you right-click an item in the new taskbar.

In Windows 7, it is very easy to clear or disable these features. Just follow these steps:

1. Right-click the Start button and select Properties.

2. Clear the two check boxes under the Privacy section on the Start Menu tab, as shown in Figure 19-7.

3. Click OK to save and activate your changes.

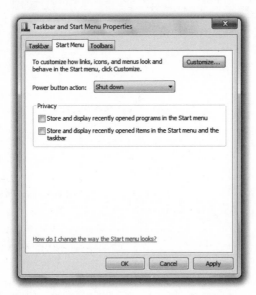

Figure 19-7: Clearing the program list on the Start panel

Both types of recent access data will now be cleared and the feature disabled. If you just wanted to clear the stored data and then continue to use the features, you will need to go back into Properties and check both items again.

Keep in mind that if you disable Store and display recently opened items in the Start menu and the taskbar, then the recent list that appears in taskbar jump lists will also be disabled.

Removing Specific Entries from Taskbar Jump Lists

Similar to Internet Explorer and following the trend in Windows 7 to give the user more control over their privacy, Microsoft included the ability to remove single entries from the recently opened list that appears on many Jump lists.

Simply right-click an application on your taskbar such as Microsoft Word and you will see a list of recently opened documents. To remove a specific entry, just right-click it and select Remove from this list as shown in Figure 19-8.

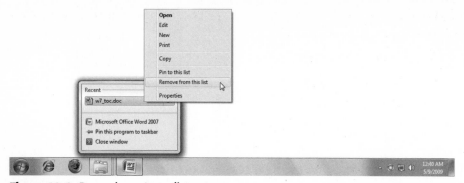

Figure 19-8: Removing a Jump list entry

Removing Temporary Files from Your Hard Drive

Over time, your hard drive can become cluttered with temporary files left behind from applications and the operating system. These files not only take up space, but they can be tracks of activity on your computer. Removing the temporary files is a great way to clean up any garbage information that is left behind, increase your privacy, and free up some disk space.

The complexity of Windows has increased over the years. In the early versions of Windows, there was just one temp folder in which all temp files were located. With Windows 7, temp folders are all over the place. To remove the files, you could go to all the different folders and manually erase the files, but there is a better way.

To clear my temporary files from my hard drive, I like to use Disk Cleanup. Disk Cleanup is a utility that comes with Windows Vista that makes it easy to remove your temporary files. It works by automatically checking the known temporary file locations for you and removing the files. With Disk Cleanup, you do not have to worry about where to navigate on your hard drive to delete the files. Instead, just execute the program.

To get started using Disk Cleanup, follow these steps:

1. Click the Start button, type **Disk Cleanup** in the Search box, and then press Enter.

2. If your computer has multiple hard drives, you will be prompted to select which drive you want to clean. Select the drive you want to clean and press OK.

3. After the utility has analyzed your computer, it gives you a report of various types of files that it can clean, as shown in Figure 19-9. Scroll through the list and make sure that only Temporary Internet Files and Temporary files are checked.

4. Click OK to run the cleanup.

5. Hit Delete Files on the confirmation screen. The utility will now run and exit automatically when it is finished cleaning your hard drive.

Figure 19-9: Using Disk Cleanup to remove temporary files

Disk Cleanup is the perfect way to easily clean up your temporary files. Now that you know how to use it, I recommend that you run it at least once a month to keep your temporary files under control.

After you have cleaned your user files you can also use Disk Cleanup to delete temporary system files. On the main Disk Cleanup screen, just click Clean up system files and then follow the previous steps starting with Step 2.

TIP Another method to clear temporary files on your computer is to use a third-party utility that is designed to delete files in known temporary folders all over your computer. My favorite utility for this task outside of using Disk Cleanup is called CCleaner by Piriform. CCleaner is a very helpful and free utility that will clear temporary files from your computer with just a few clicks. Visit www.ccleaner.com to learn more.

Removing Saved Passwords with Credential Manager

When you visit a web site that requires authentication or attempt to connect to remote computers, you are given the option to save your password so that the next time you visit the page or attempt to access a remote resource you do not have to re-enter your password. This feature can be a huge convenience, especially if you access a particular web site or resource frequently. The downside to this convenience is the potential for horrible security and privacy problems that it creates. Essentially, you are taking the password off all the sites and resources for which you saved a password. Anyone who has physical access to your computer can get in using your username and password, even if they do not know your password.

Removing your saved passwords from your computer is a very good idea because doing so will protect your accounts. In Windows 7, saved passwords can be removed using the new Credential Manager.

1. Click the Start button, type in Credential Manager, and hit Enter.

2. All your saved accounts will be listed under Windows Credentials and Generic Credentials. Next to each listed account, click the down arrow as shown in Figure 19-10.

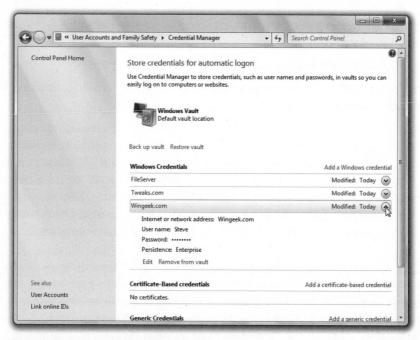

Figure 19-10: Using Credential Manager

3. The account details will be shown including the option to delete the account. Click Remove from vault to delete the account.

4. Click Yes on the verification screen.

You can also use the Credential Manager to add more usernames and passwords to your computer. If you have a web site or resource for which privacy isn't a concern, such as a news web site, just click Add a generic credential and fill in the account information.

Setting File and Folder Permissions

Windows 7 runs on the NTFS file system, which allows users to set file and folder permissions. These permission settings enable you to specify the users that can view a particular file or a whole folder on your computer. In fact, file permissions in Windows 7 are so detailed that you can even specify whether a person has the ability only to read your files while preventing them from saving any changes. For the sake of privacy, file permissions are very helpful because they allow you to prevent other users from even being able to gain access to your private folders.

Setting the permissions on files and folders is easy to do. Just follow these steps:

1. Right-click any file or folder for which you want to modify permissions and select Properties.

2. Click the Security tab and press the Edit button.

3. Make sure that your username is added to the list and that you give yourself Full Control. You can do this with the Add button.

4. Remove all users from the group or username list that you do not want having access to this file. It is a good idea to remove the Everyone group because this includes everyone that can access your computer, including guests. Make sure that you do not accidentally remove your username from the list. Also watch out for the SYSTEM account. This is one account the operating system uses to access files but can be safely removed unless you experience problems with a specific application or service.

TIP If you are having difficulties removing users from the username list, this could be because the user is inherited from a parent folder. Permissions are passed down to all subfolders and files. If you want a user to have access to a folder but not its subfolders, then you have to click the Advanced button on the Security tab of the Properties window. After the Advanced Security Settings window loads, click Change Permissions and then clear the option that says Inherit from parent the permission entries that apply to child objects. A Security notification box will pop up. Click the Remove button to remove all the inherited permissions so that you have full control of the folder.

5. Now that you have the list of users and groups taken care of, set the specific permissions that the user has on the file or folder. Select the name of the user that you want to modify, and then check the corresponding boxes in the Permissions for list for the activities that you want them to be able to do, as shown in Figure 19-11.

6. When you have finished setting the permissions for all the users, click OK to exit the permissions screen.

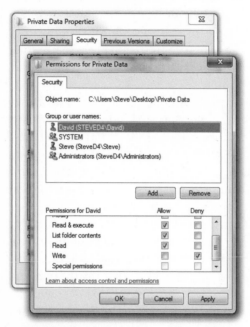

Figure 19-11: Adjusting the permissions for David, who now has permission to read files in the folder, only

After you have set the permissions for all sensitive directories, you will have greatly increased your security and privacy. Also keep in mind that file permissions are inherited. Every folder within a folder inherits the permissions of the parent folder unless they are specifically removed. Therefore, if you set the file permissions for a folder, all the subfolders and files will be automatically set with the same permissions.

File and folder permissions can be very useful. If you have a program on your computer that you do not want anyone else running, simply set the permissions on that folder so that only you can read and execute.

Summary

Throughout this chapter you found out how to increase your privacy when using Internet Explorer. The information that Internet Explorer leaves behind can be very sensitive, so I showed you how to clear your history and delete temporary files to protect your privacy. Then, I showed you how to configure Internet Explorer so it cleans up after itself when you close the browser.

The second part of this chapter addressed the privacy concerns of the Windows interface. Just like Internet Explorer, Windows records many of your computer activities. Clearing those records is an essential part of protecting your privacy. First, I showed you how to remove sensitive items that may appear in Jump Lists on the taskbar and then you learned ways to further protect your privacy with file permissions.

You have now finished reading the last chapter of Windows 7 Tweaks. I guided you through selecting the right version of Windows 7 and then install-ing and basic tips to tweak your computer safely in Part I. In Part II, you were shown how to customize just about everything that can be customized in Windows 7 to make Windows appear that it was designed just for you. In Part III the focus turned to performance and I covered tweaks that can help speed up Windows 7 on any computer by optimizing the various aspects of the operating system. In Part VI the topic shifted to securing your computer. You learned how to protect your computer from attackers, defend against spyware and viruses, and protect your privacy. Now that you have completed the final chapter your Windows 7 experience has been fully personalized, optimized, and secured.

Index

Index